SAMUEL E. LOEWENSTAMM

THE EVOLUTION OF THE EXODUS TRADITION

PUBLICATION OF THE PERRY FOUNDATION FOR BIBLICAL RESEARCH
IN THE HEBREW UNIVERSITY OF JERUSALEM

SAMUEL E. LOEWENSTAMM

THE EVOLUTION OF
THE EXODUS TRADITION

Translated from the Hebrew by
BARUCH J. SCHWARTZ

THE MAGNES PRESS, THE HEBREW UNIVERSITY, JERUSALEM

Distributed by The Magnes Press,
P.O.B. 7695, Jerusalem 91076

ISBN 965-223-784-1

Printed in Israel
Typesetting: Keterpress Enterprises, Jerusalem

CONTENTS

TRANSLATOR'S PREFACE

The Evolution of the Exodus Tradition is a translation of Samuel E. Loewenstamm, *Māsōret Yĕṣīʾat Miṣrayīm bĕHištalšĕlūtāh* (English title page: *The Tradition of the Exodus in its Development*), Jerusalem: The Magnes Press, The Hebrew University, first edition 1968, enlarged edition 1987.

The translation is identical in content to the enlarged Hebrew edition (1987). For reasons of clarity, the following stylistic modifications, all of which are of a formal, technical nature, have been made:

1. The internal divisions of the text have been more clearly demarcated. Sections of chapters have been clearly captioned and numbered, and the predominantly continuous Hebrew text has been generously re-paragraphed in accordance with the demands of English style.

2. All bibliographical references, and all internal cross-references, including those which, in the Hebrew version, were included in the text, have been placed in the footnotes. The method of cross-referencing in the footnotes themselves has been simplified, so that there is no longer any need to consult a bibliographical index. All other indexes, including the index of authors cited, have been retained.

3. The four Excursuses (which were added in the 1987 edition) have been incorporated more fully into the translation. They have been transferred from the end of the volume to the chapters to which they pertain, and they have been more frequently cross-referenced.

A few words concerning the quotation and citation of sources, both ancient and modern, are in order.

Quotations from the Hebrew Bible are according to *Tanakh — A New Translation of the Holy Scriptures According to the Traditional Hebrew Text,* Philadelphia: The Jewish Publication Society, 1985. Only such deviations as were necessitated by the author's own view of the meaning of a scriptural passage have been made. One example — which goes beyond the realm of quotations of actual passages — is the word *pesah*, referring to the paschal sacrifice. Loewenstamm's discussion of this term concludes unequivocally that the English "passover" is a misnomer, which is why, though this term appears in all English Bibles, it has generally been avoided in the present volume.

Since the Hellenistic Jewish literature was cited in the original edition in Hebrew translation, it was considered most in accord with the author's intent to make use of the existing English translations of this material wherever possible. These sources are first introduced in Chapter Four, where the reader will find the English versions used fully documented in the accompanying notes.

Scholarly works, including those by the author, which were originally published in English but were translated by Loewenstamm into Hebrew for quotation, have been reconsulted and quoted here according to their original English versions. Non-English works, again including those by the author, which are also available in English translation have been quoted *and cited* in their English versions, the original version appearing, when necessary, in parentheses. This procedure has been followed even when the publication of the English version followed that of Loewenstamm's work.

The system of abbreviation and citation used is essentially that found in the *Journal of Biblical Literature,* 107 (1988), pp. 579ff., with occasional divergences for the sake of simplicity.

It is a pleasure to acknowledge the tireless efforts of the director of the Magnes Press, Dan Benovici, without whom this work could never have been carried out, and the diligent labors of Rebecca Toueg, who capably applied herself to the tasks of proofreading and editing. The translation of particularly difficult passages was often facilitated by consulting an earlier draft prepared by Joseph Frank. Finally, I am grateful for the encouragement and assistance provided by Professor Joshua Blau.

Though the translation was conceived, and was to have been overseen, by the author, his untimely demise has made the labor of translation and of editing the sources a difficult and lonely one, and I have not always been certain that Professor Loewenstamm would have approved of the results. I can only hope that he would have regarded them as an honest attempt to convey to the English reader the full intent of his work, and that the reader will regard them as a tribute to his memory.

Baruch J. Schwartz

Jerusalem, 1991

INTRODUCTION

All of biblical historiography is sacred historiography, presenting the annals of the Israelite nation as the product of God's providential care of His people. This statement, however, does not apply with equal validity to each and every episode comprising the corpus of biblical historiography. While there are episodes which, despite their theological transformation, were never entirely separate from the realm of secular history, other events were so thoroughly absorbed into the domain of the sacred that they served to form Israel's religious and national consciousness throughout subsequent generations. These latter are the events which tend to be included in the Bible's didactic texts, which expound Israel's history as a means of strengthening her faith. Paramount among the events included in these texts is the story of Israel's Exodus from Egypt, a fact in no sense surprising, since the story of the Exodus celebrates, more than any other, God's direct intervention in the redemption of His people from the house of bondage, with a strong hand and an outstretched arm, with signs and wonders.

In the present study I have endeavored to examine the evolution of this central tradition. In so doing I have made use of dialectical, typological analysis, a method which differs from the method employed by the Wellhausenian school just as the latter differs from harmonistic interpretation. The material included in my study is not restricted to the account of the Exodus as it appears in the canonical book of Exodus, nor even to the references to the Exodus dispersed throughout the Bible; rather, it embraces Hellenistic, Apocryphal, Pseudepigraphical and midrashic sources as well.

The original version of this study was a doctoral dissertation presented to the Senate of the Hebrew University of Jerusalem. In writing it, I profited greatly from the guidance of Professor I. L. Seeligmann, whose encouragement, advice and criticism have left their mark on every chapter. I note happily that I was able to win his agreement on many issues, and that he demonstrated understanding with regard to those of my opinions from which he felt himself obliged to dissent.

This revision has not affected the basic lines of the original study, but has confined itself to matters of literary clarity and to the addition of occasional supplementary material.

I am greatly indebted to my wife Ayyala, who contributed valuable observations and undertook the arduous task of verifying the references and reading the proofs. It is a pleasure to acknowledge the diligence and devotion with which the director and members of the staff of Magnes Press applied themselves to all aspects of this book's publication. Finally, I offer sincere thanks to the Perry Foundation for Biblical Research for its support and for its decision to include this work among its publications.

Samuel E. Loewenstamm
1968

CHAPTER ONE

METHODOLOGICAL APPROACHES TO THE STUDY OF THE EXODUS TRADITION

The principal aim of the Pentateuch is to recount the prehistory of the Israelite people prior to the conquest of its land. This narrative reaches its climax in the episode most abounding in manifestations of God's miraculous acts, namely, the account of the Exodus from Egypt. In this story a group of slaves becomes an independent nation, henceforth enslaved to the LORD their God alone. The LORD, by bringing His people out of the house of bondage, becomes the God of Israel, and the Israelites simultaneously become His treasured people.

The Exodus has been subjected to two essentially different types of scholarly scrutiny. One is historical study, which investigates the date of the Exodus and the historical circumstances which enabled it to take place. In particular, it poses the question whether the tradition that all the Israelites participated in this event is historically reliable or whether preference should be given to the conjecture that some segment of Israel had never been in Egypt and therefore could not have left. This line of inquiry raises the additional question whether the historian is justified in accepting the Pentateuchal tradition that all those who left Egypt departed at one and the same time, or whether he should distinguish between various waves of departure.[1] Since the resolution of these issues cannot be accomplished on the basis of the actual Pentateuchal accounts of the Exodus, the plagues of Egypt, the

---

1 S. E. Loewenstamm, s.v. "*Yĕṣīᵓat Miṣrayīm*", *ᵓEnṣīqlōpedīā Miqraᵓīt*, III, Jerusalem 1965, pp. 754-759, with detailed bibliography to which S. Yeivin, "*Yĕṣīᵓat Miṣrayīm*", *Tarbiz*, 30 (1961), pp. 1-7 should be added.

Pesah night and the parting of the sea, the historian is not obliged to analyze them. He is concerned only with the Pentateuchal narratives of events preceding the Exodus, the historical nucleus of which can be rather clearly and definitively determined.

The second method is the quite separate task of investigating the history of Israel's traditions. Here the concern is to determine the role of the Exodus traditions in shaping the Israelite people's collective consciousness. For this purpose an attempt must be made to reconstruct as far as possible the history of these traditions, to distinguish between primary and secondary motifs, and to separate, within the corpus of finalized traditions, the originally independent elements which were assembled together in various ways to comprise the traditions as we have them. Further, an effort must be made to determine the motivating forces which were active at each stage in this complex process.

Now just as historical study cannot be conducted on the basis of an analysis of the Exodus traditions, neither can historical reconstruction contribute to the study of the literary motifs characteristic of Israel's traditions concerning this episode in its history. At most, historical investigation may cast some light on the prehistory of the account (whose importance for the study of the history of the Exodus traditions themselves must also be recognized).

The study here presented is devoted to elucidating the formation of the Exodus traditions among the Israelite people. For this reason, historical treatment will be confined to a brief survey of the events preceding the Exodus, which are of interest here only insofar as they can illuminate the background against which the Exodus traditions took shape. The range of inquiry into the Exodus traditions, however, will be as wide as possible, embracing, apart from the narratives in the book of Exodus, references to the Exodus from Egypt found throughout the rest of the Bible, the Apocrypha and Pseudepigrapha, and the Hellenistic and midrashic literature. The determination of this broad frame of reference involves methodological assumptions which require some explanation.

The classical school of criticism, which assumed its characteristic form during the nineteenth century, actually restricted the study of

Israel's ancient traditions to the internal analysis of the Pentateuch. This restriction resulted from a number of factors. In the first place, it must be borne in mind that even Christian scholars were influenced in their research by the fact that the Pentateuch is the first book to have won recognition as Holy Scripture and that its accounts are characterized by a wealth of detail and by narrational continuity. To this one must add that research carried out by the classical school was entirely devoted to unraveling the Pentateuchal sources, and that scholarly interest which focused entirely on this aim was necessarily diverted from the consideration of any other literature, outside of the sources of which the Pentateuch was composed, bearing on Israel's early history. Scholarly judgment of all such literature was predetermined by the general assessment that it was either derived from the Pentateuch or, when it presented new material, that this was to be regarded as the result of the influence of later generations.

The chief contribution of this school was that biblical scholarship directed its attention to the great variety of tradition which is reflected in the body of the Pentateuch. For this reason, even opponents of the method join with its adherents with regard to many of the questions which it raised. Yet the elaborate, dogmatic structure erected by the proponents of this method in the nineteenth century cannot now carry conviction to the same extent as in the past — and this applies not only to the Scandinavian school, which, with absolute certainty, denies the existence of any written sources prior to the Pentateuch, and in whose opinion the Pentateuch originated directly from oral traditions. One can sense even within the classical critical camp a feeling of acute embarrassment, to the extent that a scholar like de Vaux, raised in the classical German school, expressed clear reservation: "We must give up referring to 'documents' and speak rather of written and oral 'traditions', with all the greater vitality, but also greater vagueness and fluidity, that this term implies".[2] Furthermore, even such a prominent representative of this school as von Rad

---

2 R. de Vaux, "À propos du second centenaire d'Astruc — réflexions sur l'état actuel de la critique du Pentateuque", *VTSup*, 1 (1953), p. 187. See the same author's remarks in English in "Method in the Study of Early Hebrew History", in: J. P. Hyatt (ed.), *The Bible in Modern Scholarship*, London 1965, p. 20.

criticized its basic principles, observing, "On almost all sides the final form of the Hexateuch has come to be regarded as a starting-point, barely worthy of discussion, from which the debate should move away as rapidly as possible in order to reach the real problems underlying it".[3]

This uneasiness is a result of several factors. The naive belief that by dividing the Pentateuch into a few sources it is possible to arrive at texts marked by absolute uniformity has long been abandoned. This bold claim has been superseded by the more modest assumption that source-division is merely a separation into "schools", each of which is comprised of a number of sub-strata. This, of course, impairs the certainty that duplications of language or subject-matter must necessarily be evidence of different sources, since, in theory, these duplications might merely be evidence of different sub-strata. Similarly, doubts have been felt as to whether prolixity of style is always evidence of the composite character of the text or whether it might sometimes be assigned to a single author. Moreover, the crucial question arises whether variation in tradition is identical to multiplicity of sources. It is surely possible for the account given by a single author to have been influenced by numerous traditions which reached him, either orally or in writing, and which would still not justify our regarding such an author's work as that of a redactor. Our analyses of Jewish Hellenistic literature, to be presented later in the course of this study, will corroborate this. Furthermore, even if we should succeed in distinguishing, in one or another Pentateuchal narrative, between original sources and later accretions, this would still be no proof that the Pentateuch was preceded by a literary source, within whose narrative only the later tradition was incorporated and from which early traditions were expunged. For there are times when the alternative explanation is to be preferred — that from the outset, later elements were combined with the earlier ones, as a means of explaining them in the spirit of a later author's viewpoint. More importantly, a method

---

3 G. von Rad, "The Form-Critical Problem of the Hexateuch" (1938), in: *The Problem of the Hexateuch and other Essays*, trans. by E. W. Trueman Dicken, New York 1966, p. 1 (= *Gesammelte Studien zum Alten Testament*, München 1958, p. 9).

which begins the inquiry by dividing the text into sources provides no opportunity to analyze its present literary structure, since the given text has ceased to be a subject for scholarly research. Hence biblical scholarship is apt to ignore a clearly marked literary scheme. Classical source-division is also likely to ignore the nature of religious dialectic, as it is expressed in the continuous process by which varying traditions evolve from one another and unite with one another — a process which is the life force of all tradition-history. This approach also suffers from a shortcoming discussed earlier: it attaches no importance to sources outside the Pentateuch, sources which are themselves the product of multiple traditions such as are to be found in the Pentateuch itself. Thus, the classical method of Pentateuchal criticism, in the course of isolating the assumed sources from one another, at the same time isolates the Pentateuch itself from other available sources which could serve as an important basis for reconstructing the principles of the dialectic which shaped the image of Israel's tradition.

A second school, which claims to complement the source-critical method, originated in Gunkel's doctrine of the *Sitz im Leben* of ancient literature. Gunkel asserted that ancient literature was never simply literature for its own sake but was meant to be recited or sung on some typical, recurring occasion, whether secular or liturgical, in the life of the people.[4] Von Rad reasoned on this basis that the original nucleus of the tradition is to be found in brief formulations whose *Sitz im Leben* can be recognized, and that the detailed narratives for which no such *Sitz im Leben* can be found developed later.[5] Hence the exaggerated importance which von Rad attached to the ritual "credo" contained in the "Declaration of the Firstfruits" (Deut 26:1-10). A similar approach is manifested by many scholars who assign to the Song of Miriam (Exod 15:20-21) a date earlier than the formation of the other traditions concerning the Exodus from Egypt, arguing that this song is not merely a literary work but was originally associated with a festival at which women danced and played

4 H. Gunkel, *Einleitung in die Psalmen*, ed. J. Begrich, Göttingen 1933, p. 10.
5 von Rad, *op. cit.* (above, note 3), pp. 1-8.

timbrels.[6] Von Rad's approach met with the approval of Noth, though the latter found it necessary to develop it, and, in certain respects, to modify it.[7] There is, however, no need to deal with Noth's observations in detail, since the method itself is untenable. The statement that "the LORD freed us from Egypt by a mighty hand, by an outstretched arm and great terror, and by signs and portents", which occurs as part of the "Declaration of Firstfruits" (Deut 26:8), is devoid of all substantive content if we assume that the person who originally pronounced it was not acquainted with a cycle of narratives dealing with the events to which he makes only brief allusion. Likewise, the Song of Miriam becomes meaningless if it is detached from its context — especially in light of the proposal, to be advanced below, that the tradition concerning the parting of the sea is actually earlier than that concerning the drowning of the Egyptians therein.[8]

Other methods of research come closer to our own. The first scholar who was not content with the source division of the Pentateuch and attempted to describe the history of Israel's traditions within a wider framework was H. Gunkel, who, in his *Schöpfung und Chaos in Urzeit und Endzeit*,[9] put forward the assertion, revolutionary in its time, that the books of the prophets and the Hagiographa allude repeatedly to traditions about Creation which antedate the Pentateuch, and according to which God shaped the likeness of His world by doing battle with mighty powers. Gunkel contended further that these early

---

6 Gunkel. *op. cit.* (above, note 4), p. 16; see below pp. 256–257.
7 M. Noth, *A History of Pentateuchal Traditions*, trans. by B. W. Anderson, Englewood Cliffs, NJ 1972, pp 46ff. (= *Die Überlieferungsgeschichte des Pentateuchs*, Stuttgart 1948, pp. 53ff.). To von Rad's theory Noth adds that the most ancient of the later motifs is that of the slaying of the firstborn, which is based on the ritual of Passover night. He believes this to be the primal tradition underlying the plagues of Egypt, from which the motif of competition between Moses and Aaron and the magicians eventually evolved. Though Noth basically accepts von Rad's approach, he nevertheless attempts to moderate it by observing that the "credo" pertaining to an historical event inspired, by its very content, both prosaic and hymnic formulations. Hence, he concludes, the cultic "confessionals" in which the Exodus was periodically retold included, apart from the main theme of the drowning of the Egyptians, introductory material concerning the enslavement and the account of Israel's flight from Egypt.
8 See below, pp. 236-264.
9 Göttingen 1895.

traditions have left their mark not only on the Bible but on post-biblical literature as well.

Gunkel's line of argument was fully developed by U.M.D. Cassuto in "The Israelite Epic",[10] a study which actually adduced further support for Gunkel's claim by citing midrashic passages and the evidence of the Ugaritic texts. Cassuto's study is important not only by virtue of the extremely precise manner in which the content, and the pre-Israelite origins, of the mythological traditions which were current in Israel are determined, but also by reason of Cassuto's success in dealing with the phrases which recur repeatedly in the mythological sections of the Bible, the direct source of which he sought in a proto-Israelite epic poem. Cassuto considered this epic to be the link between the Canaanite epos and the Pentateuch, in which ancient, mythological foundations are either reduced to minimal proportions or else eradicated entirely by the spirit of rational theology.

The scope of inquiry was extended in another direction by A. Jirku in *Die älteste Geschichte Israels im Rahmen lehrhafter Darstellungen.*[11] The author made the first attempt to compare the narratives of the first four books of the Pentateuch (the Tetrateuch) with didactic accounts of Israel's history occurring elsewhere in the Bible and in Jewish literature from the Hellenistic and Roman periods. Here, Jirku first arrived at the important axiom that the common basis of the didactic histories was to be found in the period of history extending from the period of the Exodus until the Conquest, although additional episodes might have been annexed to this base. Jirku believed the source of these didactic histories to be an oral tradition which is alluded to in many scriptural passages,[12] which implies that he viewed these passages as independent sources not necessarily derived from the narrative tradition of the Tetrateuch. But Jirku did not stop there: he went on to define the relationship between the briefer didactic histories and the more lengthy narratives as a genetic one. In this regard,

---

10 First published in Hebrew in 1943; see U. Cassuto, *Biblical and Oriental Studies*, II, trans. I. Abrahams, Jerusalem 1975, pp. 69-109.
11 Leipzig 1917.
12 Exod 10:1-2; 12:26-27; 13:8, 14-15; Deut 4:9; 6:20-25; 11:18-19; 32:45-46; Josh 4:6-7; Judg 5:11; Isa 8:16; Jer 6:16; Joel 1:2-3; Pss 44:2; 78:1-4.

his approach resembles that of von Rad: both scholars took the brief encapsulations to be the nucleus from which the narratives evolved. But where Jirku regarded the didactic histories, and not the Pentateuchal passages, as the core of the tradition, von Rad believed that the nucleus was to be found in specific Pentateuchal passages possessing a *Sitz im Leben*. Jirku's preference for the didactic histories failed, however, to take account of the nature of homiletics, which is to select from among the traditions current among the people only those which serve the didactic purpose of the passage, while omitting other motifs which have no immediate homiletical value. Since the traditions included in a didactic passage are thus a tendentiously motivated selection, there is no justification for assigning a late date to a tradition appearing in the narratives merely because it does not appear in the didactic histories. The "Bloody Bridegroom" episode (Exod 4:24-26) illustrates the point. This story does not recur either in the didactic histories or even in the detailed historical recitals found in later literature. But the conclusion to be drawn from this silence is not that the story is late but merely that all the writers who recorded the traditions considered the story itself — that God had sought to kill Moses — to be problematic, and this attitude on their part actually amounts to evidence for the early date of the story. Another even more telling example is the fact that, while in a few of the didactic passages the history of Israel is preceded by mention of God's mighty activity in nature or in Creation,[13] not even one such passage alludes to the story of the Garden of Eden or the account of the Flood. These traditions, however, are included in the didactic history of 4 Ezra 2:6-12, which was compiled after the destruction of the Second Temple — yet no biblical scholar would claim to find in the text of this late work the nucleus from which the Pentateuchal narratives about these events evolved.

The direct influence of Jirku is discernible in A. Lauha's "Die Geschichtsmotive in den Alttestamentlichen Psalmen".[14] This study

---

13 Pss 135:6-7; 136:5-9; Neh 9:6.
14 Helsinki 1945 (= *Annales Academiae Scientiarum Fennicae*, Sarja B, 56 [1945], pp. 1-149).

is based on Jirku's theory, which assigns to the Psalms independent value for the investigation of Israel's historical and theological tradition, and in certain respects even reaches more accurate definitions of the relationship between the tradition of the Psalms and that of the Pentateuch.

A comprehensive, theoretical discussion of the problem of tradition-history appeared in 1953 in I.L. Seeligmann's "Voraussetzungen der Midraschexegese".[15] Seeligmann argued in support of the assertion that the history of the traditions was one of perpetual motion, a process whose beginning preceded the Pentateuch and which was not finally concluded until after the end of the biblical period. It follows that even late sources may reflect early traditions which have undergone metamorphoses; not as late interpretations of the Pentateuch but rather as independent transformations of the actual traditions themselves.

These basic assumptions were the foundations for my study of "The Death of Moses",[16] in which I endeavored to prove that the Pentateuchal account of Moses' death was preceded by a tradition of his ascent to heaven, a tradition preserved intact only in later literature.

In the present study the scope of inquiry has been further extended along the methodological lines described above. This does not mean that I have ignored the evident fact that most of the literature parallel to the Pentateuch has been influenced by it to some extent; one of the tasks of this study will in fact be to determine precisely the degree of such influence in each case. Nor am I unaware of the obvious fact that the divergences of later literature from the Pentateuchal narrative can be explained in part as the result of later tendencies; these too will be dealt with in the course of my discussion. Still, I cannot, in the first place, accept the assumption that all the passages in the prophetic books and the Hagiographa which refer to the Exodus are necessarily later than the Pentateuch, and secondly, I shall attempt to show that

---

15 *VTSup*, 1 (1953), pp. 150-181.
16 First published in Hebrew in *Tarbiz*, 27 (1958), 16-31; see S. E. Loewenstamm, "The Death of Moses", in: G. W. E. Nickelsburg, Jr. (ed.), *Studies in the Testament of Abraham, Septuagint and Cognate Studies*, 6 (1976), pp. 185-217.

an appreciable portion of these divergences are in fact evidence of the continued existence of the very same tension among various traditions which can be seen to exist in the Pentateuch itself.

Prior to determining, through our study of biblical as well as post-biblical sources, the nature of the traditions which make up the story of the Exodus, we shall consider the overall significance of the Exodus tradition within the framework of biblical literature.

CHAPTER TWO

THE ROLE OF THE EXODUS IN BIBLICAL HISTORIOGRAPHY

The attempt to determine the place occupied by the Exodus in biblical historiography requires an examination of the relation between the Exodus tradition and the other episodes in the history of Israel into which, both with regard to the chain of events themselves and to their theological evaluation, it is integrated.

I. The Exodus and the Enslavement

First among these related episodes is the enslavement in Egypt. Its historical background is sufficiently explained in the Pentateuchal narratives, which describe the Israelites as a group of herdsmen who left Canaan during a period of drought and were permitted to take up residence in the district of Goshen, there to live until one of the Egyptian kings finally pressed them into forced labor in one of his extensive building operations. This labor was regarded by the community of herdsmen as exceedingly strenuous, evoking their bitterest feelings of resentment. The detailed description of the actual slave-labor in the book of Exodus bears the obvious stamp of authenticity and accords perfectly with the known historical facts about the construction works of Ramses II. The historical reality of the period must therefore have been deeply impressed upon Israelite memory, as is further evidenced in Ps 81:7: "I relieved his shoulder of the burden, his hands were freed from the basket". This verse reflects faithfully what is illustrated in Egyptian depictions of the manufacture of bricks, which show, among other things, a laborer bearing upon his shoulders a receptacle heaped with wet clay, while his hands grasp it from above.[1] The very fact that the Egyptian bondage remained engraved for generations, in precise detail,[2] in Israel's memory, attests both to the shock and dismay of these herdsmen at being charged with the task of construction, a labor so different from their traditional way of life, and to their recollection of the departure from Egypt as an escape from "the house of bondage" or, in still more forceful metaphor, from "the iron furnace".[3]

Yet this simplistic view does not exhaust the full significance of the Exodus in biblical historiography. In the Bible, the Exodus is the moment at which the LORD ceased to be Israel's God in potential alone and became her God in actual fact. This idea is alluded to in both of the accounts contained in the book of Exodus which record the revelation to Moses of the divine name YHWH.[4] It is the basis

---

1 See below, Excursus I, p. 50, and in particular note 19.

2 We may dispense with the detailed analysis of Exodus 1, in which the theme of enslavement is combined with the motif of the killing of newborn sons, a motif which disappears from the book of Exodus as soon as it has served its purpose of introducing the cycle of stories about Moses. This motif does not belong to the tradition proper, as is particularly evident from Gen 15:13; Deut 26:6; Ps 81:7, all of which lack any reference to the slaying of the Israelite children and mention only the forced labor. The view of H. Gressmann, *Mose und seine Zeit*, Göttingen 1913, pp. 1-16, that the story of the slaying of the infants has been preserved by Josephus in a form closer to the original (Ant. II.ix.6, according to which Pharaoh decreed against Israelite male children because his astrologers had prophesied to him the birth of a son who would subdue Egypt), is probably correct. Yet it is still clear that in the text of Exodus 1 as it stands the decree is motivated by fear of the Israelites' proliferation (see Deut 26:5; Ps 105:24), and it is this fear which led first to the forced labor and finally to the slaying of the infants. Followed along these lines, the traditio-historical reconstruction is reasonably straightforward, since, even according to Josephus Pharaoh ordered the killing of the male children, and this decree could easily be explained as a result of his dismay at the Israelites' rapid increase and at the fulfillment of the blessings given to their ancestors (Gen 12:2; 13:6; 15:5; 22:17; 28:14; 46:3). Once this new explanation had been given for the decree against the infants, the decree of forced labor could be explained in a like manner.
The curious admixture of traditions in Josephus' account is worthy of mention. Despite the unique explanation for the decree to slay the male children (see above), Josephus does not omit the fact that the Egyptians acted out of a genocidal intent. This latter motivation is also used to account for the forced labor.

3 See below, note 8.

4 Exod 3:13-15; 6:2-3.

for all biblical historiography, which accordingly refrains throughout from presenting the Egyptian bondage in conformity with the conventional model, in which all suffering inflicted upon Israel is divine penalty for sin. The absence of this theological assessment of the enslavement is conspicuous not only in the actual account of the enslavement in the book of Exodus but throughout the Bible. No reason at all is given for the decree that the Egyptians would, in time to come, afflict Abraham's descendants for 400 years, proclaimed in the covenant made with Abraham (Gen 15:13). The decree is, however, clearly connected with the Exodus and the Conquest of Canaan, which are the main concerns of the Covenant. Whatever significance is attached to the enslavement itself consists solely in the blessings which are to succeed it. The same applies to Psalm 105, the entire purpose of which is to glorify God's acts of kindness towards His people, and which states parenthetically that "He changed their heart to hate His people, to plot against His servants" (v. 25). By referring thus to the enslavement, this line implicitly denies that the Egyptians could have enslaved the Israelites other than by God's own will. The passage bears a decidedly monotheistic character, recalling the statement in Exodus that it was God who hardened Pharaoh's heart while inflicting plagues upon the Egyptians.[5] Just as the passage in Exodus is not aimed at blaming God for Pharaoh's obduracy, the intent of the psalmist is not to imply any desire on God's part to harm His people. However, what emerges from the entire description is that the sole reason for the darkness of the enslavement was to enable the light of redemption to shine forth with redoubled brilliance.

It is not surprising, therefore, that in some of the descriptions of the Exodus, mention of the enslavement is confined to a brief allusion within the context of the redemption. This is the case in Psalm 81, in which the enslavement is touched upon only as part of the statement quoted above, "I relieved his shoulder of the burden, his hands were freed from the basket" (v. 7), and still more markedly in Psalm 78, which inserts its single, brief reference to the enslavement among its words of reproof:

---

5 Exod 7:3; 9:12; 10:20, 27; 11:10.

> Again and again they tested God,
> vexed the Holy One of Israel;
> They did not remember His strength,
> or the day He redeemed them from the foe.

(vv. 42-43)

Most instructive is Ezekiel 20, which presents the whole of Israel's history as an unbroken chain of transgressions, always followed by acts of divine deliverance performed by the LORD "for His Name's sake". To uphold the validity of the pattern, the prophet must assert what is nowhere else reported: that Israel had already sinned against its God while in Egypt. However, this exegetical innovation does not alter the theological assessment of the enslavement, since even here Israel is not accused of sinning against the LORD until after He had revealed Himself and sworn to deliver His people from bondage. Here as elsewhere, the enslavement itself remains outside of the scope of the historiosophical overview and is in fact not mentioned at all.[6]

The original tradition, that Israel was not guilty of sinning against the LORD until after the Exodus, is implied in the many passages of rebuke which charge Israel with sinfulness *ever since* they left Egypt, for instance Deut 9:7: "...you provoked the LORD your God to anger... from the day you left the land of Egypt". Similarly, God's speech to Samuel arraigns Israel for forsaking Him "ever since I brought them out of Egypt"; the same idea recurs in the oracle foretelling the fall of the Kingdom which is presented as belonging to the time of Manasseh (2 Kgs 21:15). Jeremiah too reproaches his people for their evil-hearted stubbornness "from the day your fathers left the land of Egypt until today" (7:25) — "from", but not before, that day. The explanation for this upper limit is implied in the words "For I have

---

6 Ezekiel's formulation, according to which the LORD revealed Himself to Israel in Egypt (Ezek 20:5), is more general than that of the Pentateuch, which knows only of His revelation to Moses, through whom He became known to the people. But we need not search here for differing traditions, since in Ezekiel's oracle only one fact was important for the purpose of arraignment: that the LORD had made Himself known to Israel in Egypt. The fact that He had actually done so through Moses was a detail which would not give any additional force to Ezekiel's indictment, but would rather tend to mitigate the people's guilt — which explains why the prophet made no use of it.

repeatedly and persistently warned your fathers from the time I brought them out of Egypt to this day, saying: Obey my commands" (11:7), from which the inference is clear: God has been "warning" His people only since He brought them out of Egypt, but not before.

This same rationale underlies the cautious manner in which Exod 2:23-24 expresses the cry uttered by the enslaved Israelites: "The Israelites were groaning under the bondage and cried out, and their cry for help from the bondage rose up to God. God heard their moaning, and God remembered His covenant with Abraham, Isaac and Jacob". The reason that this precisely formulated passage avoids stating simply that the Israelites cried *to the LORD their God*, and indicates merely that they groaned and cried out because of their hard labor, is that they could not yet turn to the LORD in time of trouble, since He had not yet become their God. The statement "I have now heard the moaning of the Israelites because the Egyptians are holding them in bondage, and I have remembered My covenant" in Exod 6:5 is similar; see also 3:9. In all these passages the LORD is the God of the Patriarchs, the God of Abraham, Isaac and Jacob, who remembers the covenant He had made with them, promising to bring their descendants out of Egypt. He has not yet become the God of the Israelite people, a God to whom they are able to cry out.

Still, and not surprisingly, such a fine distinction was likely to become blurred in the didactic histories, which aim at stressing the unity and continuity of Israel's history. This may be perceived in the "Declaration of Firstfruits" (Deut 26:5-10), which, referring to the cry of the Israelites, states simply: "We cried to the LORD, the God of our fathers, and the LORD heard our plea" (v. 7). The sense appears to be that they cried out to Him only in His capacity as God of their ancestors. Even this qualification is lacking in the prophetic address of 1 Sam 12:8ff: "When Jacob [LXX: and his sons] came to Egypt [LXX: and the Egyptians oppressed them], your fathers cried out to the LORD, and the LORD sent Moses and Aaron" etc. (v. 8). Yet this passage does preserve a trace of the notion that it was not until the time of the Exodus that the LORD actually became Israel's God, since Samuel goes on to recount that, after leaving Egypt, the Israelites continually rebelled against the LORD, and that He repeatedly turned them over to various oppressors until they repented and cried out to Him, after which He sent them deliverers (vv. 9-11). No similar process is alluded to with regard to God's having sent Moses and Aaron to deliver Israel initially.

Another way in which the uniqueness of the Exodus appears to have become blurred can be discerned in Judg 10:10-14. The passage relates that throughout her history, whenever Israel has cried out to the LORD He has saved her from all manner of disaster. The Exodus appears here simply as one of a series, apparently undistinguished from other acts of deliverance from later oppressors. However, even here there is no statement, nor is it in any way suggested, that the LORD subjected His people to bondage in punishment for their misdeeds. Rather, the aim of the passage is to juxtapose past and present. Though in the past the LORD has saved His people whenever, being hard pressed by their enemies, they have cried out to Him, He will not repeat this action on the present occasion: "Yet you have forsaken Me and have served other gods. No, I will not deliver you again" (v. 13). The patriarchs, the passage as a whole implies, had not forsaken the LORD or sinned against Him.

Thus, throughout the story of Israel's enslavement in Egypt, God does not admonish His people or demand their obedience. The concept of sinning against the LORD has no role, which indicates that at that time He was not yet Israel's God in deed. All of this accords well with the fact that the book of Exodus describes the enslavement as a historical occurrence arising out of Egyptian royal policy, not as an instance of divine intervention. Within the framework of biblical theology the enslavement is included only in the Covenant with Abraham, and only in order to affirm that God had foreseen and willed it as part of His plan for Israel's redemption. This is the source of the further conclusion, drawn by the psalmist in Psalm 105, that God's hardening of the Egyptians' hearts had actually begun at the time of the enslavement, causing them to oppress His people. This idea, without parallel in the Bible, does not in any event affect the basic fact: since at the time of the enslavement no real link between the LORD and Israel had yet been forged, the direct intervention of the LORD in the historical process cannot be detected.

Analysis of the enslavement episode determines, in effect, the importance of the Exodus itself within the complex of sacred historiography. It illustrates primarily the historical and sociological significance of the motif of flight from slavery to freedom and the lasting impression which this revolutionary transformation made upon the collective memory of Israel. Secondly, it reveals a turning-point, parallel to this and no less revolutionary, in the relation between the LORD and His people. Only then did the LORD become Israel's God *de facto* — no longer merely aware of Israel's plight, He became a God acting directly in history, waging war on His people's behalf and revealing, at one and the same time, both His dominion over Nature and His supremacy over the gods of mighty Egypt.

Israel's awe and wonder at the deeds performed in Egypt by her God were expressed in the Bible in recurring phrases: the LORD is spoken of as He who "brought out", "brought up", and "redeemed" his people "from the house of bondage"[7] and "from the iron furnace",[8] "by a mighty hand"[9] and "an outstretched arm",[10] "with great power",[11] "by signs and portents",[12] "with great terror"[13] and "wonders",[14] "to make Himself a name for all time".[15] These expressions[16] demonstrate that the Exodus served as the clearest evidence

---

7 Exod 13:3, 14; 20:2; Deut 5:6; 6:12; 7:8; 8:14; 13:6, 11; Josh 24:17; Judg 6:8; Jer 34:13; Mic 6:4.

8 Deut 4:20; 1 Kgs 8:51; Jer 11:4.

9 Exod 3:9; 6:1; 13:9; 32:11; Deut 4:34; 5:15; 6:21; 7:8, 19; 9:26; 11:2; 26:8; Jer 32:21; Ps 136:12; Neh 1:10; Dan 9:15.

10 Exod 6:6; Deut 4:34; 5:15; 7:19; 9:29; 11:2; 26:8; 2 Kgs 17:36; Jer 32:21; Ps 136:12.

11 Exod 32:11; Deut 4:37; 9:29; 2 Kgs 17:36.

12 Deut 4:34; 7:19; 26:8; 29:2; 34:11; Jer 32:20-21; Pss 78:43; 105:27; 135:9; Neh 9:10.

13 Deut 4:34; 26:8; Jer 32:21.

14 Exod 3:20; 15:11; Judg 6:13; Mic 7:15; Pss 78:12; 106:22.

15 Isa 63:12; Jer 32:20; Dan 9:15; Neh 9:10.

16 From the references in the preceding notes it is clear that the most complete lists are to be found in the books of Deuteronomy and Jeremiah. In both of these the term *niplā'ōt* ("wonders") is lacking, and in Deuteronomy the phrase "make Himself a name" is missing as well. A far greater number of these expressions are lacking in Exodus: "from the iron furnace"; "by signs and portents"; "with great terror"; "make Himself a name".

of the LORD's preeminence, surpassing all other deities, and of His love for Israel.

The centrality of the Exodus from Egypt in the sacred historiography of Israel is also suggested by the fact it is the only event to have left its mark on the laws of divine worship in the Pentateuch. Not only is the paschal offering, as ordained in the Pentateuch, presented exclusively as a commemoration of the Exodus, connected with it even by virtue of the date on which it is to be celebrated; even those festivals which occur at other seasons of the year are associated with the Exodus as well.[17]

II. The Exodus and Later Episodes

A. Overview

To supplement the aforegoing explanation, a more comprehensive discussion of the relationship between the Exodus and the other episodes with which it is associated in biblical historiography is in order. It might appear that this problem could be satisfactorily solved by stating simply that the LORD took Israel out of Egypt and led them through the wilderness in order to bring them to the Land of Canaan which He had promised to their ancestors. Closer scrutiny reveals, however, that such a statement does not settle all the problems involved.

According to the narrative account in Exodus, the LORD commanded that, upon leaving Egypt, Israel was to worship God upon the mountain on which He had originally revealed Himself to Moses (Exod 3:12). However, the account of Israel encamped at the foot of Mount Sinai and offering sacrifices to the LORD (Exod 24:1-11) belongs to the story of God's *revelation* at Sinai and the *ratification of His covenant* with His people. The authenticity of the link between these two motifs — the Exodus and the Covenant — is a matter of scholarly debate.

---

17 Lev 23:43; Deut 26:8.

A different sort of question poses itself regarding the problem of the relationship between the Exodus from Egypt and the conquest of Canaan. On this point it is not the antiquity of the connection which is called into doubt; rather, what requires explanation is the fact that the latter episode is left outside the scope of the Pentateuch and is consequently of less importance than the former. Surely one might have expected the opposite: that the Exodus would be presented as a transitional stage in Israel's development, reaching its conclusion in the permanent state represented by the conquest of Canaan, and that the latter would be the event more suited to occupy the foremost place in Israel's sacred historiography.

A third issue arises from the association of the Exodus theme, in writings dating from the monarchic period, with the motifs of the Davidic dynasty and the Zion sanctuary, matters far remote in time from the Exodus.

Any attempt to determine the place of the Exodus within the corpus' of Israel's sacred traditions must therefore address its relationship to these three other themes: the Sinaitic Covenant, the Conquest of Canaan, and the Davidic tradition of Zion. The ensuing discussion will take up each one in turn.

B. The Exodus and Sinai

The LORD became Israel's God when He brought them out of Egypt. This relationship, however, was secured and ratified as a legal bond by the Covenant established at Sinai. Hence, occasionally, the Exodus and the Sinai covenant are treated as a single event. In Deut 29:24 Israel is rebuked "because they forsook the covenant that the LORD, God of their fathers, made with them *when He freed them from the land of Egypt*". The same juxtaposition can be observed in the prophecies of Jeremiah, for example, in 31:31-32: "See, a time is coming — declares the LORD — when I will make a new covenant with the House of Israel and the House of Judah. It will not be like the covenant I made with their fathers *when I took them by the hand to lead them out of Egypt*, a covenant which they broke" etc. These passages, which blame Israel for having broken God's covenant with them, present the Exodus only as the background for the establishment of the Covenant.[18] In any case this assessment is of infrequent occurrence in the Bible, and, as discussed at length by Galling,[19] the act which most often serves as the basis and justification for characterizing the LORD as God of Israel is not the Covenant but the Exodus. Von Rad[20] even went so far as to assert that the connection between the Exodus and the Sinai Covenant is secondary, arguing, firstly, that the historical surveys occurring in the didactic passages (apart from the later ones in Ps 106:19-20 and Neh 9:13) omit any reference to Sinai, and secondly, that the very structure of the Pentateuchal narratives

18 This is also the case in Jer 11:3-4; 34:13; Deut 29:24; 1 Kgs 8:9. See also E. Rohland, *Die Bedeutung der Erwählungstradition Israels für die Eschatologie der alttestamentlichen Propheten*, München 1956, p. 22, who believes that even in the above cited passages from Jeremiah the sole event which confirmed the election of Israel was the Exodus, and that the Covenant merely added a more precise theological definition to this election. Rohland's main argument is the phrase "took by the hand" in Jer 31:32, which is the term used to refer to the election in Isa 41:13; 42:6; 45:1. The "Covenant" which the Israelites have broken is mentioned in Hos 6:7; 8:1 without any indication of its historical background, and thus no particular stress on the Sinaitic Covenant may be perceived there. M. Noth, *op. cit.* (Chapter One, note 7), p. 48 n. 162, is inclined to believe that the verses cited above do not allude to the Sinaitic Covenant but rather consider the Covenant to have been one and the same with the act of delivering Israel from Egypt. But this interpretation fails to take account of the formulation of Jeremiah's statement (34:13-14), "Thus said the LORD, the God of Israel: I made a covenant with your fathers when I brought them out of the land of Egypt, the house of bondage, saying, 'At the end of seven years each of you must let go any fellow Hebrew'" etc., a passage which makes a clear distinction between the Exodus and the making of the covenant. Yet, to be precise, in all the passages under discussion here, the concept of "Exodus from Egypt" does include the wilderness period. This is the case as early as Exod 16:32, in connection with the manna: "In order that they may see the bread I fed you in the wilderness *when I brought you out of the land of Egypt*". The same is true of Deut 4:45-46: "These are the decrees, laws and rules that Moses addressed to the people of Israel, when they left Egypt, beyond the Jordan" etc., and especially of 1 Kgs 8:9: "There was nothing inside the Ark but the two tablets of stone which Moses placed there at Horeb, when the LORD made [a covenant] with the Israelites when they left Egypt". See also Rohland, *loc. cit.*

19 K. Galling, *Die Erwählungstraditionen Israels*, BZAW, 48 (1928), pp. 36-37: "In the sources, the Covenant at Sinai pales in the light of the Exodus. It is not an independent tradition for the Election, but is rather associated with the Exodus....it is, in the final analysis, not an act of salvation but an expression or confirmation of such; the act of salvation is the Exodus".

20 *Op. cit.* (Chapter One, note 3), pp. 13-26; 53-54.

proves that the Sinai episode is a late interpolation, since the Israelites were at Qadesh Barnea before arriving at Mount Sinai and are again said to have been at Qadesh Barnea after having left Sinai — Massah and Meribah[21] being identical, in his view, with the Waters of Meribah.[22] Von Rad explains away the existing account by boldly assuming that it was the Yahwist who first attached the originally independent Sinai episode to the Exodus story, and that this innovation was not accepted in wider circles until after the Babylonian Exile![23] Such a theory is highly questionable when considered in the light of von Rad's own version of the documentary hypothesis, according to which the Sinai episode occupies a place in all of the Pentateuchal sources — even E, which is universally agreed to be pre-exilic. A motif appearing in all of the narrative sources must necessarily be regarded as early.

Understandably, then, von Rad's followers found it necessary to modify his thesis and to posit an earlier date for the combination of

21 Exod 17:7.

22 Num 20:13.

23 Von Rad, like M. J. Bin-Gorion, *Sinai und Garizim*, Berlin 1926, dates the Shechem covenant earlier than the Sinaitic one. Believing the former to have been renewed annually on the festival of Sukkot, he proposes to view the covenant renewal ceremony as the source of the tradition concerning the Sinai episode. This conjecture is highly questionable even if we choose to ignore the lack of any evidence connecting the Sinai theophany with the Sukkot festival and the weak and doubtful character of the allusions which supposedly prove that the renewal of the covenant was in fact celebrated annually. Furthermore, even if we assume that such a festival was celebrated at some time in ancient Israel, we must ask: what covenant was thought to be the *original* covenant which was periodically re-made? The answer that it was the covenant made by Joshua is quite unsatisfactory, since the description of the Shechem covenant (and likewise that of the ceremony on Mount Gerizim and Mount Ebal) contains no mention of a theophany, which is the characteristic element of the Sinai tradition. Its absence from the tradition which ostensibly pertains to the original covenant enactment is inexplicable. Even if we were to allow further the arbitrary conjecture that the element of theophany was transferred from Shechem to Sinai at a later date, and that this was accomplished so thoroughly that no mention of it was left in the description of the original covenant at Shechem, we are still compelled to ask what caused this transference, a question which is unanswerable. The tradition which connects the making of the covenant with the Exodus cannot be assumed to be a late construction, nor can the history of Israel's tradition be reconstructed in a manner running counter to the uniform evidence of all the sources.

the two traditions. Thus, Noth[24] sees the fusion as stemming from "G" (in his view, the common Vorlage of J and E), while Kraus[25] suggests that the Sinai tradition, having originally been connected with the cult of the Shechem sanctuary, was transferred thence to the sanctuary at Gilgal, whose cult was originally associated solely with the Exodus tradition. Kraus assumes that this took place when the amphictyonic cult center was moved from Shechem to Gilgal. Yet, if it is conceded that the Sinaitic revelation was an integral part of the Exodus tradition as early as the period of the Judges, the essential difficulty in von Rad's theory reasserts itself, and again we have no way of accounting for the omission of the Sinaitic revelation from the didactic histories. Nor can we easily explain how a tradition which did not include the Sinaitic theophany came to be preserved in the account of Israel's wanderings in the wilderness.

Apparently the solution must be sought along other lines. Indeed, the Sinaitic Covenant occupies only a very minor part in passages devoted to rebuke; in particular, only one of the two sources quoted by von Rad — the book of Nehemiah — even mentions it, while the other — Psalm 106 — refers only to the Golden Calf made at Horeb. However, as stressed above,[26] sermons of rebuke select from the totality of Israel's traditions only those episodes which suit their rhetorical purpose. Now, the legalistic argument that the Israelite nation is bound to remain loyal to the LORD in respect of having assumed this as a covenantal obligation is not nearly as effective rhetorically as the historical argument that Israel is bound to keep the LORD's commandments because He manifested His love for Israel, and His might and power in the world, when he freed Israel from Egypt with signs and wonders. An example of this ancient rhetorical technique is provided in Psalm 78. Here, the psalmist expresses his repeated insistence upon Israel's duty to keep God's law by means of an historical survey, in which the absolute power of the Lawgiver is communicated

---

24 M. Noth, *Exodus*, trans. by J. S. Bowden, Philadelphia 1962, pp. 9ff. (= *Das zweite Buch Mose*, Göttingen 1959, pp. 5f.)

25 H.-J. Kraus, "Gilgal — Ein Beitrag zur Kultusgeschichte Israels", *VT*, 1 (1951), pp. 193f.

26 See above, p. 20.

through His deeds in history. There is no reference to the dry, legal argument that Israel should observe God's commandments because it had accepted them in a covenant which it had made with Him. The rationale for admonishing Israel to keep the LORD's commandments, the yoke of which they had recently cast off, is His powerful might as manifest in His acts, both loving and punitive, throughout Israel's history. The giving of the Law is not a powerful enough example either of God's lovingkindness or of His strength: not all the Israelites imbibed the words of the Law with the same thirst with which they drank up the waters from the rock in the wilderness! The salvation-history is reviewed in the didactic passages in an effort to inculcate faith in God and observance of His laws, arguing not from the nature of the laws themselves but rather from the attributes of the Lawgiver.

Only secondarily, and perhaps later, does the praise of the Law itself combine with this motif, in such a passage as Deut 4:8: "What great nation has laws and rules as perfect as all this Teaching that I set before you this day?". The earliest historiographical oration to emphasize the giving of the Law is Ezekiel 20, which is constructed entirely upon the idea that, though Israel has broken the LORD's statutes time after time, He has continually spared them for His name's sake.[27] This thought recurs throughout the chapter in monotonous repetition, and all mention of God's mighty deeds, so prominent in earlier passages, is absent. This scheme necessitates the use of a story according to which the Law was given in the wilderness, a story couched in Ezekiel's characteristic style of generalities which omit all superfluous detail:

> I brought them out of the land of Egypt and I led them into the wilderness. I gave them My laws and taught them My rules, by the pursuit of which a man shall live. Moreover, I gave them My sabbaths to serve as a sign between Me and them, that they might know that it is I the LORD who sanctify them.
>
> (Ezek 20:10-12)

A sort of fusion of this later type of sermonic technique with the ear-

27 See below, pp. 67-68.

lier kind, which glorified God's mighty deeds, is exhibited in the
lengthy oration of Nehemiah 9, which places the giving of the Law
at Sinai in general, and in particular the gift of the Sabbath, on the
same plane as God's mighty acts of deliverance:

> You led them by day with a pillar of cloud, and by night with
> a pillar of fire, to give them light in the way they were to go. You
> came down on Mount Sinai and spoke to them from heaven;
> You gave them right rules and true teachings, good laws and
> commandments. You made known to them Your holy sabbath,
> and You ordained for them laws, commandments and Teach-
> ing, through Moses Your servant. You gave them bread from
> heaven when they were hungry, and produced water from a rock
> when they were thirsty...
>
> (Neh 9:12-15)

The inclusion of the lawgiving, and the Sabbath, in a didactic
historiographical address is without parallel in the Bible. It recurs in
the Passover Haggadah: "If He had fed us manna and not given us
the Sabbath, that would have sufficed; if He had given us the Sabbath
and not brought us to Mount Sinai, that would have sufficed; if He
had brought us to Mount Sinai and not given us the Torah, that would
have sufficed; if He had given us the Torah and not brought us into
the land of Israel, that would have sufficed..." This hymn of praise
and gratitude concludes by mentioning the building of the Temple,
from which scholars have recently deduced that it must have been
composed before the destruction of the Second Temple.[28] Still,

---

28 On this and other questions raised by the poem "*Kammā Maʿălōt Tōbōt
(="Dayyēnū")* in the Passover Haggadah, see D. Goldschmidt, *Haggādā šel Pesaḥ
wĕTōlĕdōtehā*, Jerusalem 1960, pp. 48-51. This hymn is comprised of two parts,
parallel both in content and sequence, the first containing an enumeration of the
benefits bestowed upon Israel by God, in which each separate kindness is followed
by the refrain "It would have sufficed"; the second opening with the rhetorical
"How much more, then, must we praise Him since He..." and then merely
re-enumerating the same kindnesses in sequence. Goldschmidt maintains that the
two parts must be distinguished, since the shorter (second) version is stylistically
simple, whereas the longer (first) version is illogical, occasionally running counter
to common sense (e.g. "If he had divided the Sea for us and not brought us through
it on dry land, it would have sufficed"). Hence Goldschmidt concludes that the

despite the thematic similarity, the Passover hymn was not derived from Nehemiah's oration. Not only is its style completely different; its content too speaks for its independence. Nehemiah begins with Creation and the lives of the Patriarchs (9:6-8) and concludes with a reference to the Conquest (v. 15), whereas the Passover hymn embraces the period from the Exodus to the building of the Temple. Furthermore, the divine cloud and pillar of fire, which Nehemiah treats at length (v. 12), are entirely absent from the hymn. The two selections are thus two literarily independent expressions of a characteristic Second Temple outlook. At the time that they were composed, it would have been unthinkable to enumerate the benefits conferred by the LORD upon Israel's ancestors and to omit just those events which continued to confer blessing upon Israel in the present, namely, the giving of the Law and the Sabbath. As will become apparent, after the destruction of the Temple the book of 4 Ezra went to even greater lengths in the same direction, and in words reminiscent of Ezekiel, who reflected the spirit of the similar period following the destruction of the First Temple, emphasized only the giving of the Law.

The didactic passages, as shown by the foregoing survey of their development, cannot therefore be adduced in support of the theory denying the original connection between the Exodus episode and the Sinai theophany tradition.

Nor can decisive importance be attributed to the order of these episodes as they occur in the Pentateuch, which gives the impression that

shorter form antedates the longer one and that the combination of the two versions is the work of a redactor. His argument is not entirely compelling, even if we accept his basic premise, since it could be maintained that the longer, illogical version is the earlier text and that a later redactor found it necessary to compose a simpler version. In any case it is preferable to assume that the two parts of the hymn were written at one time; the first pauses between the successive acts of kindness in order to glorify each one separately, while the second enumerates them in succession so as to stress their great number. The pattern itself should not be called into question since it is entirely appropriate to a popular hymn of praise; indeed, part of what appears illogical in the first half of the hymn is due to the very existence of the pattern, the purpose of which is to mark off each single event. But the general idea conveyed by the pattern, that one must be thankful for each and every one of God's bounties, is straightforward and logical enough, and this is all that the reader perceives in it.

the encampment at Qadesh Barnea preceded the arrival at Mount Sinai, as it is highly probable that the precise order was fixed only at a very late date. The admittedly late Psalm 106, unlike the Pentateuch, places the Dathan and Abiram episode before that of the Golden Calf at Horeb, and contains no reference to Massah and Meribah (Exod 17:1-7). The Psalm mentions only the "Waters of Meribah" (Num 20:2-13), here following the Pentateuchal order and placing the episode after the Calf story. Most probably, as held by several scholars, the events of Massah and Meribah and those of the Waters of Meribah are two versions of the same event, from which it follows that the final redaction of the Pentateuch placed one of these episodes before the Sinai pericope and one thereafter, in order to allow an interval between two events so strikingly similar. Such redactional details need not call into question the original association between the Exodus and the Sinai theophany.

Attempts to differentiate between the origin of the Exodus tradition and that of the Sinai tradition utterly fail to convince. The purpose of the Covenant made at Sinai was the legal concretization of that relationship between the LORD and His people which had in fact existed since the Exodus. The close parallel existing between the Decalogue Covenant and the treaties made by the Hittite kings with their vassals, so aptly seen by Mendenhall[29] and Beyerlin,[30] makes this all the more apparent, since the Hittite treaties too include an historical preamble which set forth the development of the relationship between the two parties which had led to the making of the treaty and in which the Great King demanded, in clear apodictic terms, that the vassal be subject to him alone.

29 G. E. Mendenhall, "Covenant Forms in Israelite Tradition" (1950), in: *The Biblical Archeologist Reader*, 3, Garden City, NY 1970, pp. 25-53.

30 W. Beyerlin, *The Origins and History of the Oldest Sinai Traditions*, trans. by S. Rudman, Oxford 1961, pp. 49-67 (= *Herkunft und Geschichte der ältesten Sinaitraditionen*, Tübingen 1961, pp. 60-78).

C. The Exodus and the Conquest

The fact that the Exodus from Egypt and the Conquest of Canaan do not seem to have had equal importance attached to them, since the former occupies the central position in the Pentateuch while the latter was not deemed worthy of inclusion in the Pentateuch at all, is another matter entirely. On this point too, scholars have become so perplexed that they have come up with a hypothesis which questions the authenticity of ancient Israel's own tradition, and have proposed exchanging the view that the Pentateuch is a literary unit for the concept of the Hexateuch. This theory, in its original form, maintained that the very same sources which go to make up the Pentateuch are found in the book of Joshua as well, and, this being so, the separation of the latter from the former is quite artificial, and nothing could be simpler than to restore the book of Joshua to its rightful place. The Hexateuch hypothesis thus endeavored to "re-attach" the book of Joshua to the books of the Pentateuch, whence it had ostensibly been severed at some late period.

Support for this optimistic approach,[31] however, has for some time now been eroding. As early as Wellhausen[32] the view that the book of Joshua *in its present form* is actually part of the Pentateuch was denied in favor of the more moderate conjecture that only at a stage which preceded the redaction of the biblical books was the story of the Conquest regarded as a part of Israel's prehistory but not thereafter; this view was later accepted by Noth[33] as authoritative. But neither the proponents of the extreme view nor those of the more moderate theory have explained what factors could have caused the

---

31 See, for example, F. Bleek, *Einleitung in das Alte Testament,*[3] Berlin 1870, pp. 125ff. A survey of earlier adherents of this view may be found in K. F. Keil, *Manual of Historical-Critical Introduction to the Canonical Scriptures of the Old Testament,* I, trans. G. C. M. Douglas, Grand Rapids 1952, pp. 203f.

32 J. Wellhausen, *Die Composition des Hexateuchs und der historischen Bücher des alten Testaments,* Berlin 1899, pp. 116f.

33 M. Noth, *Das Buch Josua,*[2] Tübingen 1953, p. 16: "Thus, on the basis of the literary evidence found in the book of Joshua, the continuation of any of the ancient Pentateuchal 'sources' in this book must be denied...the question of what may have become of the early account of the Conquest, in which the Pentateuchal sources did reach their conclusion...is another matter entirely".

account of the Conquest to be detached from the Pentateuch, especially in view of the far-reaching effect this amputation had upon the Samaritan community, which accepted only the Pentateuch. Furthermore, neither theory takes into account that the death of Moses is the only fitting conclusion to the Pentateuchal narrative, in which he, the greatest of the prophets, occupies the most prominent place.

The notion of the Hexateuch also fails to pay any regard to the fact that, as a rule, the didactic texts which review the early history of Israel make reference to identifiable passages in the Torah while they describe the period of the Conquest only in general terms. In not one such text does the name Joshua appear, and even allusions to events recounted in the book of Joshua are extremely rare. Moreover, such infrequent allusions are not independent elements in the text but are rather appended, in brief and non-specific terms, by a process of association, to episodes which appear in the Pentateuch. In this category we would include the passages in Psalms in which the parting of the sea appears in poetic parallelism with the division of the Jordan (Pss 66:6; 114:3,5). In most of the didactic histories, of course, only the parting of the sea is mentioned, and this event occupies considerably more space in these passages than the division of the Jordan.[34] Two further cases are the two hortatory passages in which reference to the victories over Sihon and Og — a theme well-attested in the Pentateuch — is followed by a general mention of victories over all the Canaanite kings (Ps 135:11; Neh 9:24); the point is clearer still in Psalm 136, where mention of the two Transjordanian kings alone is apparently sufficient. The only oration which makes specific mention of one of Joshua's victories is that delivered by Joshua himself, in which he recalls the conquest of Jericho (Josh 24:11), and it is only natural that Joshua's own valedictory address could not pass over all his personal achievements. This single exception, then, only serves to confirm the rule: passages from the book of Joshua describing the Conquest made only a minute contribution to the formation of the didactic tradition; this tradition, as a rule, reviews exclusively those events which are contained in the Pentateuchal account.

34 See below, pp. 236-254.

It is further evident that these meager contributions cannot be regarded as part of the nucleus from which the didactic tradition arose. Hence the inescapable conclusion, that only the bare fact of the Conquest, and not a detailed account of the Conquest, belongs to the nucleus of Israel's tradition, to which scholars have given the name *Heilsgeschichte*. This distinction is entirely to be expected: though the Conquest was, on the one hand, the basis for the history of the nation, it was not, on the other hand, completed until the time of David. The fact that this complex process was so protracted in time prevented it from being included in the Pentateuch, which describes the prehistory of Israel as the realization of a pre-ordained divine plan. Thus, the focal point of Israel's national tradition, which, as has been obvious all along, could not possibly be the patriarchal narratives, since they are no more than a kind of prologue to the history of the LORD's people, and, as is now clear, cannot be sought in the Conquest of Canaan, is none other than the Exodus tradition itself.

D. The Exodus and the Davidic Period

The fact that Israel did not complete the process of conquest and taking possession of Canaan until the monarchic period may also serve to explain the tendency to append the establishment of the Davidic monarchy to the sacred history and even to associate it with the Exodus episode itself. This tendency, to be sure, encountered certain obvious difficulties. The span of time intervening between the Exodus and the United Monarchy prevented the latter from being inserted in the Pentateuch, particularly as this episode was bathed in the clear light of history and was never deemed worthy of being expressed in the same legendary, theological terms in which the Exodus was celebrated.

All this notwithstanding, the monarchic period did serve as a basis for the belief in the perpetuity of the House of David and of the Zion Temple; it came to be regarded as the culmination of Israel's salvation, the beginning of which was rooted in the Exodus. When Nathan the prophet came to David with the message that Israel would enjoy tranquility in its land and that the House of David would endure forever, David reacted with words of praise which include his gratitude to God who "went to redeem His people, winning Himself renown and doing great and marvelous deeds..." (2 Sam 7:23). This view of events is the basis of Psalm 78, which opens its description of Israel's history with the Exodus from Egypt and concludes it with the election of the Davidic dynasty and the building of the Zion Temple. And whereas in Psalm 78 we find between these two terminal points a lengthy description of the intervening vicissitudes, even this does not appear in the Song at the Sea which, in brief, hymnic style, depicts as a continuous, uninterrupted process the parting of the sea, the conquest of the entire land of Canaan, the "planting" of Israel in its land, and the building of the Temple (Exod 15:8-17).

These two themes, the Exodus and the Zion tradition, are combined in a different manner in Isaiah's oracle, which begins with reference to the Davidic dynasty ("A shoot shall grow out of the stump of Jesse, a twig shall sprout from his stock", Isa 11:1) and concludes with:

> The LORD will dry up the tongue of the Egyptian sea; He will raise His hand over the Euphrates with the might of His wind and break it into seven wadis, so that it can be trodden dry-shod. There shall be a highway for the other part of His people out of Assyria, such as there was for Israel when it left the land of Egypt.
>
> (vv. 15-16)

Here it is the belief in the perpetuity of the Davidic dynasty that occupies the leading position; it is paralleled by the prophet's belief in the future glory of the Zion Temple (Isa 2:1-4). But the return of the exiles, which is to occur in the time of an eventual scion of David, is described here in a manner patterned upon the Exodus from Egypt, the very mention of which serves to strengthen faith in the final deliverance.

The same juxtaposition may be seen in Jeremiah 23. Here, at least according to the Masoretic Text,[35] the statement that the LORD will

---

35 The LXX places verses 7-8 of Jer 23 at the end of the chapter, after verse 40 of MT. See also Jer 16:14-15.

"raise up a true branch of David's line" in whose days Israel will be delivered (v. 5) is followed by the words

> Assuredly, a time is coming — declares the LORD — when it shall no more be said, "As the LORD lives, who brought the Israelites out of the land of Egypt", but rather "As the LORD lives, who brought out and led the offspring of the House of Israel from the northland and from all the lands to which I have banished them", and they shall dwell upon their own soil.
>
> (vv. 7-8)

Jeremiah's meaning is clear: the future redemption which the LORD will bring about for Israel through the agency of a descendant of David will be a greater event than the Exodus from Egypt.

The questions we have been addressing in this chapter are most instructively illustrated in a hortatory passages contained in the book of 4 Ezra. The passage (2:13-34) opens with a review of the history of Israel, beginning with the covenant with Abraham but omitting all mention of the Promised Land motif, after which it briefly narrates the stories of the patriarchs and the descent into Egypt. It refers to the Exodus in the briefest terms, and all this is a prelude to the glowing description of the Lawgiving at Sinai, from which, omitting all reference to the Conquest, the text proceeds directly to the divine command to David to build the Temple, thence to the Temple's destruction (which was caused by Israel's sins), and finally to a prayer that God weigh Israel's sins against those of the other nations. The ancient motif, namely, the glorification of the LORD's mighty deeds and His acts of lovingkindness, has been set aside; the focus of the entire passage is God's commandments. The Exodus is overshadowed by Sinai; the Conquest gives way to the theme of David, and the latter consists solely of reference to the building of the Temple. All the emphasis is placed on the theme of Israel's destruction and the hopes of its restoration.

PSALM 81 — A DECREE UPON JOSEPH*

The account of Israel's departure from Egypt in the book of Exodus occupies a central position in the pre-history of the Israelite people. Nevertheless, despite the strenuous effort expended in the scholarly attempt to investigate the historical background of the biblical account, no consensus has been reached. Each scholar maintains his own theory, adducing his own evidence to contradict that of his opponent, and the authenticity of every single piece of evidence has been called into question.[1] Without going into the various arguments, we would agree with the majority of modern scholars who view as reliable the biblical report that Israelite corvée-laborers were employed in the construction of the Egyptian cities of Pithom and Raamses (Exod 1:11), and who conclude from this report that the story of Israel's enslavement refers to the reign of Ramses II.[2] This first king of the Eighteenth Dynasty was engaged in the construction of cities in the area of the Nile delta, approximately where the Hebrews are

---

* This Excursus was originally published in the B. Mazar Volume, *Eretz-Israel*, 5 (1958), pp. 80-82. The version reprinted in the Hebrew edition of the present volume (pp. 164-168) unfortunately contains numerous typographical errors. The translation has been made from the original.

1 See the comprehensive survey in H. H. Rowley, *From Joseph to Joshua*, London 1950, as well as: R. de Vaux in *RB*, 58 (1951), pp. 278ff.; M. Noth in *VT*, 1 (1951), pp. 74ff.; E. Drioton in *Revue d'Histoire et de Philosophie Religieuses*, 35 (1955), pp. 36ff.; M. B. Rowton in *PEQ*, 85 (1953), pp. 46ff.; H. H. Rowley in *Orientalia Suecana*, 4 (1955), pp. 77f. Detailed evaluation of the different approaches may be found in Loewenstamm, *op. cit.* (Chapter One, note 1), pp. 756-758.

2 Evidently 1224-1290 B.C.E.; see M. B. Rowton in *Journal of Egyptian Archeology*, 34 (1948), pp. 57ff.

reported to have settled, and in particular the city of Pe-Raamses ("House of Ramses").[3]

This important piece of knowledge, however, does not provide a solution to all of the historical problems. In particular, no answer is forthcoming to the question whether the tribes of Joseph were enslaved along with the others or whether, as proposed by Albright, they left Egypt before Ramses II took the throne. While Albright assigns the biblical account of the Exodus to the reign of this Pharaoh, he dates the departure of the Joseph tribes at c. 1400 B.C.E. This proposal is based in part on the account of the conquest of Shechem, reported to have taken place in the time of Jacob (Gen 34 and 48:22) and viewed by Albright as evidence for early Josephite conquests, and in part on the brief notice in Chronicles of Ephraim's mourning for his sons who had been killed by the men of Gath (1 Chr 7:21-24), which Albright takes as proof that the Ephraimites had fought in Canaan during Ephraim's own lifetime.[4] Along the same lines, Mazar writes that "the archeological evidence from Jericho allows us to postulate that the city was destroyed in the middle third of the fourteenth century, and that this was none other than one link in the chain of campaigns and conquests made by the tribes of Joseph (Rachelite group) who penetrated from southern Transjordan to the steppes of Moab (Gen 33:41-49)".[5]

Both of these proposals share in common the idea that events

---

3 Since the city was called Pe-Raamses for only about two centuries, the biblical report cannot be dismissed as anachronistic; see W. F. Albright, *From the Stone Age to Christianity*, Baltimore 1946, p. 194. A. H. Gardiner has collected the pertinent documentary evidence; see *Journal of Egyptian Archeology*, 5 (1918), pp. 179ff., 242ff. On whether Pe-Raamses should be identified with Tanis, or with Qantir which is situated about 20 km. to the south, see idem, *Ancient Egyptian Onomastica*, Oxford 1947, pp. 171ff., 278f.; P. Montet, *Les énigmes de Tanis*, Paris 1952, pp. 101ff.; B. Courvoyer in *RB*, 60 (1953), pp. 111ff.

4 W. F. Albright in *BASOR*, 35 (1929), p. 6; 58 (1935), pp. 10f.; 74 (1939), pp. 11ff.

5 B. Mazar, s.v. "ʾereṣ yiśrāʾel" in *ʾEnṣiqlōpedīā Miqrāʾīt*, I, Jerusalem 1950, p. 694. See also idem, s.v. "bĕmidbar pereq l"g" in II, Jerusalem 1954, pp. 144f.; cf. Rowton, *op. cit.* (above, note 2), who contends that the Josephites left Egypt during the thirteenth century B.C.E. and that they were treated amicably throughout their sojourn there as well as at the time of their departure. This, he argues, is in contrast to the Levites, who left Egypt in the twelfth century after encountering severe hostility.

which involved only a portion of the Israelites were eventually transformed into a legendary framework for the entire people's history. Nevertheless, though it is theoretically possible that a tale of limited scope might expand into a national legend, no decisive conclusion should be reached before it is determined whether the tribes of Joseph are considered to be included among the Israelite tribes only in the Pentateuch, or whether outside of the Pentateuch as well there exists independent evidence that they were so regarded. The historicity of such evidence, even if it can be found, would certainly be subject to critical scrutiny, but it will still be of some weight in the final analysis.

The following discussion is an attempt to establish that at least one such piece of evidence exists, namely Psalm 81. This psalm, it will be argued, reflects the Josephite tribes' own tradition of their enslavement in Egypt. Such an evaluation is in direct opposition to the prevailing dating of the psalm, which places its composition after Deuteronomy and Jeremiah.[6] The accepted view rests upon the assumption that v. 17 "He fed him the finest of wheat; I sated you with honey from the rock" is a quotation from Deut 32:13-14 "He fed him honey from the crag, and oil from the flinty rock, curd of kine and milk of flocks; with best of lambs etc.", and that v. 14 "If only My people would listen to Me, if Israel would follow My paths" is but a reformulation of Jer 7:24 "they followed their own counsels, the willfulness of their evil hearts". On this basis the psalm has been assigned to the end of the First Temple period, or even to the end of the Persian period. However, this entire method of searching for stylistic influences of one passage on another has been undermined by the discovery of the Ugaritic texts, which reveal the antiquity of the literary tradition reflected in the Bible.[7] Further, even if we were to admit that in this particular case literary influence remains a possibility, we would have no a priori way of knowing which text influenced

---

6 Z. P. Chayes, *Pērūš ῾al Sēfer Tēhillim*, Kiev 1908, pp. 178ff.; C. H. Briggs, *Psalms*, ICC, Edinburgh 1902, pp. 209ff.; F. Bäthgen, *Die Psalmen*, Göttingen 1904, pp. 253f.; K. Kittel, *Die Psalmen*, Leipzig — Erlangen 1922, pp. 271ff.; A. Bertholet, *Die Heilige Schrift des Alten Testaments*, II, Tübingen 1923, p. 210; H. Herkenne, *Das Buch der Psalmen*, Bonn 1936, pp. 277ff.
7 U. Cassuto, *The Goddess Anath*, trans. by I. Abrahams, Jerusalem 1971, p. 41.

which. Conclusions concerning the relationship of Psalm 81 to the Pentateuch can be reached only after the entire psalm has been thoroughly analyzed.

The psalmist opens with a call, couched in first person, to celebrate a festival (vv. 1-2b), and continues with a divine speech of rebuke which recalls past acts of deliverance (vv. 2c-17). The psalmist, it would thus appear, has followed the prophetic tradition of arraigning Israel on festive occasions (Amos 5:21ff.; Isa 1:10ff.; 28:7ff; 29:1ff.) and accompanying rebuke with the recollection of past events[8] (Amos 2:9ff.; Hos 11:1ff.; Jer 2:1ff.; Mic 6:3ff.; Ezek 16:1ff.; cf. Deut 32).

From the opening verses, in which the psalmist's first-person address to his people alludes to an existing tradition of observing the present festival, the psalm's antiquity is apparent:

> For it is a law for Israel,
>   a ruling of the God of Jacob;
> He imposed it as a decree upon Joseph
>   when He went forth against the land of Egypt
>
> (vv. 5-6)

Most exegetes infer nothing at all from the word "Joseph" here, viewing it as no more than a poetic parallel to "Jacob". Gunkel, however, has noted that such a usage is inconceivable in any other than a Northern setting.[9] It was the northern tribes which regarded Joseph as the core of Israel and the other tribes as his inferiors; just as in the territory of Judah — and specifically there — the name "Judah" could appear as a synonym of "Israel" (Pss 76:2; 114:2). This is indisputable evidence for the psalm's early date, since, in view of the constant struggle between Judah and Joseph, it cannot be imagined that a Judahite poet would ever refer to the Israelite people in general by the name "Joseph", neither during the time of the divided monarchy,

---

8 H. Gunkel, *Die Psalmen*, Göttingen 1926, pp. 353ff.

9 *Ibid.*; Likewise H. Schmidt, *Die Psalmen*, Tübingen 1934, pp. 154f.; cf. B. D. Eerdmanns, *Psalms*, Leiden 1949, pp. 390ff. and also O. Eissfeldt, "Psalm 80", in: W. F. Albright, *et al.* (eds.), *Geschichte und Altes Testament — A. Alt zum 70. Geburtstag*, Tübingen 1953, pp. 48ff, who conducts a similar investigation of questions arising from Psalm 80.

nor after the destruction of the Northern Kingdom, when Joseph had ceased to be of any significance whatsoever. The psalm must therefore have been composed in the North, before the fall of Samaria, and it would seem to have preserved a tradition which was current among the Josephite tribes.

The unsuccessful attempts at identifying the festival referred to in the opening verses of the psalm with one of the Pentateuchal festivals attest to the independent nature of this Josephite tradition. No explanation of the words "Blow the horn on the new moon, on the *kese* for our feast day" (v. 4) brings them into accord with the Pentateuch. The traditional interpretation that they refer to the New Year (since this is a "feast day" on which the moon is "covered" [*mitkasse*])[10] does not explain what the New Year has to do with the departure from Egypt, whereas the text states explicitly: "It is a law for Israel, a ruling of the God of Jacob; He imposed it as a decree upon Joseph when He went forth against[11] the land of Egypt" (vv. 5-6), that is, the God of Jacob ordained this festival in commemoration of the occasion on which He went forth against Egypt to deliver His people. The Rabbis, aware of this difficulty in their interpretation, explained it away variously.[12] Even less in accord with the Pentateuch is the interpretation

10 This tradition is evidently reflected in the LXX as well: ἐν εὐσήμῳ ἡμέρᾳ ἑορτῆς ἡμῶν "in the propitious day of our festival". Similarly, the Talmudic interpretation of Prov 7:20 "'He will return at the *kese*ᵓ: The *kese*ᵓ is a time, as in 'on the *kese* for our feast day'" (b. Sanh. 96b); Tg. Jonathan at Prov 7:20 also renders *kese*ᵓ with ᶜēdā "time". The rabbinic attempt to provide a linguistic basis for the connection between *kese* and the New Year is apparently a later stage: "On which feast day is the moon covered (*mitkasse*)? On New Year's day" (b. Roš Haš. 8a-b; Beṣa 16a; Sanh. 11b); Tg. Jonathan to our psalm, *bĕyarḥā dĕmitkasse* "at the covered moon", is derived from this.
11 The LXX translates ἐκ γῆς Αἰγύπτου "*from* the land of Egypt", making Joseph the subject of the clause. In light of the fact that the psalm goes on to speak of God's beneficent acts, MT is preferable.
12 "...On New Year's day Joseph was freed from prison...on New Year's day our fathers' labors in Egypt ceased...in Nisan they were redeemed...but the future redemption will be in Tishre...R. Joshua says, in Nisan they were redeemed and the future redemption too will be in Nisan" (b. Roš Haš. 11a-b). The first of these statements is certainly based on the notion that the subject of "went forth against the land of Egypt" is Joseph. The second statement, though it is a bit unclear, at any rate conveys the idea that the New Year is somehow associated with the Exodus. However, no historical weight should be attached to these interpretations, as they are merely attempts at explaining away a problematic text.

found in the versions of Aquila and Symmachus, where *kese* in v. 4 is taken to mean "full moon":[13] "Blow at each new moon; [sound] the horn at the full moon on your feast-day".[14]

Nor have modern critics, who also take *kese* to mean "full moon", arrived at any persuasive explanation of the verse. Schmidt maintains that there is simply an internal contradiction in the psalm, between the observance of a festival at the new moon and its observance at the full moon.[15] Most critics adhere to the view that all of the holy days observed in the seventh month comprised one long festival, extending from the New Year through the feast of Tabernacles, and that, since the latter feast is explained in the Pentateuch as a reminder of the wanderings in the wilderness (Lev 23:43), it is indirectly connected with the departure from Egypt. The main problem with this theory is that the psalm seems to allude to a festival in which the actual Exodus was explicitly commemorated. Further, the Pentateuchal legislation distinguishes quite clearly between the New Year, the Day of Atonement, and the feast of Tabernacles, and does not represent them as points along a continuous festival season extending from the new moon to mid-month. The latter point is what impelled Herkenne to interpret the words "Blow the horn on the new moon" in v. 4 to mean "Blow the horn in the seventh month, which is the month of the horn",[16] implying that the horn is to be blown only on Tabernacles. Tur-Sinai, on the other hand, believes that the horn is sounded on the New Year but is intended to proclaim the advent of Tabernacles. Maintaining that *kese* can refer only to the fifteenth of the month, the day on which the Tabernacles festival occurs, he reads the verse as follows: "Blow the horn on the new moon, *in advance of the approaching festival which occurs* on the full moon for our feast day".[17]

---

13 In accord with Syr. *ksꜣꜣ* "full moon"; see Peshitta to 1 Kgs 12:32 where "on the fifteenth day of the month" is translated *bksꜣꜣ bh byrḥꜣ*; the same appears in the Peshitta to our verse. See N. H. Tur-Sinai, *HaLāšōn WĕhaSēfer*, III, Jerusalem 1956, p. 24.

14 ἠχήσατε ἐν παση νεομηνίᾳ χερατίνη ἐν πανσαλήνῳ ἐν ἠφέρᾳ ἑορτῆς ὑμῶν,

15 *Loc. cit.* (above, note 9).

16 *Loc. cit.* (above, note 6).

17 *Op. cit.* (above, note 13), II, Jerusalem 1951, p. 24.

In all this confusion it has even been suggested that the festival referred to in the psalm is the Pesah-feast, since its connection with the Exodus is apparent. Yet this proposal effectively removes all possibility of advancing the harmonistic conjecture that the festival extended from the beginning to the middle of the month. In sum, there is no way of reasonably reconciling the festival in the psalm with the Pentateuch. Its author must have made use of an extra-Pentateuchal tradition; perhaps, as suggested by Gunkel, a uniquely northern Israelite festival tradition.[18]

Following the brief mention of the acts of deliverance performed by the LORD "when He went forth against the land of Egypt" (v. 6), the psalm enumerates a few specific acts which obligate future generations to believe and trust in the LORD. These require close examination and comparison with the Pentateuchal account. In its most general formulation, the psalm states "I am the LORD your God who brought you up from the land of Egypt" (v. 11). This statement corresponds to the Pentateuchal tradition both linguistically and substantively (Gen 50:24; Exod 3:8,17; Lev 11:45; Num 14:13; Deut 20:1). More detailed is the description of the redemption from Egypt: "I relieved his shoulder of the burden, his hands were freed from the basket" (v. 7), and here too we are reminded of verses in the book of Exodus which speak of the "burdens" of the enslaved Israelites (Exod 1:11; 2:11; 5:4,5; 6:6,7). Yet the reference here is remarkably graphic, and its intent has become clear in light of Egyptian illustrations depicting the various stages of the manufacture of bricks, which show, among other things, a laborer bearing upon his shoulders a receptacle heaped with wet clay, while his hands grasp it from above.[19]

The beginning of v. 8, "In distress you called out and I rescued you; I answered you from the secret place of thunder", is obscure. Rashi regards this too as a reference to the Exodus, in which case it must allude to some tradition unattested in the Pentateuch, since the Pen-

18 *Loc. cit.* (above, note 8).
19 See the drawings in the *ʾEnṣīqlōpedīā Miqrāʾīt*, II, Jerusalem 1954, p. 152; G. E. Wright (ed.), *The Westminster Historical Atlas to the Bible*, Philadelphia 1945, p. 37.

tateuch nowhere speaks of God responding in thunder to the cries of the Israelites in Egypt. Most modern critics, however, agree with Ibn Ezra, holding that the psalmist is speaking of the pillar of fire and cloud which led the Israelites through the desert, and adding that the reference is particularly to the role played by the cloud at the parting of the sea (Exod 14:19,20). Even according to this harmonistic view, however, the theophany in the psalm remains quite an independent tradition, since Exodus 14 makes no mention of thunder. In fact, the only portion of v. 8 which can easily be associated with the Pentateuchal account is the last line "I tested you at the waters of Meribah", and even this deviates radically from the Pentateuch, since in the Pentateuch it is the Israelites who test the LORD[20] (Exod 17:1-7; Num 20:1-13; cf. Pss 95:8,9; 106:32). This divergence from the Pentateuch adds even more weight to our contention that the tradition employed by the psalmist is indeed an independent one.

To recapitulate the results of our investigation, we have seen that Psalm 81 reflects an Exodus tradition which was current among the Josephites. Although this tradition is independent of the Pentateuch,

---

20 It should be remarked that the manna episode too is twice presented as a "test", once as a trial by which God tested Israel and once as an occasion on which the people tried their God. Deuteronomy says that God "fed you manna in the wilderness...in order to test you by hardships only to benefit you in the end" (Deut 8:16). Psalm 78, on the other hand, speaks of a period in which Israel tested God by questioning His ability to feed His people in the wilderness, and relates that God both "passed" the test, by providing ample food, and punished those who tested Him for their lack of trust (vv. 17-28). Both of these sermonic motifs originate in the crisis of faith which occurs when men are beset by some misfortune. Such a crisis is often presented as a "trial" of God. God, of course, always "passes" the test, and occasionally He also punishes the doubters; the didactic aim of such a motif is obvious. Another response to such declines in Israel's faith in God is the belief that present suffering has in fact been brought about by God Himself, "to test them and to benefit them in the end". The words "I tested you at the waters of Meribah" in this verse imply just that: I afflicted you with hardship in order to test you and to benefit you in the end. The memories of such hardships would be adduced by the poet in a time of oppression (v. 15), when the faith of many has been strained almost to the point of apostasy (v. 10). The psalmist intimates to his listeners that their present suffering, which has come about due to their "willful hearts" (vv. 12, 13) is none other than a divine test, and that if only they would listen to Him and follow His paths (v. 14), He will once again deliver them (vv. 14, 15) and satiate them abundantly (v. 17).

differing from it even in a few specifics which affect the theological assessment of events, the divergences do not detract from the basic unity of the historical-religious viewpoint common to the Pentateuch and the psalm. Both maintain that the Josephites were forced to work with mortar and bricks, that they were brought up from Egypt by the LORD, and that during their journey they encamped at Meribah where they were beset by a serious crisis. The scholar is now free to decide whether he chooses to attach historical reliability to the tradition reflected in the psalm, or whether he would prefer to view it as influenced by the traditions of other tribes and to hold that it was actually they who experienced the events described. In either case, he may not disregard it in the final analysis of the evidence for the Israelite departure from Egypt. For even if it is decided that the tradition we have examined here is historically unreliable, its value for tracing the evolution of the historical consciousness which shaped the Pentateuchal account of the Exodus cannot be denied.

CHAPTER THREE

THE EXODUS AS A DIDACTIC MOTIF IN THE BIBLE

We referred above to Jeremiah's prediction that the words "As the LORD lives, who brought the Israelites out of the land of Egypt" will no longer be spoken (Jer 23:7).[1] It can safely be assumed that the prophet was alluding to an oath-formula current among his contemporaries, and the formula itself indicates that the Exodus was an article of belief which found expression in everyday speech. The Bible actually emphasizes this tenet not only when speaking of the Exodus itself; it interpolates the Exodus theme in the historiography of subsequent periods as well. In this manner, for instance, the story of the quails served, among other purposes, to impart the lesson that Moses and Aaron had not brought Israel out of Egypt on their own initiative and that the real Redeemer was the LORD Himself (Exod 16:6). The same belief is manifest, though from a different point of view, in the story of the Golden Calf in Exodus (32:4) and in the account of Jeroboam's calves in 1 Kings (12:28). The calf-worshippers' cry: "These are your gods, O Israel, who brought you out of the land of Egypt!" is based on the assumption that the deliverance from Egypt was indeed a divine act and that, by performing it, the deity who did so had become Israel's god. The sin of the calf-worshippers was thus that they had declared this god of Israel to be the calf. The same theme recurs in God's command to Moses to build the Tabernacle: "And they shall know that I the LORD am their God, who brought them up out of the land of Egypt that I might abide among them" (Exod 29:46).

Decisive proof of the LORD's mighty deeds was provided in state-

1 See above p. 43.

ments which the historiographical literature attributes to non-Israelites, who express their admiration for God's might as manifested in the Exodus from Egypt. For example, the words of Jethro: "Blessed be the LORD who delivered you from the hand of the Egyptians and from Pharaoh, and who delivered the people from under the hand of the Egyptians. Now I know that the LORD is greater than all gods, yes, by what they schemed against them" (Exod 18:10-11). The powerful effect of God's might is even more forcibly conveyed in the words of Balaam, who is reluctantly compelled to glorify the LORD: "God, who freed them from Israel, is for them like the horns of the wild ox. They shall devour enemy nations, crush their bones and smash their loins.[2] They crouch, they lie down like a lion, like the king of beasts; who dare rouse them?" (Num 24:8-9). In the same manner the Gibeonites, when they explain their arrival to Joshua, do not begin by mentioning what the LORD did to Sihon king of the Amorites and Og king of Bashan; they precede all this by mentioning the fact that they had heard of what God had done to the Egyptians (Josh 9:9). The same is true of Rahab the harlot, who accounts for the dread fear which has taken hold of the Canaanites by stating first: "for we have heard how the LORD dried up the waters of the Sea of Reeds for you when you left Egypt" and only afterwards "and what you did to Sihon and Og" etc. (Josh 2:10), though, to be sure, since this passage immediately precedes the story of the division of the Jordan, it places special stress on the parting of the sea rather than simply mentioning the Exodus from Egypt in general terms.

Even more remarkable is the impression which God's mighty deeds are reported to have made upon the Philistines, who exclaim: "Woe to us! Who will save us from the power of these mighty gods? These are the gods who struck the Egyptians with every kind of plague in the wilderness!" (1 Sam 4:8). Even though the final "in the wilderness" is unintelligible and probably a corruption,[3] there can be no

---

2 Reading *hlṣyw* for MT *hṣyw* "his arrows"; see Peshitta.

3 LXX has "and in the wilderness"; similarly the commentary of Isaiah of Trani, ed. A. Wertheimer, Jerusalem 1959 ("a *wāw* is missing; the meaning is 'and in the wilderness'"). This explanation, however, is forced; some emend MT *bmdbr* to read *bdbr* "with pestilence".

doubt about the general sense of these words: that the same mighty gods who smote the Egyptians are liable to strike the Philistines.

These feelings of awe and amazement which are attributed to non-Israelites are expressed by Israelites as well, in those hymns of praise and thanksgiving which include the sermonic enumeration of the LORD's mighty acts. Such is the case in Psalm 136, where the mention of God's deeds in Creation (vv. 5-9) is followed immediately by mention of His deeds at the time of the Exodus (vv. 10-19). A similar structure can be observed in Psalm 135, which begins by glorifying the LORD's activity in nature (vv. 5-7) and continues immediately with the signs and wonders which He brought upon Egypt (vv. 8-9). Even in Psalm 105, though its hymnodic character is somewhat weakened by its extremely detailed, sermonic nature, what stands out is the signs and wonders brought upon Egypt. This is so despite the lengthy recapitulation of Israel's history, extending from the period of the Patriarchs to the Conquest of Canaan. And as in hymns, so too in prayers of thanksgiving: grateful mention is made of the Exodus, such as that made by David upon hearing the prophet Nathan's oracular promise that his dynasty would endure forever (2 Sam 7:23). This is of course also true of those didactic prayers which include some kind of survey of Israel's history, such as the prayers of Jeremiah (32:20-21) and Nehemiah (9:2-10).

Most often, however, the Exodus from Egypt is employed in passages of rebuke. These can take many forms, but two basic types can be discerned: those which argue that the deliverance which the LORD granted His people when He brought them out of Egypt imposes upon them an obligation to keep faith with Him, and those which stress that when the LORD performed these acts of deliverance in ancient times He undertook to save His people thenceforth and forever. The lengthy prose sermon of Deut 4:32-40 belongs to the former type, as it presents the Exodus from Egypt primarily as a basis for belief in the LORD. The Exodus is a more persuasive argument for belief than is Creation, which is mentioned parenthetically in this passage but receives no emphasis.[4] In glowing language, this sermon, by means

---

4 As noted in the work of the twelfth-century philosopher and poet Judah haLevi in

of a henotheistic adoration of the mighty works of the national God of Israel, inculcates the belief in the one God in heaven and on earth beside whom there is no other. It embraces the entire prehistory of Israel from the Patriarchs to the Conquest of Canaan, including the Sinai theophany, but the central point is the deliverance from Egypt, which is referred to in the rhetorical question "Or has any god ventured to go and take for himself one nation from the midst of another by prodigious acts, by signs and portents, by war, by a mighty hand and an outstretched arm and awesome power, as the LORD your God did for you in Egypt before your very eyes?" (Deut 4:34). Still, though the dramatic election of Israel becomes a proof of the oneness of the God beside whom there is no other, all this is not theosophy for its own sake — it leads up to a warning: "Observe His laws and commandments, which I enjoin upon you this day, that it may go well with you" etc. (v. 40).

Simpler from the ideological point of view is the exhortation in Deut 6:20-25, since it is tailored to the level of intelligence of the

---

his treatise *The Kuzari* (trans. by H. Hirschfeld, New York 1964). The Rabbi in haLevi's work places great stress on the fact that "God commenced his speech to the assembled people of Israel: 'I am the God whom you worship, who has led you out of the land of Egypt' but He did not say 'I am the Creator of the world and your Creator'" (I:25; p. 46) because he too, in his attempt to convince the King of the Khazars of the truth of Israel's belief, adduces the Exodus tradition and not that of the Creation (see further I:25-27; pp. 46-47). God the Creator, he states, is the concern of "religion based on speculation and system, but open to many doubts" (I:13; p. 45); i.e., Creation is a debatable philosophical issue, while the wonders which transpired at the Exodus are not. These were witnessed by an entire people, and faithfully recounted from generation to generation, leaving no room for controversy or doubt. HaLevi's approach originates in the philosophy of Saadya Gaon, see *The Book of Beliefs and Opinions*, trans. by S. Rosenblatt, New Haven 1948, pp. 16-25; 138-141.

Though haLevi's words reflect the assumptions peculiar to medieval Jewish philosophy, tending even to diminish the impact of those Scriptural passages which glorify the LORD as Creator of the universe, they are nevertheless of interest for the elucidation of the plain sense of the biblical text, where the Exodus is indeed regarded as more decisive evidence for the truth of Israel's belief than the Creation. There would appear to be two reasons for this greater emphasis placed on the Exodus: it is a *national* tradition and therefore closer to the hearts of the people than the *universal* tradition of the Creation, and (essentially as stated by haLevi himself) in the biblical account, no one was present to witness Creation, while the miracles accompanying the Exodus were beheld by the entire people.

child who asks: "What mean the decrees, laws and rules that the LORD our God has enjoined upon you?" In reply to this question, a simple and restrained historical explanation is given, concluding with a warning to obey the divine laws. Another such general exhortation is to be found in Psalm 78, the whole intent of which is to demonstrate, through a re-telling of Israel's history, the necessity of walking in the ways of the LORD: "That a future generation might know — children yet to be born — and in turn tell their children, that they might put their confidence in God and not forget God's great deeds, but observe His commandments" (vv. 6-7). Moreover, even Psalm 105, a psalm of thanksgiving, does not refrain from declaring that the LORD favored Israel with His mighty acts "in order that they might keep His laws and observe His teachings" (v. 45).

Mention of the Exodus is not, however, confined to general exhortations to observe the LORD's commands; it is also employed to give the laws additional force. This is the case most significantly in the Decalogue, which opens with the words "I am the LORD your God who brought you out of the land of Egypt, the house of bondage" (Exod 20:2; Deut 5:6). These words, which serve to connect the Sinai theophany to the Exodus, also provide the rationale for what follows, the connection between vv. 2 and 3 being: Since "I am the LORD who brought you out" etc., "you shall have no other gods besides Me" (Exod 20:3; Deut 5:7). The same association of themes occurs in the rationale given for the prohibition of worshipping astral deities, a prohibition which applies to Israel only: "You, however, the LORD took and brought out of Egypt, that iron blast furnace, to be His very own people" (Deut 4:20). Similarly, the law concerning the false prophet who entices his people to serve foreign gods ends with the words "for he urged disloyalty to the LORD your God, who freed you from the land of Egypt and who redeemed you from the house of bondage" (Deut 13:6).

Such expressions are not peculiar to passages forbidding idolatry; they occur in laws pertaining to matters of holiness as well. The collection of laws of purity in Leviticus 11 concludes with the formula "For I the LORD am He who brought you up from the land of Egypt to be your God; you shall be holy, for I am holy" (v. 45). In the same fashion, the sacrificial law of Lev 22:26-30 is followed by the concluding statement: "You shall faithfully observe My commandments: I am the LORD. You shall not profane My holy name, that I may be sanctified in the midst of the Israelite people — I am the LORD who sanctify you, who brought you out of the land of Egypt to be your God; I am the LORD" (Lev 22:31-33). The concluding verse of the command to attach fringes to the garments (Num 15:27-40) is similar: "Thus you shall be reminded to observe all My commandments and to be holy to your God. I am the LORD your God, who brought you out of the land of Egypt to be your God; I am the LORD your God" (v. 40).

The Exodus appears as the rationale for each of the two laws aimed at ameliorating the condition of the Hebrew slave (Lev 25:35ff and Deut 15:12ff): "For it is to Me that the Israelites are servants; they are My servants, whom I have freed from the land of Egypt; I am the LORD your God" (Lev 25:55); "Remember that you were a slave in the land of Egypt and the LORD your God redeemed you; therefore I enjoin this commandment upon you today" (Deut 15:15).[5] The command "You shall not subvert the rights of the stranger or the fatherless; you shall not take a widow's garment in pawn" in Deut 24:17 is provided with the very same rationale: "Remember that you were a slave in Egypt and that the LORD your God redeemed you from there" (v. 18). This formulaic conclusion, typical of social ordinances, appears again in connection with usury: "I am the LORD your God, who brought you out of the land of Egypt, to give you the land of Canaan, to be your God" (Lev 25:38).[6] Somewhat exceptional is the mention of the Exodus in the law forbidding dishonest weights and measures: "You shall have an honest balance, honest weights, an honest ephah and an honest hin; I am the LORD who freed you from the land of Egypt" (Lev 19:36). More easily understood is the mention of the Exodus following the command "The stranger who resides with you shall be to you as one of your citizens; you shall love him as yourself, for you were strangers in the land of Egypt; I am the LORD your God" (Lev 19:34).

5 See also Lev 25:42; Deut 5:15.
6 The concluding words of this law are notably the only such reference to the Exodus which is followed by mention of the Conquest.

Returning to the command to free the Hebrew slave, which concludes with "Remember that you were a slave in the land of Egypt and the LORD your God redeemed you" (Deut 15:15), we note the intentional ambiguity of the verb *pdh* "redeem", which here connotes both "rescue", i.e., deliverance in general, and "redemption", i.e., the emancipation of a slave. The LORD is depicted as having freed a slave from the possession of an oppressive master,[7] and thus His act is a fitting example for Israel to follow. The same logic is present in the parallel formula in Deut 24:18, in connection with the treatment of the stranger, the fatherless and the widow. This ambiguous use of *pdh* suggests itself even when no reference is made to the slave or the poor, as in the law of the false prophet who "urged disloyalty to the LORD your God who freed you from the land of Egypt and redeemed (*pdh*) you from the house of bondage" (Deut 13:6). In this manner the underlying idea, that in return for having been redeemed from Egypt Israel is obligated to obey God's commands, is strengthened by the force of the analogy which compares the relationship of a people to its God to that of a former slave to his emancipator. No wonder that Deuteronomy makes use of this motif even in general hortatory contexts, explaining to Israel that "it was because the LORD favored you... that the LORD freed you with a mighty hand and rescued you from the house of bondage, from the hand of Pharaoh" (Deut 7:8). As noted by Yaron,[8] this passage exhibits a rhetorical agglomeration of two juridical formulae, "redeem from the house of" and "redeem from the hand of", which are used alternatively in Ancient Near Eastern contracts. In Micah too, the LORD reminds Israel: "I brought you up from the land of Egypt; I redeemed (*pdh*) you from the house of bondage" (6:4). We should add that even when the verb used is *hōṣīʾ* ("bring out", "free"), as in the passage cited above "For it is to Me that the Israelites are servants; they are My servants, whom I have freed (*hōṣēʾtī*) from the land of Egypt" (Lev 25:55), the legal concept

---

7 On the comparison of God to a person redeeming a slave, see D. Daube, *Studies in Biblical Law*, Cambridge 1947, pp. 48ff; idem, "Rechtsgedanken in den Erzählungen des Pentateuch", *BZAW*, 77 (1958), pp. 35ff.

8 R. Yaron, "Redemption of Persons in the Ancient Near East", *Revue Internationale des Droits de L'Antiquité*, 3è Série, 6 (1959), pp. 168f, note 24.

of emancipating a slave is present. The homiletical value of the passage is in the idea that the Israelites are not subject to enslavement by a human master, since they are now the property of God who redeemed them from Egypt. Apparently *hōṣī'* too can convey the same ambiguity as *pdh*, connoting both the legal idea of emancipation and the notion of deliverance. This too has been noted by Yaron,[9] who points to the parallel ambiguity of Akkadian *šūṣû*, which is used both in the general sense of "take out" and in the particularized sense of "free from slavery".

The prophet who attempts to lead his people into idolatry is punished, as we have noted, because "he urged disloyalty to the LORD your God, who freed you from the land of Egypt and who redeemed you from the house of bondage". Since this prophet is condemned to death (Deut 13:6), it follows that the Exodus serves as the rationale for the penalty inflicted by God on those who would deny His commandments.

Sermons of this type are usually addressed to the entire people. In Deuteronomy the Israelites are warned that if they grow haughty and forget the LORD their God who brought them out of the land of Egypt and the house of bondage and who led them through the wilderness, they will perish (8:11-20). A similar reproof can be found in Hosea 11, an oracle of doom against a sinful Israel: "When Israel was still a child I fell in love with him; ever since Egypt I have called him my son. Thus they were called, but they went their own way; they sacrifice to Baalim and offer to carved images" (vv. 1-2). The reproof is followed by the threat of the sword which will come down upon Israel's cities (v. 6). Elsewhere Hosea declares:

> I the LORD have been your God
> Ever since the land of Egypt;
> You have never known a God but Me
> You have never had a helper other than Me.
> I looked after you in the desert,
> In a thirsty land.
> When they grazed, they were sated;

9 *Ibid.*, pp. 165-166.

When they were sated, they grew haughty;
And so they forgot Me.
So I am become like a lion to them,
Like a leopard I lurk on the way.

(13:4-7)

Likewise Micah, when reproaching the Israelites for not following the
LORD's demands — doing justice and loving mercy — and threatening
them with utter failure in every endeavor, begins his words of rebuke
with the words "My people! What wrong have I done you? What hardship have I caused you? Testify against Me. In fact, I brought you up
from the land of Egypt. I redeemed you from the house of bondage,
and I sent before you Moses, Aaron and Miriam" (6:3-4). Jeremiah
describes the misfortune which befalls Israel in his day (2:14-16) in
a rebuke which opens similarly: "What wrong did your fathers find
in Me, that they abandoned Me and went after nothingness and
became nothing? They never asked themselves, 'Where is the LORD,
who brought us up from the land of Egypt'" (vv. 5-6; he goes on to
speak of God's leading Israel through the wilderness and into the land
of Canaan [vv. 6-7]). Even in prayer, Jeremiah admits that the misfortune which has befallen Israel is justly deserved; he addresses God

Who displayed signs and marvels in the land of Egypt...and won
renown to this very day. You freed Your people Israel from the
land of Egypt with signs and marvels, with a strong hand and
an outstretched arm, and with great terror. You gave them this
land that You had sworn to their fathers to give them, a land
flowing with milk and honey, and they came and took possession of it, but they did not listen to You or follow Your
teachings...therefore You have caused all this misfortune to
come upon them...

(32:20-23)

The prophetical source which explains the downfall suffered at the
time of Jephthah (Judg 6:8-10) does so in the very same manner.

In sum, the Exodus from Egypt was a tenet well-suited for use in
rebuke, since it is the very basis of the belief that Israel is subject to

the commands of the LORD and hence that Israel will be subjected to punishment if it fails to observe these commands.

The Exodus was equally well-suited for use in teaching more optimistic lessons. It was, after all, also the grounds for the belief that the LORD, who brought His people out of Egypt, will continually save them from the hand of their adversaries, and that in all times of trouble and sorrow, Israel can expect God's salvation.

The Law of War in Deuteronomy 20 opens with the exhortation "When you take the field against your enemies and see horses and chariots — forces larger than yours — have no fear of them, for the LORD your God, who brought you from the land of Egypt, is with you" (v. 1). More significantly, the Exodus is invoked when appeal is made to the LORD for salvation lest He appear as a god who has abandoned his people and ceased to be their god. This rather naive aspect of popular theology stands out in Gideon's plea to the messenger of the LORD: "Please, my Lord, if the LORD is with us, why has all this befallen us? Where are all His wondrous deeds about which our fathers told us, saying 'Truly the LORD brought us up from Egypt'? Now the LORD has abandoned us and delivered us into the hands of Midian!" (Judg 6:13).

Not far from this point of view is that found in Psalm 80, in which God is beseeched to rescue Ephraim, Benjamin and Manasseh from distress (vv. 1-8). The petition is bolstered by the graphic depiction of the Exodus from Egypt and Israel's settlement in its own land (vv. 10-12), followed by the bitter complaint that the LORD has abandoned His people (vv. 13-14). In the plea for His assistance which follows, the psalmist includes the promise "We will not turn away from You; preserve our life, and we will invoke Your name" (v. 19).

Though like Gideon, the psalmist does not state that disaster has befallen Israel because of its sins, the psalmist is more optimistic than the author of Judges. The latter, despairing of salvation from the LORD who delivered His people in the past but has forsaken them in the present, believes that it is no longer of any use to invoke God's name in prayer, whereas in the psalmist's heart the confident hope still beats that he may succeed in rousing the LORD to renew His deeds as of old; he even suggests that a renewed display of God's might could perhaps put an end to the heretical thought that the LORD has forsaken His own people whom He brought out of Egypt. If the LORD will deliver Israel, so the psalmist believes, Israel will continue to invoke His name rather than turning away from Him.

The antiquity of the view that the memory of the Exodus provides the grounds for belief in God's ever-present help is also attested, indirectly, in the prophetic reproof of Amos. Amos has no use for the conventional argument that Israel's misdeeds amount to ingratitude in return for God's kindness; instead he interprets the significance of the Exodus in ways both revolutionary and paradoxical, ways likely to undermine the very basis for the people's confidence, namely, their assumption that the God who brought them out of Egypt will never forsake them. And while his first reproof at least recognizes the election of Israel ("You alone have I singled out (*yāda͑tī*) of all the families of the earth"), the implication of the election is the surprising "*therefore* I will call you to account for all your iniquities" (3:2). Amos' second rebuke goes even further, denying the very principle of God's having "singled out" Israel of all the nations; it asserts that in His eyes the Israelites are of no greater importance than the Ethiopians: just as He brought Israel up from Egypt, so did He bring the Philistines from Caphtor and the Arameans from Kir (9:7). This poignant invective, without parallel in the Bible, in which Amos contradicts the idea expressed in Deuteronomy's question "Has any god ventured to go and take for himself one nation from the midst of another..." (4:34) which serves as grounds for the doctrine of election,[10] openly expresses Amos' own view while indirectly providing eloquent testimony of the view held by his contemporaries, which he rejects.[11]

10 Taking the word ͗*ĕlōhīm* as a common noun; cf. Rashi. Alternatively, "Has God ever ventured..." etc. Along with the preceding verse ("Has any people heard the voice of God/a god"), in any case, the general intent of the passage is still the same: to exclude any possibility that any deity whatsoever, much less the God of Israel, ever acted towards another nation as the LORD acted towards Israel.

11 On the interpretations suggested for Amos 3:2, and on the relation of the passage to Amos 9:7, see A. Weiser, "Die Prophetie des Amos", *BZAW*, 53 (1929), pp. 118-124. While correctly observing that the technique employed by Amos to

Even after this simplistic theology has been demolished, mention of the Exodus remains the source of hope that the LORD will cease from His anger, relent and redeem His people again. And so, as we have seen above,[12] messages of consolation and awaited salvation which appear in the prophecies of Isaiah and Jeremiah combine the memory of the Exodus with the belief that the House of David will last forever. Micah consoles Israel with the words "I will show him wondrous deeds as in the days when You sallied forth from the land of Egypt" (7:16). For the same reason, the Exodus is mentioned in prayers which recount God's wondrous deeds of old in order to arouse Him to repeat them, as in the recollection of the LORD's leading Israel through the depths of the sea (Isaiah 63:11-13) or in Psalm 77, in which the general statement "You are the God who works wonders; You have manifested Your strength among the peoples. By Your arm You redeemed Your people, the children of Jacob and Joseph" (vv. 15-16) is followed directly by a description of the parting of the sea. To this category belongs also the prayer for the LORD's help in Psalm 80, which begins its review of past salvation with the words "You plucked up a vine from Egypt; You expelled nations and planted it" (v. 9).

A few motifs which were originally independent of the Exodus tradition are adapted for use in interpreting the Exodus and even in describing the events of the Exodus themselves. One such motif is the petition that God act for His own name's sake, which often appears

---

develop his ideas is that of antithesis and paradox, Weiser unnecessarily compounds the difficulties in the logical contradiction between the two passages. Further, in his attempt to mitigate them, he is forced to conjecture that the prophet was familiar with a popular saying "You alone have I singled out of all the families of earth, therefore I will *overlook* all your iniquities" and that in 3:2 he has substituted "I will call you to account" for "I will overlook". The supposed contradiction to 9:7, however, need not be explained away by such arbitrary conjecture. Both passages are meant to convey the same idea — that the LORD will call Israel to account for her sins even though He is the God who brought her out of Egypt. Moreover, both are marked by the same stylistic technique of startling the listener with the unexpected.

12 Above, pp 42-43.

in individual petitionary psalms[13] even when not contextually appropriate. It recurs in Jeremiah's prayer of intercession: "Though our iniquities testify against us, act O LORD, for the sake of Your name"; "We acknowledge our wickedness, O LORD — the iniquity of our fathers — for we have sinned against You. For Your name's sake, do not disown us; do not dishonor Your glorious throne" (Jer 14:7; 21-22). In Isa 48:9-11 this idea is translated from the language of prayer to that of consolation. Most noteworthy though are those passages in which the plea that God act for His name's sake is associated with the Exodus, as in Moses' plea following Israel's worship of the Golden Calf:

> Let not Your anger, O LORD, blaze forth against Your people, whom You delivered from the land of Egypt with great power and with a mighty hand. Let not the Egyptians say, "It was with evil intent that He delivered them, only to kill them off in the mountains and annihilate them from the face of the earth". Turn from Your blazing anger, and renounce the plan to punish Your people. Remember Your servants, Abraham, Isaac, and Jacob, how You swore to them by Your Self...
>
> (Exod 32:11-13)

As grounds for his plea, Moses argues that the Egyptians are liable to conclude that the LORD is not a God of truth and lovingkindness but rather one of evil. To this main point Moses adds a second: his reminder of the oath God has sworn to the patriarchs; it has been rightly pointed out by Galling[14] that each of the two arguments can in fact stand alone. Another version of the same prayer is found in Deuteronomy:

> O LORD God, do not annihilate Your very own people, whom You redeemed in Your majesty and whom You freed from Egypt with a mighty hand. Give thought to Your servants,

---

13 See Pss 25:11; 31:4; 104:21; 143:11.
14 Galling, *op. cit.* (Chapter Two, note 19), p. 60.

Abraham, Isaac, and Jacob, and pay no heed to the stubbornness of this people, its wickedness, and its sinfulness. Else the country from which You freed us will say, "It was because the LORD was powerless to bring them into the land that He has promised them, and because He hated them, that He brought them out to have them die in the wilderness". Yet they are Your very own people, whom You freed with Your great might and Your outstretched arm.

(Deut 9:26-29)

Here the main argument is that the Egyptians might cast aspersions upon the LORD's ability to free His people. To this is added the point made in Exodus as well: the Egyptians may conclude that the LORD brought the Israelites out of Egypt in order to do them harm. In Deuteronomy the mention of the patriarchs is placed at the outset of the prayer, whereas in Exodus it serves as its conclusion.[15]

Deuteronomy's version of Moses' prayer following the calf episode closely parallels the prayer he offers in Numbers following the return of the spies:

When the Egyptians, from whose midst You brought up this people in Your might, hear the news...they will say, "It must be because the LORD was powerless to bring that people into the land He had promised them on oath that He slaughtered them in the wilderness".

(Num 14:13-16)[16]

---

15 These differences between the two passages make it impossible to accept Galling's view (*ibid.*, p. 63) that Deuteronomy's version of the prayer is an imitation of that found in Exodus. The two variants are independent.

16 The Numbers passage is not completely intelligible; it would seem to be a conflation of two versions. In the original version the supposed speakers are the inhabitants of Canaan, who have heard about the LORD's acts of salvation in the wilderness, while in the later version it is the Egyptians who recall — here as elsewhere — Israel's departure from their land. The variant readings in v. 14 attest to the conflation: MT sees the Egyptians as addressing the Canaanites, while LXX has "All the inhabitants of the earth have heard" etc. — i.e., both the Egyptians and the Canaanites have heard of God's acts. The variants are evidence of differing attempts to combine the two originally independent versions of the prayer.

The apprehension that Egypt might fail to recognize God's benevolent intent in redeeming His people from Egypt, only alluded to in Deuteronomy, is here completely suppressed, but in all other respects the two passages are thematically similar.

The very same idea is repeated in Psalm 106 in connection with the parting of the sea: "Our forefathers in Egypt did not perceive Your wonders; they did not remember Your abundant love, but rebelled at the sea...Yet He saved them, for His name's sake, to make known His might" (vv. 7-8).

Most extreme in this regard is Ezekiel 20, which, as noted earlier,[17] presents Israel's entire history as one continuous and unbroken chain of transgressions against God, paralleled by repeated acts of salvation which God performed for His name's sake, extending from the moment at which He made Himself known to them in Egypt to the future envisaged by the prophet. This pattern explains even the redemption from Egypt itself, contending that it was performed despite Israel's refusal to heed the LORD's command to cast away the idols of Egypt, a command spoken when he appeared to them in Egypt and swore to set them free. In view of their refusal, the prophecy continues:

> Then I resolved to pour out My fury upon them, to vent all My anger upon them there, in the land of Egypt. But I acted for the sake of My name, that it might not be profaned in the sight of the nations among whom they were. For it was before their eyes that I had made Myself known to them to bring them out of the land of Egypt.
>
> (Ezek 20: 8-9)

The theme of God's acting for His own name's sake is thus integrated into the Exodus tradition in various ways. While the prayer of Moses expresses the idea that the act of redemption from Egypt obligates the LORD to save His people for His name's sake, Psalm 106 states that the LORD acted for His name's sake at the parting of the sea, and

17 See above, p. 35.

Ezekiel attributes this motivation to God from the very moment of the Exodus.

Another motif, which has been woven into the very fabric of the Exodus narrative, is the idea that Israel is the LORD's son, in particular His "firstborn", or that the Israelites are His children. This motif too originated outside the Exodus tradition,[18] but it has been incorporated in it, appearing as the basis for the LORD's demand that Pharaoh free Israel: "Thus says the LORD: Israel is My first-born son. I have said to you, 'Let My son go, that he may worship Me,' yet you refuse to let him go. Now I will slay your first-born son" (Exod 4:22-23).

This element adds flavor to Hosea's statement of God's tender love for Israel: "When Israel was still a child I fell in love with him; ever since Egypt I have called him my son" (11:1). Surely it is no coincidence that the utterances of the very same prophet also contain the bold image of Israel as the LORD's wife, an image which, at least in its more developed form, belongs to the stock of prophetic symbols — even though it may be that the Pentateuchal warnings against "whoring after" foreign deities stem from the same notion. In any case, the very same prophet who added an emotional chord to the Exodus tradition by combining with it the idea that Israel is the LORD's beloved son did not hesitate to make use of the image of the young wife, faithful to her husband, in the words "I will give her her vineyards from there, and the Valley of Achor as a plowland of hope. There she shall respond as in the days of her youth when she came up from the land of Egypt" (Hosea 2:17).

---

18 For an attempt to trace the source of this motif, see S. E. Loewenstamm, "Man as Image and Son of God", *Tarbiz*, 27 (1957), pp. 1-2 [Hebrew].

CHAPTER FOUR

THE PLAGUES OF EGYPT

I. The Sources

The literary sources for the tradition of the plagues of Egypt fall into two categories: detailed narratives and brief didactic passages.

The former category includes, first and foremost, the Pentateuchal narrative in Exodus (7:26-11:10 + 12:29-36), to which the following, arranged in chronological order, are to be added: (1) The account of Artapanus in his Ἰουδαικά or περί Ἰουδαίων, preserved in Eusebius' *Praeparatio Evangelica*, Book IX, Chapter 27, para. 28-33; (2) Philo's narrative in *Vita Mosis* (=VM) Book I, Chapters xii-xxvi; (3) Josephus' account in Jewish Antiquities (=Ant.), Book II, Chapters xii-xiv.[1]

To the latter category belong, most importantly, those texts which include an actual enumeration of the plagues in sequence. The biblical texts are Pss 78:43-51 and 105:26-38, and the post-biblical sources are: (1) the book of Jubilees;[2] (2) the account of Ezekiel the Tragedian in his drama Ἐξαγωγή, preserved in Eusebius,

---

1 Artapanus' work will be quoted according to the translation by J.J. Collins, in J. H. Charlesworth, *The Old Testament Pseudepigrapha*, II, Garden City, NY 1985, pp. 898-903; for texts and bibliography see pp. 889, 896. Quotations from Philo will be from Volume VI of the Loeb Classical Library edition, translated by F. H. Colson, London 1935, pp. 309-353 (page numbers refer to the Greek text of L. Cohn, P. Wendland and S. Reiter, *Philonis Alexandrini Opera Quae Supersunt*, Vols. I-VI, Berlin 1896-1915). Josephus' Antiquities too will be cited according to the Loeb edition, Volume IV, translated by H. St. J. Thackeray, pp. 279-303. Occasionally, for reasons of content, it has been preferable to diverge from the English versions cited in this and the following notes.

2 The English version used is that of O. S. Wintermute, in Charlesworth, *op. cit.* (above, note 1), pp. 52-142; for texts and bibliography see pp. 41-43, 51.

Praeparatio Evangelica, Book IX, Chapter 29;[3] (3) the account in Pseudo-Philo's *Liber Antiquitatum Biblicarum* (=LAB).[4]

To the above may be added the apocryphal Wisdom of Solomon (=WS), which differs from the other sources in that it refers to the plagues only parenthetically, within its sermonistic treatises on divine providence.[5]

Two other passages, Pss 135:8-9 and 136:10, refer to the plagues but make mention only of the slaying of the firstborn. In addition we should mention a number of prose sermons: Deut 11:3, Josh 24:5; Neh 9:10, Jdt 5:12; 3 Macc 2:6; Acts 7:36. These, however, are of limited value for traditio-historical study, since their references to the plagues consist of no more than allusions of the most general nature.

The nature of the sources themselves thus dictates that the study of the plagues tradition be divided into (1) an examination of the traditions which are common to the detailed narratives and the didactic passages and (2) an examination of those traditions which are peculiar to the detailed narratives. Our purpose will best be served by beginning with the common traditions — those attested in all the sources — and then proceeding to discuss those which are peculiar to the detailed narratives. In this latter stage the focus of our attention will be on determining whether these "added" traditions are to be viewed as an extension or an embellishment of those traditions also attested in the didactic passages, or whether they may in fact exhibit early elements simply omitted in the didactic passages, which aimed merely to glorify God's acts and not to narrate them.

---

3 English translation, and line nos., according R. G. Robertson in Charlesworth, *op. cit.* (above, note 1), pp. 807-819; for texts and bibliography see pp. 803, 807. We have included Ezekiel's account of the plagues among the didactic works since, even though it is part of a drama on the Exodus from Egypt which follows the same line as the Pentateuch's detailed narrative, the description of the plagues is of the same type as that found in the didactic psalms.

4 The edition primarily used was G. Kisch, *Pseudo Philo's Liber Antiquitatum Biblicarum*, Notre Dame, Indiana 1949. The English translation to be quoted below is that of D. J. Harrington in Charlesworth, *op. cit.* (above, note 1), p. 317.

5 The English version is J. Reider, *The Book of Wisdom*, in *Jewish Apocryphal Literature*, Dropsie College Edition, New York 1957.

II. The Plagues

The common denominator of all the texts — detailed narratives and didactic passages — is that they contain an account of the plagues themselves: their nature, their number and their sequence. In order to facilitate our survey, we shall begin with a discussion of those sources which are contained in the Hebrew Bible. This discussion, which aims at elucidating the fluctuations of the early traditions, will, at the same time, serve as a preface to our analysis of later traditions evidenced in the Hellenistic literature, each of which will be discussed in a separate section of this chapter.

A. The Biblical Sources

1. The Dating of Psalms 78 and 105. In view of the fact that even a casual glance at the three sources for the plague episode — the Pentateuch, Psalm 78 and Psalm 105 — is enough to reveal discrepancies in the number of plagues and their sequence, as well as in their essential nature, it is needless to dwell on the importance of a systematic comparative study. In theory, the appropriate way to begin such a study would be with a discussion of the character and dating of all three of the sources in question. In fact, however, we must confine our preliminary remarks to the two psalms, whose clear literary unity makes it possible to engage in a study so general in nature, whereas the complex and composite nature of the Pentateuchal account does not allow for a general survey in advance of the detailed textual analysis.

The precarious nature of the attempts at dating each psalm in the Psalter are among the best-known maladies of biblical scholarship. Today it is agreed that the problem cannot be solved by general statements, such as the pronouncement that the book of Psalms was "the hymnal of the post-exilic community". For some time now scholars have recognized the striking resemblance between certain poetical passages in the El-Amarna writings and the poetry of the Psalter, irrespective of whether the former were believed to be early Canaanite hymns[6] or translations from Egyptian.[7] In addition, the discovery of the Ugaritic texts provided a basis for the overall perception that, from a literary standpoint, Hebrew literature in general is nothing less than the direct continuation of Canaanite literature. Still it should be clear that this novel view of Israelite literature, which in principle enables the composition of a psalm to be dated earlier than was hitherto possible, does not by any means exclude the possibility that some psalms were composed in later periods, and in particular in Second Temple times. Hence, only through analysis of each individual psalm can we hope for progress in this area.

Of the many obstacles confronting the scholar in pursuit of the date of a psalm, one requires mention here: the difficulty in dating a psalm based on its religious outlook. In making such an attempt the scholar is forced to rely upon his own views of the stages in Israel's religious development, which in turn are founded upon the historical-critical analysis of the Pentateuch and Former (to some extent also the Latter) Prophets, an analysis which, based on conjecture, distinguishes various historical strata in these books. Since it is this conjecture that provides the scholar with a historical frame into which he places the psalm, the determination of the psalm's date becomes a conjecture erected upon conjecture. For all its weakness, such a method is a necessity not to be decried, so long as the psalm itself contains no historical data which might aid in the dating process. It has, however, no justification at all when the historical contents of the psalm open up the possibility of dating it. In such a case the scholar is bound to base his dating of the psalm solely on the historical evidence, after which he must assign its religious outlook to the period in which the historical evidence has fixed the psalm. He may not proceed in the reverse order, first fixing the date of the psalm on the basis of a particular hypothesis concerning the evolution of Israel's religious beliefs

---

6 F.M.T. de Liagre Böhl, "Hymnisches und Rhythmisches in den Amarnabriefen aus Kanaan", *Theologisches Literaturblatt*, 35 (1914), pp. 337-340 [=*Opera Minora*, pp. 375-379]; A. Jirku, "Kanaanäische Psalmenfragmente in der vorisraelitischen Zeit Palästinas und Syriens", *JBL*, 52 (1933), pp. 108-120.

7 W. F. Albright, "The Egyptian Correspondence of Abimilki, Prince of Tyre", *Journal of Egyptian Archeology*, 23 (1937), pp. 196-201.

and then forcing the historical data into the Procrustean bed of his preconceived theories of religious development.

Most scholars base their dating of Psalm 78 on the pragmatic model according to which the psalm recounts the history of Israel, that is, sin followed by divine retribution. This is referred to as the "Deuteronomic" model, and is marked by the repeated stress it places upon Israel's obligation to observe the LORD's commands. By super-imposing upon this view the assumption that the book of Deuter-onomy is a composition of the seventh century B.C.E., a *terminus a quo* is obtained for the composition of the psalm.[8] A modification of this basic calculation is provided by Junker,[9] who dates the psalm at the end of the eighth century B.C.E., assigning to the same period the first stages of the formation of the book of Deuteronomy and, pro-ceeding from this hypothesis, surmises further that the psalm shows the impress of the fall of the Northern Kingdom. Only a minority of scholars oppose this approach, assigning the psalm, on the basis of its historical content, to the early days of the United Monarchy. This school of thought has recently been supported at length by Eissfeldt.[10]

To arrive at the historical background of Psalm 78 we must com-pletely ignore all those elements which aim at adducing the moral les-son of the Exodus and Israel's wanderings in the wilderness, and concentrate entirely on those sections which the psalmist has added in the way of recent history. For our psalmist, the starting-point for

---

8 These scholars disagree on the exact dating of the psalm. Though we may dispense with the detailed account of the opposing views, mention should be made of the extreme position taken by L. Finkelstein, "Pre-Maccabean Documents in the Pass-over Hagadah", *HTR*, 36 (1943), pp. 24-27, who dates Psalms 78 and 105 in the Ptolemaic period, supposing that the pro-Egyptian bias of these psalmists caused them to omit some of the plagues enumerated in the Pentateuch.

9 H. Junker, "Die Entstehungszeit des Ps. 78 und des Deuteronomiums", *Biblica*, 34 (1953), pp. 487-500; see also J. Schildenberger, "Psalm 78 (77) und die Pentateuchquellen", *Lex Tua Veritas — Festschrift H. Junker*, Trier 1961, pp. 233-256.

10 O. Eissfeldt, *Das Lied Moses — Deuteronomium 32,1-43 und das Lehrgedicht Asaphs Psalm 78 samt einer Analyse der Umgebung des Moses-Liedes*, Berlin 1958, pp. 31-41; see also the detailed bibliography given there. Eissfeldt's opinion is accepted by W. F. Albright, "Some Remarks on the Song of Moses in Deuteronomy XXXII", *VT*, 9 (1959), p. 345 n. 1, and M. Tsevat, "Studies in the Book of Samuel", *HUCA*, 32 (1961), p. 208 n. 93.

this recent history is some serious crisis in Israel's recent past which occurred because the Ephraimites "played false in the day of battle" (v. 9). The psalmist uses this detail as a programmatic introduction, even before he opens his survey of Israel's history,[11] while at the same time stressing that the disaster experienced by Israel occurred because they had repudiated God's covenant (vv. 10-11).

When, in the course of his subsequent, more detailed account of Israel's history, the psalmist returns to this event, it becomes clear that he is referring to the defeat which eventually led to the destruction of the Shiloh sanctuary by the Philistines (vv. 60-64). Furthermore, the detailed description includes an openly theological, pragmatic explanation for Ephraim's military collapse, in which it is emphasized that the defeat was divine retribution for Israel's iniquity, that Israel's sins had caused God to spurn the Shiloh sanctuary and the tribes of Joseph. Moreover, the psalmist adds, when the LORD arose to His people's aid, He did not restore the tribes of Joseph to

---

11 The confused chronological order observable in the psalm has aroused some scholarly suspicion, calling into question the integrity of the text. But such disorder is typical of the structure of the entire psalm, in which historical events and homiletical matter are quite freely combined. The psalmist, after bringing grave accusations against the descendants of Ephraim, inhabitants of Canaan (vv. 9-10), moves on to begin an account of Israelite history with the words "They forgot His deeds and the wonders that He had showed them" (v. 11). The account opens with a brief reference to the plagues: "He performed marvels in the sight of their fathers, in the land of Egypt, in the plain of Zoan" (v. 12). The psalmist goes on to recount the parting of the sea and the journey in the wilderness, emphasizing Israel's sins (vv. 13-41), after which he returns to the actual Exodus: "They did not remember His strength, or the day He redeemed them from the foe; how He displayed His signs in Egypt, His wonders in the plain of Zoan" (vv. 42-43). Clearly, v. 43 is the chronological continuation of v. 12. Only then does the psalmist enumerate the plagues — which preceded the parting of the sea and the wilderness journey; after describing the plagues he briefly summarizes once again the story of the journey (vv. 52-53), alludes to the conquest of Canaan (vv. 56-58), relates the sins committed there (vv. 54-55) and then returns again to the punishments inflicted by the LORD upon the descendants of Joseph (vv. 59-64). Similarly, towards the end of the psalm, the psalmist places the building of the Temple on Mount Zion before the election of David (vv. 70-71). Obviously, he has made no attempt at preserving the chronological order in his account of Israel's past; he has even intentionally blurred the distinction between the history of Israel in general and that of Joseph and Ephraim. There is thus no reason to suspect that the text of v. 9 is corrupt.

their special destiny, choosing instead the tribe of Judah and erecting His everlasting sanctuary on Mount Zion (vv. 65-69).[12]

After depicting the course of history in these broad terms, the psalmist goes back and details the divine election of David, whom the LORD "took from the sheepfolds...from minding the nursing ewes, to tend His people Jacob, Israel, His very own. He tended them with blameless heart; with skillful hands he led them" (vv. 70-72). Now it stands to reason that the express mention of David as founder of Judah's royal house is a clear indication that the choice of an eternal dynasty is analogous to the eternal choice of the Temple on Mount Zion. Thus, what the psalmist celebrates with this paean of victory is the transference of hegemony from Joseph to Judah. The tremors of the days when God punished His people for sinning against Him belong to the past; by now the united Israelite people have arrived at "haven and inheritance" under the leadership of the tribe of Judah and the House of David, chosen by the God everlastingly enshrined on Mount Zion. At this glorious juncture all that remains for the Davidic king is the tranquil task of shepherding the Israelite people "with blameless heart". Such confidence in the stability of the Davidic monarchy and such boundless joy at the transference of hegemony from Joseph to Judah reflect faithfully the mood of the tribesmen of Judah at the time of the United Monarchy, that brief period when Judah rose from its lowly tribal status and became leader of a mighty kingdom to which even Joseph was subservient. This

---

12 V. 69 "He built His Sanctuary like the heights, like the earth that He established forever" is a clear allusion to the building of the Temple; Eissfeldt's doubts on this point (*op. cit.* [above, note 10], p. 36), and his suggestion that the word *miqdāš* here may refer to the city of Jerusalem or to Mount Zion, the place of the Ark, are groundless. Nowhere in the Bible is either the Holy City or the Holy Mountain called a *miqdāš*, and from the whole tenor of the psalm it is evident that the Jerusalem Temple is referred to, in contradistinction to the sanctuary in Shiloh. The expression "He built" proves further that this is no reference to the Tent in which the Ark was housed but to an actual building. To the rhetorical style of the psalm, compare the prologue to Codex Hammurabi (col. 1, ll. 20-26; *ANET*[2], p. 164), which relates how Anu established for Marduk in the midst of Babylon an everlasting kingdom, the foundations of which are as strong as the heavens and the earth. The words *kēmō rāmīm*, lit. "like the heights", in v. 69 are a reference to the heavens; some critics emend to *kammērōmīm* "like the heavens".

mood cannot be imagined after the schism, which turned our psalmist's hopes to naught. If the psalmist, so intent on advocating the Judahite cause, had known of the schism, he would not have passed it over in silence; he would have inveighed all the more bitterly against Joseph's disloyalty to David.

The psalm must therefore have been composed during the Solomonic period, when the Jerusalem Temple had been completed. It was this, not the destruction of the Shiloh sanctuary, that gave the stamp of irrevocable divine judgment to the transfer of power from Ephraim to Judah. By erecting His sanctuary on Mount Zion the LORD proclaimed publicly that He had chosen David and his tribe forever, and that He would never again dwell in the midst of Ephraim. This feeling of elation echoes in the psalm's self-assurance. The psalmist's attitude toward recent history determines his view of the distant past. Though the psalm ends on an optimistic note, the account of recent events stresses a dreadful national disaster which the LORD has inflicted upon His people in return for their sins. The psalmist insists that such an occurrence is not unique in the annals of Israel; in fact as early as the wilderness period Israel had shown its characteristic ingratitude and had repeatedly aroused the divine wrath (vv. 17-36). Thus, the psalmist combines his description of the LORD's acts of salvation in the distant past with an account of His harsh judgments; recent events and ancient history become inseparable parts of an integrated whole.

The so-called "Deuteronomistic" outlook which determines the psalmist's description of history is thus of incontestable antiquity. Indeed, as rightly observed by Eissfeldt, it is by no means peculiar to Israel; the same pragmatic assessment of history is suggested in the Mesha stele which accounts for Israel's dominion over Moab by claiming that Chemosh was angry with his land (ll. 5-6).[13] Even the

13 See above, note 10; compare the prayer of the Hittite king Mursilis, who regards the sins of his father Suppiluliuma as the cause for a pestilence which afflicted the land of the Hittites in his time; see A. Goetze in *ANET*[2], pp. 394-396 and A. Malamat, "Doctrines of Causality in Hittite and Biblical Historiography: A Parallel", *VT*, 5 (1955), pp. 1-12.

seemingly Deuteronomistic phrase "observe His commandments" (v. 7) cannot be cited as proof of Deuteronomic influence on the psalm, since this phrase is contained in the larger expression "that they might put their confidence (*kislām*) in God, and not forget His great deeds (*ma'ălēlē 'ēl*) but observe (*yinṣōrū*) His commandments". None of these expressions — neither the noun *kesel*, nor the idiom *ma'ălēlē 'ēl*, nor the verbal phrase *nṣr miṣwōt* — occurs anywhere in Deuteronomy, which prefers *šmr miṣwōt* "*observe* commandments".

Thus, the only similarity between Psalm 78 and Deuteronomy is the noun *miṣwā*, and this is misleading — particularly to present-day scholars — since only in post-biblical Judaism did the noun *miṣwā* become a fundamental term used when referring to adherence to the laws of the Torah in all their specifications. One must therefore be certain not to ignore the fact that the original meaning of the term *miṣwā* is simply "an order", as is evident from passages which use this term for the thoroughly secular concept of "royal order" (1 Kgs 2:43; 2 Kgs 18:36). The psalmist's urgent pleading with his people to keep God's *miṣwōt* is to be understood as a contrast to those violations of divine *miṣwōt* which the Psalm itself mentions — such as playing false in the day of battle (v. 9) and failing to rely on the LORD's deliverance (v. 22). The only charge which bears any relation to *standing* ordinances occurs in verse 58: "They vexed Him with their high places; they incensed Him with their idols" — i.e. they worshipped foreign gods. But the prohibition of idolatry, since it is tantamount to the denial of the LORD's absolute sovereignty over the Israelite people, a principle which had been the ultimate basis for Israel's faith since its inception, cannot be regarded as being on the same plane with the rest of the Pentateuchal legislation. Hence there are no grounds for the claim that Psalm 78 echoes the spiritual climate of later Judaism. The psalmist does not argue that the LORD's Law is better than the laws of the Gentiles. His only concern is with the mighty power of Israel's God, His acts of deliverance and retribution. Further, the idea that a people is enjoined to keep the commands of its god is in any case a widespread religious concept. One can, for example, compare the Akkadian *Ludlul bēl nēmeqi*, in which the righteous prince attests

(II:29) *"ušar ana mātija mê ili naṣari,* that is: "I have instructed my countrymen to keep the commands of the god".[14]

More important in this context are the similarities noted by Mendenhall between the Sinai covenant and Hittite treaties.[15] The striking resemblance between the language in which the Hittite king warns his ally to observe his orders and the sermonic style of the book of Deuteronomy is undeniable. Compare the words in which the Hittite king Suppiluliuma addresses the Ugaritic king Niqmadu: *u šumma atta niqmandu amâte annâti ša šarri rabî bēlika tašamme u tanaṣṣaršina u šarrumma tamar dumqa ša šarru rabû bēlka udammiqakku*[16] ("If you, Niqmadu, will heed the words[17] of the Great King, your master, and will observe them, you, O king, will see all the beneficent acts wherewith the Great King, your master, will reward you".

To be sure, this sort of speech, in which the listener is exhorted to hear and observe the words of the LORD, is most fully developed in Deuteronomy. Still, it cannot be assumed that the author of Deuteronomy was the original creator of this style of address, nor can we say that such exhortation was originally connected with the theological sphere — any more than the concept of a theological covenant, which also has known secular origins. Psalm 78 thus represents an instructive example of the early form of admonition which urges the people to keep faith with the covenant of their God. At the same time it affords us a view of the prehistory of the Deuteronomic type of address.

The dating of Psalm 105 is far less clear. Its historical content is confined to a description of episodes in history which appear repeatedly in didactic histories dating from all periods. The manner in which these are depicted in Psalm 105 differs essentially from that in Psalm 78, in that Psalm 105 consists entirely of thanksgiving for

---

14 W. G. Lambert, *Babylonian Wisdom Literature,* Oxford 1960, p. 40.

15 See above, p. 38.

16 *Ras Šamra,* 17, 132 ll. 14-18; J. Nougayrol, *Le Palais Royal d'Ugarit,* IV, Paris 1956, p. 36, ll. 14-18.

17 This is the basic significance of the Akkadian word *amātu,* which is frequently used in the pregnant sense of command or order; see *CAD* A/II, pp. 29ff.

acts of divine kindness. In Psalm 105 there is no room for mention either of Israel's sins or of the divine retribution which followed them. And while the psalmist cannot entirely ignore the fact that from time to time God brought evils upon Israel (vv. 17-19; 25), it is still apparent from the general tenor of the description that these ills were sent only in order to benefit Israel at a later date; in other words, the evils have no significance in themselves but are merely part of a necessary transition to the blessings which followed.

It is difficult to imagine that this unqualified thanksgiving, which contains not a single reference to the confession of sin or the acceptance of divine justice, could have been composed at a time later than the destruction of the First Temple. Most probably, therefore, the psalm expresses the mood of some peaceful era during First Temple times. Clearly, however, this line of reasoning does not lead to a definite conclusion, particularly because the psalm contains no precise chronological data. On the other hand, there is no evidence whatsoever for the view which posits a late date for the psalm on the basis of a supposed connection to the admittedly late Psalm 106 which follows it in the Psalter.

2. The Number of Plagues in the Psalms. Because the account of the plagues in the Pentateuch distinguishes clearly between each plague and the one which follows, there is no doubt at all that, according to this account, the number of plagues is none other than ten. This is true despite the fact that the Pentateuch does not expressly mention this number. In the psalms, however, the division of the plagues is much less certain, and depends to a great extent on the approach adopted by the scholar. He may, if he so wishes, assess what is recorded in the psalms in the light of the Pentateuch, but he may just as easily elect to evaluate the psalms solely on their own terms.

The former method is adopted by Jirku and Lauha,[18] who enumerate the following *seven* plagues in Psalm 78: blood, swarms, frogs, locusts, hail, pestilence and the slaying of the firstborn. However, since the plagues of frogs and swarms are mentioned in a single verse

18 Jirku, *op. cit.* (Chapter One, note 11), p. 110; Lauha, *op. cit.* (Chapter One, note 14), pp. 49-51; see below, Excursus III.

(v. 45: "He inflicted upon them swarms to devour them, frogs to destroy them"), the view that this verse speaks of two distinct plagues is actually based on the Pentateuchal narrative, which distinguishes clearly between the plague of frogs and that of swarms. And even this harmonistic interpretation leaves a noticeable discrepancy between the two passages, since in the Pentateuchal narrative the plague of lice intervenes between frogs and swarms.

It is surely preferable to explain the psalm on its own terms and to admit that only one plague is spoken of in v. 45, since the words "frogs" and "swarms" appear in parallelism just as do "grubs" and "locusts" in the following verse (v. 46: "He gave their crops over to grubs, their produce to locusts"). Just as the grubs and the locusts are one and the same plague, so too the swarms and the frogs. On the other hand it is equally logical to conclude that the following *two* verses speak of *two* plagues: "He killed their vines with *hail*, their sycamores with frost. He gave their beasts over to *hail*, their cattle to lightning bolts" (vv. 47-48). Even if we maintain the Masoretic reading, these may still be two distinct plagues, since the hail which smites the vines (v. 47) is the appropriate sequel to the locust which smites the crops (v. 46), while the destruction of the cattle by hail (v. 48) is an entirely separate affair. This would explain why the psalmist has devoted two separate verses to the hail.

The contention that vv. 47-48 speak of two separate plagues is even more compelling, however, if we prefer the reading of Symmachus in verse 48: "He gave their beasts *to pestilence*" (*ldbr*) rather than MT "to hail" (*lbrd*). There are several readings why we should: First, the parallelism "pestilence // lightning bolts" (*dbr/ršpym*) is strongly supported by the occurence of the same pair in Hab 3:5,[19] whereas the pair "hail/lightning bolts" (*brd/ršpym*) is not attested. Second, there is extra-biblical evidence that Rešep was considered the god of pestilence. In a Greek-Phoenician inscription from Idalium, Cyprus,[20] a

19 This argument has already been raised by A. Bertholet, *Das Buch der Psalmen*, Tübingen 1923, p. 206; Lauha, *op. cit.* (above, note 18), p. 52 n. 2, rejects his suggestion while agreeing to the distinction between *rešep* (sg.) and *rĕšāpīm* (pl.).

20 H. Donner and W. Röllig, *Kanaanäische und Aramäische Inschriften*, I, Wiesbaden 1962, pp. 8f.

god "to A-po-lo-ni to A-mu-ko?-lo-i", evidently meaning the Greek god Apollo, who was the god of pestilence, is paired with *ršp mkl*. It has recently been established that *Rešep* was identified in Ugarit with the Assyrian god of pestilence, Nergal.[21] Nor does the fact that *ršp* appears in Psalm 78 in the plural (*ršpym*) militate against the proposed reading, since the plural is found occasionally in Egyptian and Ugaritic as well.[22] A similar usage appears in Hos 13:14 "Where, O Death, are your plagues (pl.: *dēbāreykā*)? Your pestilence (sg.: *qāṭobkā*), O Sheol?", even though the same pair occurs in Psalm 91:6[23] "the plague that stalks in the darkness, or the scourge that ravages at noon", where both are in the singular: *deber/qeṭeb*.

A third reason to prefer Symmachus' reading here is that verse 48 opens with the verb "He gave over" in the converted imperfect (*wayyasgēr*), and the same verb reappears in the simple perfect (*hisgīr*) at the end of the pestilence (*deber*) which afflicted humans (v. 50). Such an *inclusio* apparently suggests an interconnection between the two plagues enclosed within the frame (vv. 48-50).

From both a natural and a literary perspective, it should be noted, the cattle pestilence is also the fitting transition to the pestilence among humans. With its artfully calculated gradation, the text indicates that the LORD did not content Himself with merely delivering their cattle to hail; He sent forth the fierceness of His anger upon humans as well: "He did not stop short of slaying them, but gave their life over to pestilence" (v. 50). The exegetical history of this verse provides the key to understanding how "hail" and "pestilence" have come to be confused. "Their life" is without a doubt the correct sense in which *ḥayyātām* is used, in synonymous parallelism with *napšām*. The same synonymous parallelism recurs in Ps 143:3 "The foe has hounded me (*napšī* "my life"); he crushed me (*ḥayyātī*) to the ground" as well as in Job 33:22 "He (*napšō*) comes close to the Pit; His life

---

21 Lists of Ugaritic deities are found in Ugaritic and Akkadian, and in both lists the gods appear in the same order. See for the present J. Nougayrol, "Nouveaux textes d'Ugarit en cunéiformes babyloniens", *Comptes-Rendus de l'Académie des Inscriptions et Belles-Lettres*, 1957, p. 83.
22 W. K. Simpson, "Reshep in Egypt", *Orientalia*, 29 (1960), p. 70.
23 On *deber* "pestilence" and *qeṭeb* in these writings see J. Blau, "Ueber Homonyme und angeblich Homonyme Wurzeln II", *VT*, 7 (1957), p. 98.

(*ḥayyātō*) to death". The earliest interpreters, however, understood *ḥayyātām* in our psalm to mean "their *cattle*", and it is this misunderstanding that gave rise to the Septuagint reading κτήνη. A copyist, misunderstanding *ḥayyātām* to mean "their cattle", was faced with an absurd text, in which cattle were smitten twice in the same plague (pestilence). Recalling the Pentateuchal account, in which the cattle were smitten by the plague of hail, he was forced to conclude that *deber* in the same verse must be a metathesized corruption of *bārād*, and on the strength of this convincing assumption he made the paleographically simple emendation.

Thus our analysis, like that of Jirku and Lauha, arrives at seven as the number of plagues in Psalm 78. Our sequence, however, differs from theirs: blood, swarms and frogs, locusts, hail which smote the trees, cattle pestilence, pestilence among humans, and the slaying of the firstborn.

In Psalm 105, both Jirku and Lauha[24] enumerate eight plagues: darkness, blood, frogs, swarms, lice, hail which smote the trees, locusts and the slaying of the firstborn. Here too their line of reasoning has been influenced unduly by the Pentateuch, ignoring the psalm's own structure. The verse "He spoke and there came swarms; lice throughout their country" (v. 31) does not, as these two scholars imagine, indicate two plagues but only one, as can be seen clearly from the obvious similarity between this verse and one closely following: "He spoke, and there came locusts; grasshoppers without number" (v. 34). Psalm 105, it is now apparent, also enumerates seven plagues: darkness, blood, frogs, swarms (including lice), hail, locusts and the slaying of the firstborn.

3. The Seven-Plague Tradition and the Ten-Plague Tradition. The very fact that the Pentateuchal series of ten plagues is paralleled in the Psalter by two sets of seven plagues provides an opportunity for typological study. From the outset it should be clear that both seven and ten are typological numbers signifying completeness. The similarity in the typological significance of the two numbers explains to some extent the tendency to interchange them. Deuteronomy speaks

---

24 Jirku, *op. cit.* (above, note 18), p. 113; Lauha, *op. cit.* (above, note 18), p. 55.

emphatically of "seven nations much larger than you" (7:1) whom the LORD displaced before the Israelites, but in the account of the covenant with Abraham (Gen 15:19-21) *ten* such nations are enumerated. One might add that the same type of interchange is found in Rabbinic literature. Compare: "Rab said, By ten things the world was created: by wisdom, understanding, knowledge, power, rebuke, might, justice, judgment, kindness and mercy" (b. Hag. 12a); "By seven things the Holy One, blessed be He, created His world: by knowledge, understanding, might, kindness, mercy, justice and rebuke" (Abot deRabbi Nathan, A, 37[25]). 2 Enoch 20:1 enumerates seven firmaments, but an addition found in some manuscripts at 20:3 enumerates ten.[26] In this respect, then, the seven-plague tradition is on a par with the ten-plague tradition; both express the desired idea, that the Egyptians were smitten with a *complete* series of plagues. An interesting combination of both typological numbers in one tradition is to be found in Rev 12:3, which describes the dragon as having "seven heads and ten horns".

There is, however, another consideration, also typological in nature, which inclines us in favor of viewing the seven-plague tradition as the primary one. The number seven signifies not only completeness but also the climax of successive and parallel events which build up to a single entity and in which the final event is the decisive one. Seven as the climactic number has early roots in the tradition of the Ancient Near East. There are, for example, Akkadian omen texts constructed on the pattern "If the oil raises one bubble, two, three...if it raises seven bubbles, this is the position of the coun-

---

25 Ed. S. Schechter, Wien 1887, p. 110.
26 See the edition of F. I. Andersen in Charlesworth, *op. cit.* (above, note 1), p. 134. On the use of both seven and ten as symbols of plenty and perfection, see Schildenberger, *op. cit.* (above, note 9), p. 253. He believes the number seven to be peculiar to J, and assigns the number ten to the Priestly redactor (=P), even though he correctly points out that Psalm 105 also enumerates seven plagues — rightly regarding the plagues of lice and swarms as a single plague in the psalm (*ibid.*, p. 224) and denying any connection between the psalm and the J narrative.

selor".[27] This primitive pattern occasionally varies in Akkadian, assuming a later form in which each single member bears its own particular character. A remarkable example is to be found in Šurpu.[28] In the original, underlying text, the burning of seven objects indicates the lifting of the curse which afflicts the patient. The seven texts which accompany the burning are all different, but they are all worded according to one and the same formula and all have the same ending: "The curse shall depart and I shall see light". But the seventh text is amplified by a solemn introduction which has no parallel in the other texts, in order to stress the special importance of the seventh act, the act which is to bring about the patient's complete cure.

The best-known such pattern is that of an action lasting six days and culminating or changing on the seventh. This pattern appears as early as the Gilgameš Epic,[29] which recounts that the mountain held the ship for one day, for a second day, for a third, for a fourth, etc. until, on the seventh day, Utnapištim sent forth the dove. The same pattern recurs several times in the Ugaritic epic writings, as in story of the building of Baal's temple.[30] As recorded in identical words repeated six times, the building operation lasted six days, until, on the seventh day, the task was completed. It is needless to mention that this pattern was developed to perfection in the Pentateuchal account of Creation (Gen 1:1-2:3), in which each separate member of the series bears its own particular character and marks a new stage in the completion of the work of Creation.

The climactic series of seven members is based therefore upon

---

27 J. Hehn, *Siebenzahl und Sabbat*, Leipzig 1907, p. 18; British Museum 22446 (CT V, 4-7): Certain phenomena are to be explained by oil-divination: "If one *šaršarru* comes out of the oil; if two *šaršarru* come out, if 4, 5, or 6...if the oil flows away towards the east and seven *šaršarru* come out, this is the position of the *kūbu*-ghost for the counselor". Likewise seven forms the conclusion (pp. 48-55): "If the oil gives off one, two, three bubbles" etc.; "If seven bubbles, this is the position of the counselor".

28 Tab. 8, ll. 143-160; see Erica Reiner, *Šurpu*, Graz 1958, pp. 31-34.

29 XI.141-146; see *ANET*², p. 94.

30 C. H. Gordon, *Ugaritic Manual*, Rome 1955, Text 51, VI, ll. 24-32, p. 142 (*ANET*², p. 134); on the history of this pattern in the Ugaritic epic and its dependence upon Akkadian literature, see S. E. Loewenstamm, "The Seven-Day Unit in Ugaritic Literature", *IEJ*, 15 (1965), pp. 121-133 (= *Tarbiz*, 31 [1962], pp. 227-235).

ancient literary tradition.[31] This is not the case with the climactic series of ten members, of which there is no known example apart from the plague narrative in the Pentateuch.[32] Though ten Words — a number indicating completeness — were spoken at Sinai, the literary structure of the Decalogue shows no perceptible gradation, no progress from less weighty commands to those of greater import. This would seem to lead to the hypothesis that the ten-plague tradition in Israel was developed from an original series of seven, and that the origin of the ten-plague tradition is to be sought in the fusion of two seven-plague traditions.

In light of the ancient literary pattern discussed above, it should not be surprising that both of the seven-plague series we have identified in Psalms 78 and 105 are indeed of a graduated nature, while the ten-plague series in the Pentateuch, though ultimately climactic, is not. The plagues in Psalm 78, as aptly observed by Lauha, "begin with distressing natural phenomena, proceed to devastation of the countryside and the destruction of livestock, culminating in myriad human

---

31 There is indeed some evidence in the Hebrew Bible — and only there — for an alternative pattern, in which the number eight forms the final member of an ascending series. Aaron's investiture lasted seven days (Lev 8:33), and on the eighth day he was installed in the service of the Sanctuary (9:1). Another illustration is the oracle of Amos against eight nations, which reaches its climax in the eighth oracle, which is pronounced against Israel (Amos 1:3-2:16). Here, however, the authenticity of the seventh oracle, that regarding Judah, is contested by some scholars; if it is indeed not original then the oracle against Israel originally occupied the seventh place. We may also add the passages in Samuel which assign seven sons to Jesse and in addition a younger son, David (1 Sam 16:10-11; 17:12), unlike Chronicles which enumerates seven sons of Jesse including David (1 Chr 2:13-14). As has been rightly pointed out by C. H. Gordon, "Ugarit as a Link Between Greek and Hebrew Literatures", *Rivista degli Studii Orientali*, 29 (1954), p. 168, the origin of this variation may be sought in the form of a proverb of ascending numbers in Canaanite literature, in which the number eight is used as an exaggeration for the number seven, as in the Ugaritic epic which displays the parallelism "seven ʿlmk" // "eight hnzrk", and likewise "seven šnt" // "eight nqpt"; Gordon, *Ugaritic Manual* (above, note 30), text 67, V, ll. 8f., p. 149 (*ANET*[2], p. 139); text 75 II, ll. 45f., p. 151. So too in the Bible: "We will set up over it seven shepherds and eight princes of men" (Mic 5:4), and similarly "Distribute a portion to seven, or even to eight" (Qoh 11:12).

32 The ten generations from Adam to Noah cannot be adduced here, since, Noah's great importance notwithstanding, it is clear that Adam was not inferior to him in importance.

fatalities".[33] A climactic structure is likewise perceptible in Psalm
105, though it is less evident here than in Psalm 78 since here there
is no plague which is fatal to livestock. Still a certain progression,
from alarming plagues (darkness, blood, frogs, swarms and lice) to
those which destroy vegetation (hail smiting the trees, locusts) and
thence to the slaying of the firstborn, can be observed. By contrast,
no similar progression can be detected in the Pentateuch. The clearest
indication of this is that in the Pentateuch the cattle pestilence (fifth
plague) *precedes* the locusts (eighth plague). Thus, in this respect as
well, the plague traditions in the psalms fit into recognizable literary
patterns from which the Pentateuchal narrative diverges. This is a
further reason to date the tradition of the psalms earlier than that of
the Pentateuch. Lauha's attempt to reverse this logic, contending that
Psalm 78 is based on the J account (this, Lauha believes, also contains
seven plagues but in this sequence: blood, frogs, swarms, cattle [!] pestilence, hail, locusts, slaying of the firstborn) which the psalmist has
rearranged in order to achieve a graduated series, is without foundation.[34]

---

33 Lauha, *op. cit.* (above, note 18), p. 51.
34 Schildenberger, *loc. cit.* (above, note 9), who reads, as we do, *dbr* "pestilence" rather
than *brd* "hail" in Ps 78 : 48, has stressed the similarity between the J narrative and
the psalm. In his view, this similarity confirms the existence of the J document,
which, he believes, is reflected in the wording of the psalm. The differences between
the assumed J document and the text of the psalm as we have it cannot, however,
be ignored:

Psalm 78	J
Blood	Blood
Swarms with frogs	Frogs
Locusts	Swarms
Hail	Cattle pestilence
Cattle pestilence	Hail
Pestilence among humans	Locusts
Slaying of the firstborn	Slaying of the firstborn

This table reveals that the psalm and the J account differ on no fewer than four
essential points: (1) The psalm recognizes a plague of pestilence among humans;
J does not. (2) The psalm counts swarms and frogs (in that order!) as a single plague,
whereas J enumerates frogs and swarms as two plagues. (3) The psalm places locusts
before hail; J has them in reverse order. (4) The psalm places the cattle pestilence

4. The Structure of the Ten-Plague Narrative. All the above notwithstanding, our analysis clearly demonstrates that the ten-plague narrative, which took shape in the Pentateuch through the fusion of two separate traditions, is not merely fortuitous coincidence. The number ten is expressive, signifying the idea that the Egyptians suffered complete and perfect punishment. Furthermore, the Pentateuch does not simply abandon the climactic form but substitutes another literary pattern, first recognized by Samuel ben Meir. In his commentary on the Pentateuch (at Exod 7:26), he writes:

> Twice Moses warned Pharaoh, the third time he did not, and so through the whole series; in every group of three, the third carries no warning. In the plagues of blood and frogs he warned him, in the plague of lice he did not; in the plagues of swarms and pestilence he warned him, in the plague of boils he did not; in the plagues of hail and locusts he warned him, in the plague of darkness [he did not].

The same idea was developed by Abrabanel (also at Exod 7:26), who added some details concerning Moses' powers of persuasion:

> I shall point out a rule in the account of these plagues: In the first plague of the first triad Moses is told "station yourself" before Pharaoh (Exod 7:15), in the second "Go to Pharaoh" (v. 25), and in the third neither expression appears, rather, the miracle is performed without warning. The same is true of the second and third triads; the sequence is maintained throughout.[35]

after the two plagues just mentioned; J places it before them. Nor does this exhaust the differences between the two sources, each of which has its own unique manner of describing even those plagues which occur in both. Thus we read in the psalm, "He gave their crops over to grubs, their produce to locusts" (v. 46), but of all this the only parallel in the book of Exodus is the word "locusts"! This difference is even more pronounced in the case of the hail, of which the psalm tells us "He killed their vines with hail, and their sycamores with frost" (v. 47), whereas in the account of the hail in Exodus there is no mention of the vine, the sycamores or the frost; once again the resemblance is limited to the name of the plague! See below, Excursus II.

35 R. Samuel ben Meir, *Pērūš HaTōrā*, ed. D. Rosin, Breslau 1882 (repr. N.Y. 1949); Don Isaac Abrabanel, *Pērūš ʿal HaTōrā*, repr. Jerusalem 1964.

Though this literary structure has been noticed in recent times by exegetes of the harmonistic school,[36] it has not been found worthy of any attention in the critical literature. The reason for this disregard is obvious: If the account is divided up among the three narrative sources of the Pentateuch, the literary structure described by the medieval commentators automatically disappears. This means that the critical method itself obstructs the path to any understanding of the literary structure of the existing text! We are faced with a kind of *deductio ad absurdum* of a method which necessarily leads to such inadmissible results.[37]

5. *The Pentateuchal Account Compared With the Psalms.* We proceed from the general comparison of the plague narrative in the Pentateuch with its analogue in the psalms to a detailed comparison, which we shall begin with the following table:

EXODUS	PSALM 78	PSALM 105
1. Blood	1. Blood	1. Darkness
2. Frogs	2. Swarms and frogs	2. Blood
3. Lice	3. Locusts	3. Frogs
4. Swarms	4. Hail (smiting trees)	4. Swarms and lice
5. Cattle pestilence	5. Cattle pestilence (or hail)	5. Hail (smiting trees)
6. Boils (man and beast)	6. Pestilence (man)	6. Locusts
7. Hail (man and beast)	7. Slaying of the firstborn (man)	7. Slaying of the firstborn (man)
8. Locusts		
9. Darkness		
10. Slaying of the firstborn (man and beast)		

36 B. Jacob, "Gott und Pharaoh", *MGWJ*, 68 (1924), pp. 268ff.; A. Šanda, *Moses und der Pentateuch*, Münster 1924, pp. 68-73; U. Cassuto, *A Commentary on Exodus*, trans. by I. Abrahams, Jerusalem 1967, p. 93.

37 Schildenberger, *op. cit.* (above, note 9), p. 251 has attempted to reply to this objection. According to his analysis, in J the first plague (blood), the third (swarms), and the fifth (hail) begin with the command *hityasṣēb* "Present yourself to Pharaoh", while the second (frogs) and the sixth (locusts) begin with *bōʾ* "Go to Pharaoh". The redactor (i.e., P) took over this ready-made pattern and added to each pair of

The Pentateuchal account, like that of Psalm 78, begins with the plague of blood. We may observe already at this stage that this is the case in all of the extra-biblical passages as well. Only Psalm 105 diverges from this fixed tradition, placing the plague of darkness before that of blood. It can safely be assumed that the placement of blood as the first plague is based upon early tradition.

The plague of blood brings a double misfortune upon the Egyptians: death of the fish and human thirst. The latter of the two is alluded to in Ps 78:44, while the former is referred to in Ps 105:29. Still it cannot be determined whether the Pentateuch has here combined two traditions, or whether perhaps in each psalm the brevity of the psalmist's style gave prominence to only one aspect of the plague. The actual description of the plague itself in the Pentateuch has, however, been viewed for some time as the result of the fusion of two traditions, one maintaining that Moses changed the water of the Nile into blood by striking it with his rod, the other maintaining that Aaron changed all the waters of Egypt into blood by waving his rod over them. We shall have reason to return to this topic when we take up such matters as the motif of competition between the LORD's emissary and Pharaoh's magicians, the question of how each plague was brought about, and the role of Aaron in the plague narrative.[38]

Here we must pause for two observations on the history of Jewish exegesis with regard to the plague of blood. Early exegetes stated unequivocally that Aaron acted alone, though it is explicitly stated (Exod 17:5) that Moses struck the Nile with his rod. The earliest appearance of this interpretation — which, it seems, is what the redactor of the Pentateuch has intended — is the LXX Codex A at Exod 7:20, which reads "And *Aaron* lifted up the rod" instead of "And he lifted", adding Aaron's name where the text is unspecific. Rabbinic exegesis took this as self-evident; note the midrashic ques-

---

plagues a third without any preliminary warning. This act of simply filling out a given pattern is not, in his view, a literary form. His theory is based on the assumption of a J narrative which enumerated seven plagues but did not arrange them as an ascending series, placing the pestilence before the hail and locusts, and this is most improbable; see also note 34, above.

38 See below, pp. 118-147.

tion "Why was the water not smitten by Moses?" (Exod. Rab. Wāʾērāʾ 9:10 and parallels[39]). Abrabanel was the first commentator not to be content with this, suggesting instead that Moses smote the Nile and Aaron the rest of Egypt's waterways.[40] Similar to this is the view of B. Jacob:[41] Moses struck the Nile, after which Aaron completed the activation of the plague by waving his rod over the remaining waterways of Egypt. In the actual text, however, this rather forced notion of "combined effort" is without foundation; from the pre-Pentateuchal, tradition-history point of view Aaron's action and that of Moses are merely variants of the same tradition. No less certain is the fact that the latter, more detailed formulation, in which the command is "hold out your arm over the waters of Egypt — its rivers, its canals, its ponds, all its bodies of water" (Exod 7:19), is intended to amplify the miracle by means of exhaustive specification.[42]

In all three biblical sources the plague of blood is followed by a plague of noxious animals. In Psalm 105, however, instead of one such plague, consisting of both swarms and frogs, which is what we have in Psalm 78, we find two plagues: frogs, followed by swarms

---

39 See below, p. 143.
40 Commentary to Exod 7:26.
41 *Op. cit.* (above, note 36), p. 271.
42 It would still appear that poetic elements underlie this latter formulation, which includes the statement that "there shall be blood in all the land of Egypt, even in wood and stone" (Exod 7:19). Though all the commentators have, quite properly, questioned the superfluous reference to "wood and stone", even modern exegesis has not been able to add to the two explanations given by the Midrash: (1) "wood and stone" mean *vessels of* wood and stone; (2) "This is an expression for idolatry — a disparaging synonym for the graven images of their gods" (Midr. HaGadol Wāʾērāʾ 7:19-21). Both are forced. Perhaps the correct meaning of the passage can be elucidated from Ugaritic writings, which exhibit the phrase *rgm ʿṣ wlḫšt ʾabn* "a word of wood and a whisper of stone" alongside *tʿnt šmm ʿm ʾarṣ thmt ʿmn kbkbm* "the speech of heaven with earth, depths with stars" (Anath III, ll. 19-22; U. Cassuto, *op. cit.* (Excursus I, note 7), pp. 127-128. Since "wood and stone" are mentioned in connection with "heaven and earth, depths and stars" as the elements which make up the whole of nature, it may be that the same poetic tradition is at work in the Pentateuch, and "even in wood and stone" may have found its way into the narrative as a relic of an earlier, poetic formulation of the story.

together with lice.[43] In the Pentateuch, moreover, there are three successive plagues: frogs, lice and swarms. Ancient tradition, it would thus appear, has fixed these plagues in literary proximity to the plague of blood and has apparently fixed their contiguity to each other as well. With regard to their number, however, ancient tradition seems not to have been consistent.

43 The exact meaning of the words *kinnīm* and ʿ*ārōb* is by no means clear. See A. W. Knobel — A. Dillmann, *Exodus und Leviticus*, Leipzig 1860, pp. 77f.; W. Leslau, Ethiopic and South-Arabic Contributions to the Hebrew Lexicon, Berkeley-Los Angeles 1959, pp. 26f.; G. Hort, "The Plagues of Egypt", *ZAW*, 69 (1957), pp. 98ff. It is at any rate clear that the noun *kinnīm* denotes some annoying insect and that the same is true of ʿ*ārōb*, as is suggested in the parallelism between the two words in Ps 105:31. This explanation is supported by the LXX rendering κυνόμυια ("dog-fly"), which is also adopted by Ezekiel the Tragedian (l. 138) and Philo (VM I.xxiii, p. 101); cf. also WS 16:9. A trace of this ancient and correct interpretation may be seen in the opinion of R. Nehemiah, who explains ʿ*ārōb* as a "mixture" *(ʿērūb)* of hornets and gnats (Tan. Wāʾērāʾ, 14), thus combining the tradition which explains ʿ*ārōb* as hornets and gnats with the linguistic theory that ʿ*ārōb* is derived from ʿ*ērūb*. Similarly Aquila translates πάμμυια "all kinds of gnats". Pseudo-Philo goes further, rendering the word by *pammixian*, a mixture of all species. It is likely that the interpretation of ʿ*ārōb* as meaning ʿ*ērūb* has given free rein to exegesis, leading eventually to the view that God was not content with sending mere flies but displayed the full force of His might by sending a mixture of mighty beasts, or even newly created monsters of unprecendented types. The history of exegesis is complicated, however, by the fact that the earliest evidence for this interpretation does not pertain specifically to the plague of ʿ*ārōb*. Thus, the Wisdom of Solomon views all the animals that God sent against the Egyptians as "measure-for-measure" punishment, arguing that since the Egyptians reverenced animals as gods and worshipped them, God chose to punish them in this way (11:15-16; 16:1-2). When, among these creatures, the author mentions the locust and the ʿ*ārōb* (μύες; 16:9), he asks: why were the Egyptians punished by means of such insignificant creatures as these, since surely God's power is unlimited and He could have sent mighty beasts of prey or even created novel monsters to instill fear and dread. "For Your all-powerful hand, that created the world out of formless matter, lacked not means to send upon them multitudes of bears or fierce lions, or new-created wild beasts, full of rage, unknown before, either breathing out a blast of fiery breath, or blowing out roarings of smoke, or flashing dreadful sparks from their eyes" (11:17-19). Dismissing these ideas, the author finally returns to the plain sense of the Pentateuch with the words "But You did order all things by measure and number and weight" (11:20). A similar question is posed by Philo regarding the plague of *kinnīm*: "Someone perhaps may ask why He punished the land through such petty and insignificant creatures, and refrained from using bears and lions and panthers and other kinds of savage beasts which feed on human flesh; and if not these, at any rate the asps of Egypt, whose bites are such as to cause immediate death" (VM I.xix, pp. 97-98). In what follows, Philo too dismisses the question, differing from the Wis-

We may further deduce that the grouping of the plagues in threes is not based upon the nature of the plagues themselves, since the plagues of lice and swarms are so closely connected in Psalm 105 that they constitute one single plague, while in the Pentateuch not only are they separate, the lice ends the first triad while the swarms belong to the second.

We have in any case concluded that the order of the first four plagues in the Pentateuch is based on early tradition. In the next two plagues, cattle pestilence and boils afflicting man, this is not the case. We note at once that these two do not bring to a close the series of bodily afflictions, since, surprisingly enough, after the plague of boils Moses appears before Pharaoh to announce, in alarming terms, the advent of a pestilence which will afflict humans (Exod 9:14-15), though immediately thereafter he retracts (v. 16)![44] Indeed, a brief

---

dom of Solomon in two main respects: (1) Philo raises only the first of the two possibilities given by the Wisdom of Solomon, namely, that God could have sent mighty beasts of prey; (2) Philo, for no apparent reason, connects his question specifically to the plague of lice! If one may hazard a guess, Philo may have inadvertently confused the ʿārōb and the lice, and, if so, one may further conjecture that the question raised in Wisdom of Solomon regarding the locusts and the ʿārōb arose originally only in regard to the plague of ʿārōb but that, by a process of abstraction, the author extended an interpretation, which had originated as a linguistic explanation of the word ʿārōb, to a general question regarding all the plagues inflicted by means of live creatures. Later literature lends some support to this view. Josephus describes the plague of ʿārōb thus: "He now sent wild beasts of every species, the like of which no man had ever encountered before, to infest their country" (Ant. II.xiv.3). He thus accepts the second of the two possibilities rejected by the Wisdom of Solomon, but applies it specifically to the plague of ʿārōb. On the other hand, the Midrash accepts the first of the two, which is rejected by the Wisdom of Solomon and Philo, that is, that the LORD could have sent lions, bears and leopards, including these beasts of prey under the general title of ʿārōb (Midr. HaGadol Wāʾērāʾ 8:17-20; compare Tan. Wāʾērāʾ 14). Actually the Midrash accepts only the content of the Hellenistic tradition but not the reason given for it, for which the Midrash substitutes its own reason: that the predators were set loose upon the Egyptians, again as a sort of "measure-for-measure" punishment, in this case, in return for having compelled the Israelites to hunt these creatures in the wilds. One may perhaps venture that the Midrash here reflects a Roman practice of hunting beasts of prey, an activity in which they may have used Jewish prisoners of war.

44 It may well be that the original text of Exod 9:14-15 began with an account of the plague of pestilence among humans. In the received text, the logic of these verses is that of unfulfilled condition: Had I not wished to spare you, I could have stretched forth My hand, etc. But the exact interpretation of the verse is fraught

look at the two psalms is enough to show that the juxtaposition of the bodily afflictions to the first four plagues has no foundation in ancient tradition, and that on this point the tradition has undergone far-reaching changes. In Psalm 105 not a single bodily affliction is mentioned, whereas Psalm 78, according to what appears to be the original reading, places a pestilence which afflicts both cattle and humans (in MT only humans) in the penultimate position. The Pentateuch, unlike either of these, places the bodily afflictions before hail and darkness.

Such a schematic view of this vast complex of variants enables us to divide them into two types: questions regarding the actual occurrence of a particular plague and those concerning the positioning of a plague within the series. And since, according to Psalm 105, the

---

with difficulties. It is universally agreed that v. 14 is a proclamation of what has yet to occur, whereas the ancient versions disagree in their understanding of v. 15. The LXX renders it too as a proclamation, explaining the verb *šālaḥtī* ("stretched forth [My hand]") as *perfectum confidentiae*, whereas Tg. Onqelos translates it as an unfulfilled condition: I could have stretched forth — a view which has commended itself to modern scholars; see GKC p.313: "I had almost put forth My hand". This leads necessarily to the conclusion that v. 14 does not refer to a plague of pestilence among humans. Indeed, Samuel ben Meir (above, note 35) and Ibn Ezra (below, note 79) both maintain that it alludes to the plague of hail, and Abrabanel (above, note 35) believes that it refers to all four of the plagues still to come. These interpretations, however, are all forced, and there are good grounds to see v. 14 as a threat of pestilence among humans. First, the words "upon your person, your courtiers and your people" must refer to a plague aimed specifically at human beings, and not to hail or the last four plagues. Second, Ps 78:49-50, before mentioning the word *deber* "pestilence", provides a general depiction in which the plague's awesome power is emphasized, and it stands to reason that the general reference in v. 14 is explained in the verse immediately following. On the other hand, accepting the view of Samuel ben Meir and Ibn Ezra would necessitate allowing three verses (15-17) to intervene between the allusion to the plague of hail and the proclamation to Moses of its impending arrival, while Abrabanel's opinion causes a cryptic allusion to become clear only some whole chapters later — not to mention that this would be the only case in which Moses departed from his usual practice of speaking to Pharaoh about the next plague only. In view of all these considerations, it can be definitely stated that v. 14, which speaks as a pronouncement, refers to a pestilence among humans, and this in turn means that v. 15 does so as well — in accord with the LXX rendering. The fact that no such pestilence will actually materialize becomes evident only in v. 16, and this structure gives the speech far more rhetorical force than if it had been phrased according to the normal scheme ("Had I not wished...")

Egyptians suffered no bodily afflictions at all, while according to the Pentateuch and Psalm 78, despite the differences of number and order, more than one such plague did occur, it stands to reason that the two types of variants are interconnected. The absence of a fixed and agreed tradition concerning whether or not a particular plague did occur led to a lack of uniformity in determining its position in the sources which record it. As will become clear,[45] this rule applies to the plague of darkness as well.

In addition to the differences between Exodus and Psalm 78 in the order of the bodily afflictions, there are discrepancies between the two sources on the very nature of the plagues themselves. Psalm 78 states that the Egyptians suffered a pestilence afflicting humans, which it describes at considerable length: "He inflicted His burning anger upon them, wrath, indignation, trouble, a band of deadly messengers. He cleared a path for His anger; He did not stop short of slaying them, but gave them over to pestilence" (vv. 49-50). The Pentateuch, however, preserves only the smallest trace of this tradition, admitting that Moses did indeed threaten Pharaoh with such a pestilence but adding that the threat was immediately withdrawn, i.e., that there was in fact no such plague.

On this point Lauha has preceded us, recognizing as he did that in order for the Pentateuch to reject the tradition of a pestilence affecting humans it must first have known of this tradition's existence.[46] Lauha's point is well taken despite his assumption that the order of plagues in the Pentateuch — to be precise, in J — is more ancient than the order in Psalm 78.[47] It follows that the redactor of the Pentateuch would not have attributed to Moses the surprising threat and even more surprising retraction, unparalleled in the plague narrative, were he not acquainted with a tradition according to which a pestilence did indeed strike the Egyptians personally. Lauha, however, has failed to appreciate why this tradition has been rejected in the Pentateuch itself. The narrative explains why Moses withdraws his threat:

45 Below, pp. 100, 106.
46 Lauha, *op. cit.* (above, note 18), pp. 52ff.
47 See above, pp. 87ff.

"Nevertheless I have spared you for this purpose: in order to show you My power, and in order that My fame may resound throughout the world" (Exod 9:16). These words leave no room for any doubt. The fact is — though early, popular tradition had not felt any need to deal with this fact — that once a pestilence has afflicted humans there can be no more plagues, particularly no slaying of the firstborn. The redactor of the Pentateuchal narrative, however, was unable to live with this difficulty; unwilling to obscure entirely the pestilence among humans, he furnished it with a new interpretation, effectively eradicating it.

The plague of boils too bears the mark of secondary tradition. This is the only plague appearing in the Pentateuchal account which is mentioned in neither of the psalms. Apparently, this plague was originally no more than a substitute for the plague of pestilence, intended to convey the idea that the Egyptians did not suffer a fatal blow at all but rather a painful, but not lethal, illness. As a corollary to this we may now posit that in a later, but still pre-Pentateuchal, tradition, the plague of boils served likewise as a substitute for that of cattle pestilence.[48] The redactor has assembled all the traditions in the maximal

---

48 Jacob, *op. cit.* (note 36, above), p. 270 advances the interesting theory that one can detect here a polemical tone against the slanderous statement made by the Egyptians to the effect that the Hebrews were expelled from Egypt because they were infected with a skin disease called σαββάτωσις (Josephus, Contra Apionem I.xiv). To this slander, according to Jacob, the Pentateuch replies that there was indeed such an infection, but that it struck the Egyptians and not the Israelites. Hence the further inference that "the Pentateuchal narrative on the Exodus is a protest against the Egyptian view, which predates the Pentateuch and thus affords proof of the historicity of the Exodus. The Egyptians could have had no reason to invent the Exodus by themselves except to distort the facts, but they nevertheless wrote about it at an early period; the words of the Pentateuch are simply a reply to them". But this theory has no real basis; all evidence for the Egyptian tradition on the subject of the Israelite Exodus belongs to the Hellenistic period (see M. Stern, "A Fragment of Greco-Egyptian Prophecy and the Tradition of the Jews' Expulsion from Egypt in Chairemon's History", *Zion*, 28 (1963), pp. 223-227 [Hebrew]). Furthermore, it must be noted that the Egyptian tradition is not uniform. The earliest source for it is Hecataeus (early Hellenistic period), cited by Diodorus (III.40). According to his account, the expulsion of the Jews was preceded by an epidemic afflicting the Egyptians, who believed that the gods had brought disaster upon them as punishment for having allowed foreigners to settle in their land, whereby they had become attached to foreign cults and had neglected to honor the gods of Egypt as was their

fashion, preserving both the early tradition of cattle pestilence[49] and the later tradition of boils, alongside of which he has even kept a passing reference to the pestilence afflicting humans.

Thus, the very fact that the Pentateuch has rejected the tradition of Psalm 78 with regard to human pestilence enables us to view the entire process whereby the Pentateuchal account evolved from that of the psalm, or, more precisely, from the underlying tradition which preceded the psalm. We are not, however, in a position to be quite so definitive with regard to the relationship between Psalm 78 and Psalm 105. We must consider two equally valid alternatives: It may be the case that Psalm 105 too rejected the tradition of pestilence affecting humans, which resulted incidentally in the rejection of the

due. The Egyptians in this account concluded that the only cure for the epidemic was to expel the foreigners, among whom were Jews. Since Hecataeus devotes to the Jews a detailed description, whereas he mentions only briefly the expulsion of the other foreigners, there is good reason to accept Stern's view (*art. cit.*) that Hecataeus' words are an Egyptian response to the Pentateuch. In the course of time this response assumed a more antagonistic and even anti-Semitic form. Thus, another tradition in Diodorus (XXXIV.1-2) states that the Jews were expelled from Egypt because they did not worship the gods, by whom they were despised on account of the leprosy with which they were afflicted. This source indicates a later stage in the development of the Egyptian tradition. Though just as in Hecataeus the Jews were despised by the gods of Egypt, here the affliction has been transferred from the Egyptians to the Jews. A third stage is reflected in the words of Apion cited by Josephus, according to which the Jews were expelled from Egypt because they were leprous, blind and lame. The source goes on to say that after they had been expelled from Egypt and were on their way, the Jews were infected by another disease called σαββάτωσις. A different response to the Pentateuch was given by Manetho (Contra Apionem I.xxvi) at the beginning of the Hellenistic period. As in Hecataeus, it was the Egyptians who were infected with disease, but, in Manetho's account, the diseased Egyptians were those who had been expelled from Egypt on account of their sickness and had joined the Hyksos, i.e., the Jews. There is, in brief, no authentic Egyptian tradition on the reason for the expulsion of the Israelites, only various Egyptian responses to the Israelite tradition.

49 The plague of cattle pestilence too raises the question of how, in the ensuing narratives, the Egyptians still had cattle, which were then smitten with boils, hail and the slaying of the firstborn. The redaction of the Pentateuch was aware of the difficulty in the case of the pestilence among humans, but not in the cattle pestilence, apparently because the focus of the narrative is on humans and the question looms much larger where men are concerned. The redactor's rejection of the tradition of a pestilence afflicting humans is nonetheless an openly hesitant one, and his decision to refrain from tampering with the plague of cattle pestilence is only natural. See below, Excursus III.

cattle pestilence — triggered perhaps by a question such as the one formulated in the Midrash: "Though men sinned, what sin did beasts commit?" (Exod. Rab. Waʾērāʾ 9:10). In this case, it would be necessary to postulate that the psalmist in Psalm 105 has made up the necessary complement of seven plagues by separating frogs from swarms and adding darkness — a known natural phenomenon in Egypt — while the psalmist in Psalm 78 omitted darkness, apparently also in order to maintain the requisite number of plagues. It may be, however, that a simpler explanation should be preferred to this dialectical reasoning, namely, that the two psalms reflect two separate, original and simultaneously existing traditions, each of them enumerating seven plagues but differing from one another with regard to the character of some of them.

The bodily afflictions are followed in the Pentateuchal narrative by hail and locusts. Nevertheless, although both psalms exhibit this same juxtaposition, even in this seemingly fixed tradition a significant number of modifications are evident. Most obvious of all is the fact that hail precedes locusts in Psalm 105 and in the Pentateuch while in Psalm 78 locusts precede hail. The rationale for the latter order is obvious: the plague of locusts is here grouped together with the other plagues inflicted by means of living creatures. Further, the locusts destroyed only the produce whereas the hail, by shattering the trees, killed them as well, so that the hail in effect completes what the locusts began yet surpasses them in severity. There is no perceptible reason for this order to be reversed in Psalm 105, since here too the effect of the hail is confined to shattering the trees. In any case it is clear that the plague of locusts is the penultimate plague, a fact which accords with the description of the plague of locusts in the Pentateuch which, as we shall see below in greater detail,[50] preserves a trace of the tradition that this plague was the penultimate one.

The order of these two plagues in the Pentateuch is self-explanatory. The shattering of trees, which in the psalms is the entire raison d'être of the hail, is only incidentally mentioned in the Pentateuchal account (Exod 9:25); in the Pentateuchal narrative the

---

50 See below, pp. 163-164, and Excursus II.

emphasis is on the destruction of all vegetation (including mention of the fact that only the early-ripening plants were affected and not the later-ripening ones [v. 31], which were thus annihilated by the locusts). The death of both livestock and humans in the plague of hail thus follows upon the death of vegetation.

The plague of hail itself, however, appears to be a later expansion, and requires further comment. The text states that Pharaoh was told by Moses at the LORD's command to bring both people and livestock indoors for safety so that they might not be smitten by the hail. The exegetical problem of why God should have desired to save the Egyptians from a plague that He Himself was about to bring upon them arises immediately. Gressmann[51] incorrectly surmised that the plague of hail was originally a mere threatening showpiece — but in fact this plague was first and foremost a disaster for vegetation; this was its original character as attested by both psalms and the Pentateuch, which express in various ways the idea that hail and locusts together completely effaced all plant life. The additional havoc wrought by the hail on man and beast served only to amplify the plague and is undoubtedly a secondary embellishment; nothing can be deduced from it about the essential nature of this plague. The unique and surprising development of this secondary motif is designed to offset the theological difficulty posed by the idea that, by taking refuge in their homes, the Egyptians could avoid being smitten by the hail. The narrative stresses that although those who took refuge indoors were indeed saved from the effects of the hail, this was possible by obeying, not by opposing, the command of the LORD.

It should be added that this entire episode is unattested outside of the Pentateuchal account in Exodus. The extra-biblical sources fall into three categories: those which give no details as to the damage caused by the hail (Pseudo-Philo), those which represent the effect of the hail as confined to the destruction of produce (Wisdom of Solomon, Jubilees, Josephus), and those according to which the hail actually smote both man and beast but which do not mention the warning (Artapanus, Ezekiel the Tragedian, Philo). It follows that the unique

51 Gressmann, *op. cit.* (Chapter Two, note 2), p. 74.

Pentateuchal formulation was prompted by a later theological consideration entirely unconnected with the original character of the plague.

The third of the triads appearing in the Pentateuch concludes with the plague of darkness, which is entirely lacking in Psalm 78 but occupies the first position in Psalm 105.[52] This confirms the rule outlined

---

52 Gressmann (see previous note), pp. 84ff., suggests that this plague too was originally a mere spectacle, since it could not have caused any serious discomfort. But this idea has no support in the sources and is improbable on the factual level as well. The darkness in Egypt was caused by dense clouds of dust which rendered breathing extremely difficult; see Knobel-Dillmann, *op. cit.* (note 43, above), pp. 94f. and Josephus' description of the plague (Ant. II.xiv.5) which, notwithstanding some hyperbole, is based on actual knowledge.

Critical studies of the Psalter have been perplexed by the position of the plague of darkness in Psalm 105. Gunkel, in his commentary on the Psalms (see above, Excursus I, note 8) deleted this plague. D.H. Müller, "Komposition und Strophenbau", in *XIV. Jahresbericht der Israelitisch-Theologischen Lehranstalt in Wien*, 1906-07, pp. 61, 67, transferred it to the penultimate position. V. 28 ("He sent darkness, it was very dark...") is also problematic: the two hemistichs are not parallel, and the second is obscure. To clarify its meaning, an observation regarding the psalm's entire account of the plagues must be made. The darkness (v. 28) is preceded by two verses which stress that the LORD produced these plagues through the agency of Moses and Aaron, whereas in the verses following the darkness (vv. 29-36) only the LORD Himself is said to have acted. It may be surmised, therefore, that the psalmist used a Vorlage which, like Psalm 78, omitted the names of Moses and Aaron. In this early text the account of the plagues began with the words "He displayed His signs and wonders in the land of Ham"; compare Ps 78:43 "He displayed His signs in Egypt, His wonders in the plain of Zoan". After this came "He sent darkness, it was very dark", completed by a hemistich which cannot be restored. The author of the psalm preceded this with the verse "He sent His servant Moses, and Aaron whom He had chosen" (v. 26), and accordingly changed the next verse "They performed among them (i.e. among the Egyptians) His signs, wonders in the land of Ham" (unless we prefer the LXX reading "he performed by them...", i.e. by means of Moses and Aaron). This revision destroyed the parallelism between "Egypt" and "the land of Ham". Even more thorough was the change which took place in the account of the darkness. Here (v. 28) the psalmist substituted for a description of the plague the words "They did not defy His word", meaning that Moses and Aaron did not rebel against the LORD's decree but performed their mission faithfully.

The LXX failed to grasp the psalmist's intent and made the second hemistich refer to the behavior of the Egyptians, rendering ὅτι παρεπίκραναν τοὺς λόγους αὐτοῦ "for they rebelled against His words". Yal. Šimʿoni contains the cryptic, composite midrash: "What is the meaning of 'did not defy (*mārū*) His word'? Since they exchanged (*hēmīrū*) His words, the Holy One, blessed be He, said to the angels: 'The Egyptians deserve to be punished by darkness!' They immediately agreed, saying 'Yes!'; not a single one of them exchanged (*hēmīr*) [the words of] the Holy One,

above,[53] that a plague which does not occur in all the traditions has no fixed position in those traditions which do contain it.

In all three biblical sources the plague series concludes with the slaying of the firstborn. The striking similarity between the two psalms in their descriptions of this plague should be noted: Ps 78:51 reads "He struck every firstborn in Egypt, the first fruits of their vigor in the tents of Ham"; Ps 105:36: "He struck every firstborn in the land, the first fruit of their vigor". To these we may also compare Ps 136:10, which, among all the plagues, mentions only the slaying of the firstborn, and Ps 135:8, which gives this last plague considerably more prominence than all of the "signs and portents against Egypt" to which it makes only brief allusion. In this connection mention should also be made of Exod 4:23, a difficult passage and one which lends support to the conjecture, to which we shall return, that some very ancient tradition was aware of one plague only: the slaying of the firstborn.

The fixed, final position of the slaying of the firstborn is intelligible also in light of this episode's close connection with the events of the night of the Exodus and with the Pentateuchal legislation, serving as it does to explain the reason for the laws concerning the firstborn (Exod 13:15; Num 3:13; 8:16-17). It is, however, uncertain whether the actual event referred to in the psalms is identical to that described

---

blessed be He". Perhaps this midrash reflects two variant readings in the biblical text: one (*mārū*) without the negative, which was meant to describe the behavior of the Egyptians, and one (*wĕlōʾ mārū*) with the negative which, the midrash says, is to be explained as referring to the reaction of the angels. The same passage occurs in Yal. HaMakiri on Psalms: "Our Rabbis say: Because they defied the word of the Holy One, blessed be He, He said to the angels: 'The Egyptians deserve to be punished with darkness'. They all immediately agreed and did not defy his word". The Yal. HaMakiri also contains the unusual interpretation that "the darkness which the Holy One, blessed be He, sent upon the Egyptians was severe. Why? Because they would not accept His word". Forced to interpret the midrash according to the MT of the psalm (*wĕlōʾ mārū*), it could be assumed that its author understood *mārū* to mean "accepted authority" — but perhaps the midrash actually reflects the reading *mārū* without the negative. Midr. Teh. is also interesting: it explains "Because they did not observe (*šāmĕrū*) the words of the Holy One, blessed be He, and rebelled against Him", recalling the view of many modern scholars (following F. Hitzig, *Psalmen*, Leipzig 1865) who read *šāmĕrū*; others delete the negative.

53 Above, p. 94.

in the Pentateuchal narrative, since the latter states explicitly that the firstborn of man and beast were slain, whereas the psalms (except for 135:8) contain no unequivocal mention of the slaying of beasts.

The description of the slaying of the firstborn differs from that of the preceding plagues. The accounts of the other plagues do not confine themselves to the plagues' results, namely, that the LORD smote the Egyptians in such-and-such manner. Rather, they give precise details of the natural phenomena (which must have been of lengthy duration) which brought about these results. The slaying of the firstborn, however, is described in a rather vague and unspecific account which stresses that the firstborn were all slain instantly and simultaneously. The narrative is shrouded in mystery in order to enhance its power. The actual manner in which the LORD slays the firstborn of Egypt is nowhere indicated; there is no natural affliction imaginable which would kill all its victims in a moment and all of whose victims would be firstborn.

It is, of course, to be posited from the outset that the lack of specificity is a function of the essential nature of this plague, and this would seem to obviate the need to search for an early tradition that may have described the firstborn dying of a pestilence. To be sure, Psalm 78 seems to suggest just this possibility:

> He inflicted His burning anger upon them,
> wrath, indignation, trouble, a band of deadly messengers.
> He cleared a path for His anger;
> He did not stop short of slaying them,
> but gave them over to pestilence.
> He struck every firstborn in Egypt,
> the first fruits of their vigor in the tents of Ham.
>
> (vv. 49-51)

It could be argued that this passage implies that the firstborn were slain in the plague of pestilence. In fact, this is just what Philo implies when he states that although all the Egyptians deserved to die in the plague of pestilence, God restricted this plague to the firstborn alone (human firstborn, of course; the firstborn of livestock were smitten in the plague of cattle pestilence).[54] But, as we have already indicated, Ps 78:48 speaks in fact of *cattle* pestilence, in which cattle in general, not just firstborn, were smitten, and the same is true, by extension, of the pestilence which struck humans. As discussed earlier, the psalm stresses the close connection of the pestilence among cattle to that among humans, by opening the description of the former with the verb *wayyasgēr* and concluding the description of the latter with *hisgīr*. The slaying of the firstborn follows after this *inclusio*, and is thus an independent topic, not a part of the sixth plague but rather the seventh and last of the series of plagues. Philo's testimony is based on his own artificial rearrangment of the plagues,[55] in which the cattle pestilence immediately preceded the slaying of the firstborn. Now Philo seems to have sensed intuitively that the cattle pestilence should have been followed by pestilence among humans; not finding this in the Pentateuchal account, he explained away the difficulty by rearranging the order of plagues. His solution is thus of no independent value. To be sure, the Pentateuchal account does in fact connect the cattle pestilence with the plague of pestilence among humans (Exod 9:16) despite the intervention of plague of boils. All of these, however, are clearly distinguished from the slaying of the firstborn. As we shall see below, Ezekiel the Tragedian records pestilence among humans as the sixth plague and the slaying of the firstborn as the ninth.

B. The Later Traditions

The process by which the plague traditions evolved, and especially the process by which these traditions were variously combined and recombined, did not come to an end with the completion of the Pentateuch but rather continued in some measure during the Hellenistic period. We shall here review each of the later sources.

1. Artapanus. Artapanus begins his account with a plague resembling the plague of blood. Moses strikes the waters of the Nile with

---

54 See below, p. 109.
55 *Ibid.*

his rod, whereupon they overflow, inundating the land of Egypt, becoming stagnant and fetid and causing the death of fish and severe thirst among humans. This plague, corresponding to the biblical plague of blood, is followed in Artapanus by the description of Moses' striking the ground with his rod and producing "some winged creature" (ζῷόν τι πτηνόν). This episode of course parallels the Pentateuchal account of the plague of lice, in which Aaron struck the ground with his rod; Artapanus, however, is speaking here of the plague of swarms, since the lice (σκνῖφες) are mentioned specifically later on in his account, among the last plagues. The interchange of lice and swarms, which are of similar origin, is easily understandable. In Artapanus' account the lice cause all the Egyptians to develop sores on their bodies (πάντας τε ἐξελκωθῆναι τά σώματα), which suggests the plague of boils. After the boils, Moses makes use of his rod to call forth the frogs, which are accompanied by locusts and lice. The series concludes with the plague of hail, which is accompanied by an earth-quake causing the collapse of all the houses and most of the temples. This is the decisive plague and leads to the expulsion of the Israelites (Eusebius IX:27, 27-34).

To this last segment of Artapanus we should compare the midrashic formulation:

> How did the hail descend? At first there were roars of thunder and flashes of lightning and the earth quaked, as it is said "Your thunder rumbled in the wheels; lightning lit up the world; the earth quaked and trembled"(Ps 77::19).
>
> (Midr. HaGadol Wā²ērā² 9:23)

In this passage the plague of hail has become a description of a theophany involving an earthquake. Obviously, such a conception of the plague of hail would easily lead to presenting this destructive theophany as the fitting conclusion to the plague narrative.

Artapanus differs from the Pentateuchal account in several important respects. (1) He omits all mention of cattle pestilence, darkness and the slaying of the firstborn; (2) The Nile, rather than becoming blood, inundates Egypt; (3) locusts and lice are combined with frogs in a single plague; (4) the swarms cause boils. Some of these discrepancies can be explained as variations which accord well with the general picture of how the tradition evolved. After all, as has already been established, cattle pestilence is lacking in Psalm 105 and darkness is omitted in Psalm 78. The combination of frogs and lice to form one plague has a parallel in the similar combination of frogs with swarms in Psalm 78. Swarms and lice, as noted above, can interchange easily. The only really new feature of Artapanus' account is the fact that locusts too become a part of this one combined plague, and even this is not particularly revolutionary when we recall that Psalm 78 has placed the locusts in immediate proximity to the combined plague of swarms and frogs.

The remaining discrepancies, however, can be understood only as tendentious deviations from authentic tradition. This is particularly true of the absence of the slaying of the firstborn, which is the last of the plagues not only in the three biblical sources but also in all of the later ones. It would seem that we are provided here with an example of the rationalistic tendency to bring the plague narrative into closer accord with the natural order, a tendency which leaves no choice but to omit a plague whose character is entirely miraculous. The same tendency is evident in Artapanus' contention that the swarms brought the boils, which means that the sting of flying insects led to skin inflammation, and perhaps in the transformation of the blood to a mere inundation of water — though, as we shall see presently,[56] here there is a further consideration: the attempt to explain away the difficulties posed by the competition between the Pharaoh's magicians and the true messengers of the LORD.

We shall be in a better position to appreciate Artapanus' tendentiousness if we compare his account with the results obtained by the Danish scholar Hort[57] in her attempt to explain the plague narrative in terms of natural phenomena. Hort too maintains that at the time of the first plague the waters of the Nile inundated Egypt; she too attributes the boils to insect bites; she too denies the slaying of the firstborn. And while it is not the case that Artapanus' has gone

---

56 Below, p. 125.
57 G. Hort, "The Plagues of Egypt", *ZAW*, 69 (1957), pp. 84-103; 70 (1958), pp. 48-59.

as far as Hort, explaining away all supernatural elements, it cannot be denied that the inclination to distort the narrative on rationalistic grounds is already present in his account.

2. Ezekiel the Tragedian. The same cannot be said of Ezekiel the Tragedian, who fuses early and late traditions in a most interesting manner. Ezekiel enumerates the following plagues: (1) blood (affecting the Nile and the other waterways); (2) frogs and lice together (βατράχων τε πλῆθος καὶ σκνῖπας ἐμβαλῶ χθονί); (3) boils ("ulcerous sores"); (4) swarms; (5) pestilence among humans; (6) hail (affecting people, livestock and crops, but not trees); (7) darkness; (8) locusts; (9) slaying of human firstborn (ll. 133-148). This account has not yet been adequately evaluated from the tradition-history point of view; even Wieneke's important monograph regards each and every deviation from the Pentateuchal narrative as an exercise of poetic license. Most characteristic is Wieneke's observation on the plague of pestilence among humans in Ezekiel: "Ezekiel fabricates the story that the Egyptians were smitten by a pestilence, whereas in the book of Exodus only the cattle are consumed by pestilence and death".[58] Ezekiel, though, did not fabricate anything here; he has, to the best of his ability, eclectically combined different traditions. On the question of the pestilence he has chosen to follow the tradition reflected in the received text of Psalm 78, in which pestilence among humans, but no cattle pestilence, is mentioned. Alongside this he took over the Pentateuchal tradition of boils affecting humans (which from the outset was a substitute for the tradition of pestilence affecting humans), but not that of boils afflicting livestock.

According to Ezekiel, then, the only plague from which beasts suffered along with men was that of hail, just as in (the MT of) Psalm 78. It is in describing this plague that Ezekiel is influenced by the Pentateuch — as evidenced by the words "Hail and fire shall fall and slay all mortal men, and cause to perish every crop and beast" (ll. 141-143). Note that this description omits all reference to the shatter-

---

58 J. Wieneke, *Ezechielis Judaei poetae Alexandrini fabulae quae inscribitur* ἐξαγωγή *fragmenta*, Monasterii Westphalorum 1931, p. 84: "Ezechiel in homines Aegyptios pestilentiam incidentem fingit, cum in Exodo solum pecudes peste et morte urantur".

ing of trees, an aspect of the hail which is so prominent in the psalms but barely mentioned in the Pentateuchal narrative.

Mention should be made of the fact that, in Ezekiel's account, the destruction of crops intervenes between the killing of humans and the killing of livestock, while the Masoretic Psalm 78 and the Pentateuch differentiate only between the destruction of vegetation on the one hand and the smiting of men and beasts on the other. Another, more striking difference between Ezekiel and the Pentateuch is to be observed in the manner in which Ezekiel, like Artapanus, combines the plagues of frogs and lice — though he does view the swarms as a separate plague — here resembling not only Artapanus but also the Pentateuch.

The history of tradition has left its mark on the order of the plagues as well. The plague of boils, of late origin, is here inserted between the plague of frogs-lice and that of swarms, and the darkness comes between hail and locusts. These extraordinary features are intelligible in light of the general rule cited above:[59] those plagues which are to be found only in some of the early traditions have no fixed position within the series.

Ezekiel's account, in conclusion, is a remarkable specimen of the tradition in its final stage, in which early and late elements are fused meaninglessly and without any independent skill of design. This assessment does not, however, detract from the obvious fact that the Pentateuch did not, in its own time, mark an end to the process by which the early traditions continued to evolve into ever-new combinations.

3. Wisdom of Solomon. The Wisdom of Solomon contains no continuous or unified account of the plagues, making only oblique references to one or another of the plagues in order to demonstrate divine providence. Nevertheless, the book must still be considered among the sources for the history of the plague tradition among Hellenistic Jews, since even the scattered references enable us to construct a general picture. For some time scholars have been aware of the fact that

59 See pp. 94, 100.

these references are for the most part[60] contained in one particular type of homiletical passage, namely, that which exemplifies the contrast between God's paternal care for Israel and the strict justice with which He treated the Egyptians. It has also been correctly observed that these comparisons are arranged according to the same order in which God visited His judgments upon the Egyptians.

The first passage (11:2-14) mentions the thirst-causing plague of blood; the second (16:1-4) a plague brought about by wild beasts;[61] the third (16:5-15) the fatal sting of locusts and "swarms"; the fourth (16:16-29) hail which devastated the land; the fifth (17:1-18) darkness; the sixth (18:5-19) the slaying of the firstborn. A seventh passage (19:1-22), speaks of the drowning of the Egyptians in the sea, which amounts to a sort of seventh plague. In the entire series, only one description is somewhat obscure — that of the wild beasts which tormented the Egyptians, appearing in the second passage. No doubt the reference is to frogs and lice, which the Israelites are later said to have recalled after the Exodus (19:10). The depiction of the locusts and swarms as creatures whose sting was fatal is somewhat exceptional, but this is a function of the context into which the author has placed this plague: a comparison between it and the biting serpents which God sent down upon Israel in the wilderness.

Another innovation is the inclusion of the drowning of the Egyptians in the sea as one of the plagues, creating a new conception of the seven-plague series in which the death of the Egyptians in the sea is the most severe, exceeding even the slaying of the firstborn. This is clear in the statement that "them who plotted to slay the infants of the holy ones...to convict them, you did deprive of the multitude of their children, and all together did destroy in a mighty flood" (18:5). On the whole, however, the description has its roots in well-attested tradition history. In omitting the plagues of pestilence and boils as well as those plagues which were inflicted by means of animals, Wisdom of Solomon resembles Psalm 105, going beyond it by leaving out all reference to the death of fish during the plague of

---

60 With the exception of WS 11:17-19; on this passage see note 43, above.
61 κνώδαλον, a generic term for all undomesticated creatures, not specifically reptiles.

blood. Nor is it surprising, in light of Ezekiel the Tragedian's account, that Wisdom of Solomon too sees the frogs and the lice as one plague. And while no other source combines locusts and swarms, we have already seen the broad range of variations in tradition regarding those plagues which were brought about by means of living creatures; we recall in particular the account in Artapanus which combines locusts, lice and frogs all in one. There is likewise no cause to assume that the placement of the plague of locusts — before that of hail — is an innovation of the author of Wisdom of Solomon; the same arrangement is found, as we recall, in Psalm 78.

4. Jubilees. This flexibility, still felt in Artapanus, Ezekiel and Wisdom of Solomon, is not present to the same extent in later literature, on which the Pentateuch imposed its authority to an appreciably greater degree. This authority is most evident in the book of Jubilees, which is the earliest source to refer explicitly to *ten* plagues (48:7), listing them according to the order they occur in the Pentateuch. The brevity of the account in Jubilees makes it difficult to determine whether the minor discrepancies in the descriptions of some of the plagues can be attributed to evolutions in the traditions, and each case actually requires individual treatment. In any case no inference can be drawn from the fact that the brief mention of the plague of blood omits the death of fish or the problem of thirst, since the mere mention of the plague suggests the suffering which it would cause. We may perhaps be more conclusive in the case of the boils, which in Jubilees affect only humans; it may be that the author here reflects a tradition in which, unlike the cattle pestilence, the boils had no effect on livestock. The same sort of conclusion is called for in the case of the hail, which in Jubilees is said to have smitten the produce of the fields (the remainder of which was subsequently destroyed by the locusts), but not trees, livestock or humans.

5. Philo. Philo too, like Jubilees, expressly places the number of plagues at ten (VM I.xvi, p. 95). His description of the plagues, too, generally accords with that of the Pentateuch, though the slaying of the firstborn does not affect beasts — just as it does not in most of the psalms and in Ezekiel. Philo further allows himself the liberty of arranging the plagues in his own order, beginning with the three plagues induced by Aaron (blood, frogs and lice), following them with the three brought on by Moses (hail, locusts and darkness), after these the plague of boils, which was brought on by both, and finally the plagues inflicted by God Himself: swarms, pestilence and the slaying of the firstborn. Philo's order is thus: blood, frogs, lice, hail, locusts, darkness, boils, swarms, cattle pestilence, slaying of the firstborn. Philo's highly developed exegetical method is not the issue here; still his interpretation of the juxtaposition of the plagues of cattle pestilence and of the slaying of the firstborn is exceptional: Philo states that the death of the cattle foreshadowed the advent of the death of humans, as is quite the norm with infectious diseases. The sudden death of mindless animals is a sort of prelude to a plague of epidemic character (VM I.xxiii, pp. 101-102). Philo adds that God confined the killing to the firstborn, rather than killing all the Egyptians, since He wished not "to make a complete desert of the country, but only to teach them a lesson" (xxiv, p. 102). Above[62] we have had occasion to discuss Philo's reasoning and to evaluate his statements from the tradition-history standpoint.

6. Josephus. Even more closely parallel to the Pentateuchal narrative is the account of the plagues given by Josephus. Josephus strictly maintains the Pentateuchal sequence, differing consistently on only one point: Josephus does not speak of a single plague affecting the livestock. Neither the pestilence, the boils, the hail nor even the slaying of the firstborn is said to have struck the cattle. Among these four, the most striking omission is, of course, that of all mention of cattle in the plague of pestilence, since, in the Pentateuch, this plague was aimed solely at livestock, whereas in the other three cases — boils, hail and the slaying of the firstborn — the effect on beasts is purely incidental. Instead of cattle pestilence, Josephus' account contains a brief and unclear passage accompanying the description of the plague of swarms and describing a sickness among humans, thus creating a single narrative episode of two plagues. Thus Josephus, similar to Wisdom of Solomon, follows Psalm 105 in not recognizing a cattle pestilence, but goes beyond the psalm — again, like Wisdom of Solo-

62 See p. 102.

mon — in his exclusion of any effect of the plagues on animals — to such an extent that he too does not mention the death of fish in the plague of blood.

Nevertheless, the tradition that animals were affected by the plagues, which Josephus systematically excludes, succeeds in burgeoning forth in his account of the negotiations between Moses and Pharaoh. He relates that following the plague of locusts Pharaoh agreed to allow the Hebrews to leave with their wives and children on the condition that their livestock be left behind for the Egyptians, since the latter's cattle had died (Ant. II.xiv.5). This demand lacks any foundation in Josephus' own account, and is intelligible only in light of the tradition that there had been a cattle pestilence. This discrepancy in Josephus is a typical result of the existence of conflicting traditions in the mind of a single author.

Josephus' omission of any effect of the hail on livestock has led to the omission of any similar effect of the hail upon humans, since hail which kills people but not animals cannot be imagined — even though the opposite sort of paradox, a pestilence which affects cattle but not men, is in fact posited by the Masoretic Psalm 78. As already established, however, the Masoretic version is probably corrupt.[63]

7. Pseudo-Philo. The most enigmatic description of the plagues to be found in the post-biblical sources is that of the *Liber Antiquitatum Biblicarum*. This work, though attributed to Philo, is generally believed to have actually been written in Hebrew at the end of the first century CE and translated, first into Greek and thence into Latin.[64] Only the Latin version has been preserved. The book describes at length several episodes in Israel's history, but its account of the plagues is as brief as that contained in the homiletical accounts discussed above:

> God sent upon them ten plagues and struck them down. Now these were the plagues: that is, blood and frogs and swarms and

63 Above, pp. 80-81. On Josephus' version of the plague of swarms, see note 43.
64 Kisch, *op. cit.* (above, note 4), p. 17.

hail and the death of cattle and locusts and lice and unbearable[65] darkness and the death of the firstborn.

(LAB, X:1)

This source, like Philo and Jubilees, expressly states that the number of plagues was ten, but it then proceeds to list only nine, omitting the plague of boils. Textual corruption is therefore the obvious solution — but should "boils" be added or "ten" deleted? The latter option commends itself since the order of plagues deviates from that in the Pentateuch: cattle pestilence occurs between the hail and the locusts, and the plague of lice is interposed between locusts and darkness. Possibly then, the author, who did not bother to retain the Pentateuchal order, was not particular about the number either. The Melk MS of the LAB does in fact omit the word *decem*. On the other hand, Kisch's observation[66] that the aforementioned MS omits individual words in many instances precludes certainty. Even the fact that all the Latin MSS agree in omitting "boils" is inconclusive, since all the MSS can be shown to derive from a single archetype.[67] The absence of "boils" is thus based on what amounts to a single, doubtful proof. Even if the word is added, it remains puzzling that a source compiled after the destruction of the Second Temple deviates from the Pentateuchal order of plagues in a fashion unattested in any other known source. Worthy as this enigmatic situation is of attention, no evidence exists which might enable us to proceed toward its solution.

III. Early Motifs in the Pentateuch Rejected in Didactic Passages

We now proceed to discuss a number of motifs which, though part of the plague tradition, are peculiar to the detailed narratives, whether found in the Pentateuch alone or in the other narrative accounts as well. Our contention is that at least some of these motifs, rather than being later, ornamental expansions of motifs appearing

---

65 Though most MSS read *tractabiles*, two read *intractabiles*, which is the more likely.
66 Kisch, *op. cit.* (above, note 4), p. 76.
67 *Ibid.*, pp. 29ff.

in the didactic passages, are in fact extremely ancient, but were omitted from the earlier, didactic passages because they were considered incompatible with their theological aims.

A. Pharaoh Deceived by the Israelites

According to the narrative account in Exodus, Moses was commanded at the burning bush, "When you have freed the people from Egypt, you shall worship God at this mountain" (Exod 3:12). Worship of God at the mountain was thus one of the aims of the Exodus. In the ensuing command, however, God charges Moses to present this as the sole purpose of his request to free the Israelites, by saying to Pharaoh: "The LORD, the God of the Hebrews manifested Himself to us. Now, therefore, let us go a distance of three days into the wilderness to sacrifice to the LORD our God" (v. 18; see 8:23). Moses was thus ordered to tell Pharaoh that the Israelites wished to leave Egypt with the intent of returning. Accordingly, Moses and Aaron tell Pharaoh: "Thus says the LORD, the God of Israel: Let My people go that they may celebrate a festival to Me in the wilderness" (5:1). The object of all this is to conceal from Pharaoh their true objective — to leave Egypt permanently. This limited demand for permission to leave Egypt temporarily is also the issue over which Moses and Aaron negotiate with Pharaoh throughout the narrrative, including the account of the plagues, as is clear from Exod 10:7-11, 24-27.

This motif of a deception practiced by the Israelites is an indication of the weakness of an oppressed people, entirely at Pharaoh's mercy. It cannot be overlooked, however, that it stands in some opposition to the central theme of the plague narrative in the Pentateuch: God's sovereign control over Egypt. This tension was acutely felt by Abrabanel (commentary to Exod 3:1):

> Concerning God's commanding Moses to say to Pharaoh "Now let us go a distance of three days into the wilderness": How can God have instructed Moses to speak falsely in His name? It would have been better for Moses simply to say "Release My people from the labors of Egypt". And what purpose is served

by this story, if in any case Pharaoh would eventually be forced to free them?

In his attempt to solve this difficulty, Abrabanel considers the solution proposed by Rabbenu Nissim — that the deception is necessary in order for the story to proceed in the desired manner; for had Pharaoh released the Israelites unconditionally he would never have pursued them. Rejecting this interpretation — which, though it accounts for the progression of the narrative does not solve the theological issue — Abrabanel explains that the deception was necessary in order to highlight Pharaoh's extreme obstinacy, as he was unwilling to grant even a modest request.

Both interpretations show the crucial place occupied by the motif of deception in the plagues account. It should be added that this is a motif which appears from the outset of the narrative: God informs Moses at the burning bush (Exod 3:19-20) that even when asked for permission to make a three days' journey Pharaoh will refuse, and will concede only after he has suffered the full extent of God's power. As noted, throughout the negotiations with Pharaoh Moses mentions only the request for permission to sacrifice and return.

Now this motif, though absent from the didactic poetical passages, cannot be considered as a homiletical intensification of the mighty and wondrous manner in which God redeemed Israel from slavery. Rather this is reliable evidence of historical memory, the memory of Israel's wretched condition in Egypt — a factor understandably passed over in the didactic passages such as Josh 24:5 ("Then I sent Moses and Aaron, and I plagued Egypt with the wonders that I wrought in their midst, after which I freed you") and Jdt 5:12 ("They cried out to their God, and He inflicted incurable plagues on the whole of Egypt"). It hardly needs mentioning that Psalms 78 and 105 omit all reference to the deception of Pharaoh. With the exception of Philo, who in this instance accepts the Pentateuchal account as totally binding, the Hellenistic sources reject this motif vehemently: Ezekiel has God tell Moses to inform Pharaoh of "the things commanded by Me unto you" (l. 111: τὰ ὑπ' ἐμου ταταγμένα), clearly referring to the divine command to free Israel from bondage permanently since this, and this only, is what is contained in God's earlier charge to Moses (ll. 107-108). Artapanus, still more emphatically, states explicitly that Moses informed Pharaoh that the Master of the Universe had commanded him to let the Israelites go (Eusebius IX:27, 22).

Josephus too, at least in the first portion of his account, follows this later tradition. Later, changing course in midstream, he reverts to the Pentateuchal version, relating that God, who had revealed Himself to Moses at the burning bush, told Moses to take the Israelites out of Egypt and to bring them to the land where Abraham had lived (Ant. II.xii.1). Josephus adds here the command to offer sacrifices of thanksgiving during the journey, at the place where God had appeared to Moses. The divine utterance does not, however, contain any suggestion that Moses was to represent to Pharaoh the offering of sacrifices as Israel's sole aim. Moses is hesitant, and argues: "How should I constrain Pharaoh to permit the exodus of those to whose toil and tasks his subjects look to swell their own prosperity?" (xii.2) — which indicates clearly that the issue at stake is the permanent release from slavery. Appearing before Pharaoh, Moses delivers God's message (xiii.2) which, if the command as given to Moses is intended, must have been the truth. Josephus' vague formulation is no accident: since, as we have stated, the same account says that Moses' second interview with Pharaoh (xiii.4) and all subsequent negotiations (xiv.3-5) were confined to the request for a brief leave of absence in order to sacrifice to God, it is likely that Josephus was attempting to obscure the lack of consistency in his account.

In short, since the deception of Pharaoh by the Israelites tends more to detract from the power of God than to enhance it, this motif cannot be seen as a later development of the traditions found in the early, didactic passages which aim at the glorification of God's power. It can only be regarded as a relic of an early tradition — either a tradition of an actual deception employed by Israel in order to obtain Pharaoh's permission to leave Egypt, or a more general tradition regarding their abject status in Egypt, which would not have admitted the bold idea that they had simply demanded to be released from bondage.

B. Egypt's Gods Struck by the LORD

Another early motif, visible in the Pentateuch yet different from the deception-motif discussed above, is that of the rivalry between the LORD and the gods of Egypt. While the deception-motif appears in the Pentateuch in fully developed form, so that it can be classed among the basic elements of the narrative, the motif of the LORD's confrontation with Egypt's gods is relegated to an inconspicuous position and does not affect the course of the story. The most characteristic aspect of this motif is that the LORD's contestation with the gods of Egypt is not mentioned until the moment He vanquishes them, that is, in the last plague (Exod 12:12; Num 33:4). This trait is reminiscent of Psalm 82, in which the assembly of divine beings is mentioned solely for the purpose of describing the harsh justice to be inflicted upon it by the LORD.[68] In both passages, the existence of foreign gods is in

---

68 The line of interpretation adopted here in regard to Psalm 82 is a subject of dispute among scholars. Y. M. Grintz, "Between Ugarit and Qumran (Deut. 32:8-9:34)", *Studies in Early Biblical Ethnology and History*, 1969, pp. 253-254, n. 41 [Hebrew] (and see references cited) argues against it, believing that "God stands in the divine assembly, among the divine beings He pronounces judgment" (v. 1) means simply that the LORD stands in the celestial entourage when giving judgment, without giving any indication of who are being judged; these, he says, are earthly rulers, whom the psalmist mocks: "I had taken you for divine beings, sons of the Most High all of you" (v. 6), in a fashion similar to Ezek 28:9. This interpretation of the words *bĕqereb ʾĕlōhīm yišpōṭ* in v. 1 is difficult to accept; see, for example, "O God my King from of old, who brings deliverance throughout the land" (Ps 74:12), where the word *ʾereṣ* cannot be forced into referring to the place from which the LORD acts but rather indicates that the earth is the place wherein His action is perceived. The passage in Psalm 82 is to be explained similarly. If, as Grintz contends, the text does not indicate to whom the words "How long" etc. are addressed, it must be defective, whereas in our interpretation (see below), these words are meant to denounce the assembly of divine beings mentioned previously.
These divine beings, the psalm's context would imply, are none other than foreign deities — not as in the Ugaritic pantheon, where *ʿdt il, bn il*, and *bn ilm* are devoid of any national color. In Israel the pantheon tends to become an assembly of the divine representatives of each nation. Thus, in Deut 4:19 the sun, the moon and the stars of heaven are made into the gods of the foreign nations. In Psalm 96 the hymnodic verse "For the LORD is great and much acclaimed, He is held in awe above all divine beings" is followed by the theological explanation "All the gods of the peoples are mere idols, but the LORD made the heavens" (Ps 96:4-5). The psalmist has also altered the phrase "sons of gods" (Ps 29:1), replacing it with "families of the peoples" (96:7), implying that he regarded the "sons of gods" as

effect admitted, but in such a way as not to conflict with the idea of God's sovereign dominion over the world, since the very passages which speak of foreign gods declare simultaneously the LORD's absolute ascendancy over them.

Now, while the Pentateuch's decision to postpone all mention of the gods of Egypt until such time as God should execute judgment upon them is clear enough, it still stands to reason that in ancient tradition the Egyptian gods had occupied a position as rivals of the LORD: only some such rivalry can account for the judgments executed against them. The existence of this tradition is suggested by the words spoken by Jethro: "Now I know that the LORD is greater than all gods, yes, by what they schemed against them" (*kī baddābār ʾăšer zādū ʿălēhem*) (Exod 18:11). Though the text is unclear and perhaps

identical to the gods of the foreign nations and preferred to mention the nations themselves rather than their gods. The same evolution in terminology can be observed in Ps 82. No purpose is served by describing the LORD's harsh judgment upon the celestial entourage which serves Him, but there is good reason to depict Him as abolishing their rule. This is what is alluded to in the words "Arise, O God, judge the earth, for You shall possess all the nations" (Ps 82:8). The word *tinhal* "possess" here is a clear contrast to the many passages which stress that Israel and its land are the LORD's *nahălā* "allotted possession" (Exod 15:17; Deut 4:20; 9:26,29; 32:9; 1 Sam 10:1; 26:19; 2 Sam 20:19; 21:3; 1 Kgs 8:51,53; Isa 19:25(?); 47:6; 63:17; Jer 2:7; 12:7-9; 50:11; Joel 4:2; Mic 7:18; Pss 28:9; 68:10; 74:2; 78:68,71; 79:1; 94:5; 106:5). This condition obtained as long as the heathen gods also had their own allotted possessions (*nahălā*); at their fall, the whole earth became the possession of the LORD.

The foreign gods are specifically mentioned in the LXX of Deut 32:8, as well as in a Dead Sea fragment which scholars have correctly accepted. Even Grintz, who defends MT (*loc. cit.*), does not suggest any interpretation for its reading "for the number of the children of Israel".

For Grintz, the main proof that Psalm 82 speaks of judgment over mortal men is the verb *niṣṣāb* ("stands") in v. 1, which elsewhere always refers to God's standing over human beings — unlike the verb *yāšab* "sit", which is always used to refer to His position whenever He is among the heavenly entourage. This reasoning is not persuasive: the LORD *sits* among the celestial beings when the entourage concerned is the assembly of His attendants who wait upon Him (1 Kgs 22:19; Dan 7:9-10), whereas in Psalm 82 the phrase "divine assembly" refers to foreign gods whom the LORD rebukes. Since the psalmist denigrates them, to the extent that he reduces them to the rank of human beings destined to die, it is not at all surprising that he has God *standing* in this assembly, just as He stands over actual mortals! Grintz's interpretation derives from his basic view that the idea of individual gods

incomplete, all the passages taken together appear to be the remnants of a tradition regarding the battle waged by Israel's God against the gods of Egypt.

It is no surprise that the judgments executed by the LORD upon the gods of Egypt are nowhere mentioned outside of the Pentateuch, with the sole exception of Jubilees, totally dependent even here on the Pentateuchal account. Jubilees modifies the motif, however, by explaining that God avenged Himself upon the *idols* of Egypt by burning them with fire and not mentioning the actual *gods* themselves (48:5). A more distant echo of the same motif is found in Wisdom of Solomon, which asserts that the LORD punished the Egyptians by means of the very animals which they had reverenced in their folly and which they worshipped (12:23-27; 16:1).

---

assigned to foreign nations was created in Israel *ex nihilo* when the book of Daniel was written. His proof consists of the well-known passages which state that non-Israelite gods are of no substance, identifying the heathen gods with their lifeless images. But the importance of these polemical statements should not be overestimated. The idea that each nation has its own god is rooted in a theological view centuries earlier than the book of Daniel, and it is this view which, on the one hand, sees the LORD as the Creator and supreme Ruler of the universe and, at the same time, as the God of Israel, whose people and land are His allotted possession. It was the monotheistic trend, however, the war against the worship of other gods and the hatred of the heathen whose might testifies to the rebellion of their gods against the LORD, which led to a longing for these gods to be annihilated. This is sometimes expressed rather vaguely, as in "In that day, the LORD will punish the host of heaven in heaven and the kings of the earth upon the earth" (Isa 24:21); "And the LORD shall be King over all the earth; in that day the LORD shall be One and His name one" (Zech 14:9). "In that day", the prophet says; not before.

One argument used in the polemic against idols is that they did not create the heaven and the earth and are therefore doomed to destruction (Jer 10:11). In Psalm 82 this argument from cosmogony is replaced by the ethical argument: these gods are not righteous judges and it is therefore only just that they should die and their allotted possessions be added to that of the LORD. This struggle with the problem of foreign deities went on for many generations in Israel, since it was woven in the very fabric of Israel's religion. For this reason one cannot address the question posed by Grintz, namely, if the "divine beings" in the psalm are the gods of the heathens and are destined to perish, how were any left to appear in Daniel and in all subsequent generations (*loc. cit.*), to the interpretation we have proposed to Ps 82:7. See further S. E. Loewenstamm, "*Nahălat* YHWH", *Scripta Hierosolymitana*, 31 (1986), pp. 155-192 (enlarged version of an earlier Hebrew study appearing in *Sefer Dim*, Jerusalem 1958, pp. 120-125).

C. Pharaoh's Magicians *vs.* Moses and Aaron

Although the motif we have been discussing, of which the Pentateuch shows only the barest traces and which the other sources have rejected entirely, namely, the LORD's defeat of the gods of Egypt, cannot be reconstructed, one can surmise that this tradition has some connection with what is recounted in the Pentateuch about Pharaoh's magicians. Presumably, the magicians of Egypt acted by the power of Egypt's gods, just as Moses and Aaron acted by the LORD's power. The exhibiting of miraculous signs too is to be considered an early motif and one worthy of comprehensive analysis.

The marvels which Moses is to perform in Pharaoh's sight are mentioned for the first time in a puzzling passage:

> And the LORD said to Moses, "When you return to Egypt, see that you perform before Pharaoh all the marvels that I have put within your power. I, however, will stiffen his heart so that he will not let the people go. Then you shall say to Pharaoh, 'Thus says the LORD: Israel is My first-born son. I have said to you, "Let My son go, that he may worship Me", yet you refuse to let him go. Now I will slay your first-born son'".
>
> (Exod 4:21-22)

From this statement one gets the impression that Moses was later to perform the three miracles with which the LORD had entrusted him at the burning bush (the rod turned to a serpent; the leprous hand; the bloody water) and that immediately thereafter the LORD would slay the Egyptian firstborn. That this is not what happens was noticed as early as Rashi, who states: "God could not have been ordering Moses to perform these three aforementioned wonders before Pharaoh, since Moses never does so; rather he was told to perform them before Israel in order that they might believe in him". Rashi therefore proposes that the three signs referred to are not those mentioned in the vision at the bush, but rather "those marvels which I will later put within your power — in Egypt". Advising the reader not to be puzzled by the wording of the text ("the marvels *that I have put* within your power"), Rashi interprets, "The meaning is: By the time you speak to Pharaoh, *I shall have put* them in your power". Rashi explains further that the slaying of the firstborn announced here "is indeed the last plague, but he warned Pharaoh of it at the outset, since it was to be the most severe".

The difficulty posed by the ensuing account, namely, that Moses does not threaten Pharaoh with the death of the firstborn at the outset of the negotiations between them, is however unavoidable. Thus it may in fact be the case that the passage quoted preserves some recollection of a tradition according to which the slaying of the firstborn followed immediately upon the performance of the three marvels which Moses had been shown at the bush. Another possibility is that the narrative has telescoped the ensuing events, reducing them to their barest essentials. In any case we are here concerned only with Moses, who, as noted by Rashi, did not in fact perform the three signs before Pharaoh. Yet, we should not ignore the striking resemblance between the first of these three signs (the rod turned to a serpent) and the turning of Moses' rod into a crocodile (Exod 7:8-12), and between the third sign (transforming some water into blood) and the plague of blood. Even according to the Pentateuchal account, then, wonders bearing a similarity to two out of the three marvels entrusted to Moses at the bush were in fact performed before Pharaoh, which indicates that there is a traditio-historical connection. Furthermore, Josephus states quite simply that Moses, at his first encounter with Pharaoh, displayed the signs which he had been given (Ant. II.xiii.3). A trace of the same tradition can be found in Philo, although he seems to have been uncertain regarding this question and kept his account vague. The very signs which, according to the Pentateuch, were performed by Aaron before the people prior to the start of the negotiations with Pharaoh were, according to Philo, shown by Moses to the people when they complained so bitterly that their yoke had been made heavier as a result of Moses' speaking to Pharaoh. Following the display of marvels in the sight of the Israelites, Philo states, "The exhibition of these wonders to the king and the Egyptian nobles followed very quickly" (VM I.xv, p. 95), which presumably implies that the very same marvels which the people had just seen were performed before Pharaoh. In what follows, however, Philo describes the crocodile episode as it appears in the Pentateuch; the inconsistency may be an indication of conflicting traditions.

Artapanus, too, it would appear, has preserved the memory of a similar tradition. He asserts that "Moses threw down the rod which he had and made a *serpent*. When all were terrified, he seized its tail, took it up and made it a rod again" (Eusebius IX:27, 27). When he describes the plague of blood, however, Artapanus adds that the magicians of Egypt repeated the miracle. There is thus no room for any doubt that there existed a Hellenistic tradition that Moses performed before Pharaoh the very marvels he had received at the burning bush. The question remains whether this is the most ancient tradition, one which took shape at a stage which knew only of these first three marvels and the slaying of the firstborn, or whether — less daring perhaps — the motif of marvels performed before the Israelites has simply led to a secondary motif, that of their being performed before Pharaoh.

The actual competition with Pharaoh's magicians is introduced in the Pentateuch in part before the plagues cycle begins and in part as a component of the plagues cycle. At both stages the power of the Egyptian magicians is equal to that of the LORD's emissary at the beginning of the episode and humbled before it at the end. The difference is that in the crocodile episode the entire process takes place within one scene, while in the plagues cycle it takes place over the course of three plagues (or four; see below). The implication is that the Pentateuchal account is based upon two separate, perhaps alternative, traditions.

The only point worthy of comment in the episode is the fact that the protagonist is not Moses but Aaron.[69] The characteristic element in Artapanus' account (discussed above) is that the Egyptians manage to emulate Moses precisely, leaving the latter with no advantage. Philo's lengthy description (VM I.xvi, p. 95), which is marked by considerable literary embellishment, does not deviate essentially from that of the Pentateuch. Even his remark that Aaron's crocodile, after swallowing up those of the magicians, became a rod once more is

69 See below, pp. 136-147.

nothing more than an interpretation of the statement in the Pentateuch that "Aaron's rod swallowed their rods" (Exod 7:12).

Josephus' account is more complex. Here, after Moses has exhibited the three marvels to Pharaoh — including, of course, the rod
which turned into a serpent — Pharaoh commands his magicians as
well to perform miracles. They cast down their rods, which become
serpents, after which Moses once again casts down his own rod and
it becomes a serpent once more, swallows the magicians' rods and
resumes its form (Ant. II.xiii.3). Josephus' rearrangement of events
recorded in the Pentateuch is necessitated by his assumption (mentioned above) that Moses had changed his serpent back into a rod
before the magicians arrived on the scene. This in turn compels him
to arrange the account which follows in such a way that when the
magicians finally arrive on the scene, it is they who initiate the action.
The combination of traditions, however, in which the story of Moses'
performing *three* marvels before Pharaoh is recorded alongside the
Pentateuchal idea that a competition took place over *one* marvel
alone, is unconvincing, since we would surely have expected to find
a triple contest in Josephus' account.

We have stated that the process by which the magicians begin as
the equals of God's agent and are ultimately humbled, a process
which is complete in one episode in the story of the crocodile,
extends, when it recurs in the plagues cycle, over three separate episodes which are integrated into the first three plagues. In the first two
plagues the magicians are successful in obtaining the same results as
the LORD's emissaries, but fail to do so in the third, going so far as
to admit their failure by declaring, "This is the finger of God!" (Exod
8:15).[70] We thus have here an ascending series of three episodes in
which the decisive event takes place in the third stage, a feature reminiscent of the Gilgameš Epic (Tablet XI, ll. 146-154), the dove episode in the biblical Flood story (Gen 8:8-12), the account of the three
delegations sent by Ahaziah to Elijah (2 Kgs 1:9-16) and, in the
plagues cycle itself, the three stages of Pharaoh's gradual capitula-

---

70 For this rhetorical figure see B. Courvoyer, "Le Doigt de Dieu", *RB*, 63 (1966),
pp. 481-495, who claims to have found an Egyptian source for the image.

tion.[71] The disappearance of the magicians after the third plague is thus perfectly understandable; what is surprising is their sudden re-appearance in the sixth. The ascending scale, complete in itself, is thereby augmented with an additional phase: while in the third plague (lice), the magicians were still able at least to launch an unsuccessful attempt at imitating the act performed by God's agent, in the sixth plague (boils) they were incapable of any action, since they too were infected by the boils. In this manner, though the story of the lice spares the magicians' dignity even while reporting their defeat, since the words "This is the finger of God!" are a wise insight and a credit to whoever utters them, in the sixth plague the magicians are the object of ridicule. All of these considerations lead us to conclude that the development of the contest motif, with the added motif of ridicule at the plague of boils, belongs to a later stage of the tradition, just as the plague of boils itself is the latest element in the entire plagues cycle, as we have seen above.[72]

While we have begun here with the unique difficulty posed by the plague of boils, there is actually another, much larger problem, namely, the extent to which the competition motif is integrated into the plague narrative. The crocodile episode is simple enough, since the rivalry between God's messenger and Pharaoh's magicians is over a mere display. Thereafter, however, even the uncritical reader will ask, why should the magicians have wished to aggravate the suffering of their countrymen by adding to the plagues? In the case of the blood, moreover, there is an even more glaring difficulty: if, as the text states

---

71 See below, pp. 154-159.
72 See p. 95. J. Pedersen, "Passahfest und Passahlegende", *ZAW*, 52 (1934), p. 173 conjectures that the magicians also belong to the tradition of the fourth and fifth plagues, explaining the fact that they are not mentioned in the Pentateuchal accounts of these plagues by assuming, without any basis, that the text is defective. But the difficulty in the text is that the magicians return in the sixth plague after having already admitted the superior power of the LORD in the third, not that they are absent in the fourth and fifth! Far from being defective or incomplete, the account in the Pentateuch endeavors to assemble, as far as possible, all the various traditions. Pedersen's theory is intelligible only as a result of his harmonistic explanation, which sees in the apparent duplication of some of the wonders, which appear both as spectacles and plagues, two aspects of the same event rather than contradictory accounts.

emphatically, all the waterways of Egypt had become blood, leaving no water at all, whence did the magicians obtain water to turn into blood?

These matters, which cannot be overlooked, refute firstly the opinion of those scholars who believe the competition motif to be a late element, introduced for the sake of embellishing the narrative. From the literary point of view, a motif which flatly and transparently contradicts the internal logic of the narrative cannot be regarded as a literary embellishment. Moreover, from the theological perspective, this motif does not enhance but rather detracts from the desired intent. The aim of the plagues narrative, to establish that the supremacy of God is absolute, is achieved by virtue of the fact that the plagues actually occurred, while the competition with the magicians of Egypt establishes only that the supremacy of God's agents is relative. No later writer could possibly have added this motif of his own accord without being aware that he was in fact doing damage to the story.

Such an action would, however, be intelligible if we were to assume that the writer had before him two traditions to which he felt obligated to do justice: one viewing the episodes of blood, frogs and lice as mere spectacles in which the parties competed and the other regarding these same events as actual plagues. In such a case it would not be the fault of the writer not to have solved a difficulty to which no solution exists. It would further appear, in view of the theological consideration noted, that the tradition containing the competition motif is the earlier of the two. A process by which the account of God's messengers competing with Pharaoh's magicians over the performance of spectacular feats gradually evolved into a story in which God's enemies are dealt fatal blows, thus revealing His absolute and unmediated supremacy over them, is easily envisaged, while the opposite process is unimaginable. A tradition which recognizes the power of the enemy and the effort entailed by the competition with him must certainly be ancient, in fact, near in time to the events it recounts. It cannot be viewed as a later addition to an alternative tradition in which the power of the enemy is utterly obliterated and all that is left is a series of dazzling victories.

Our view also requires assuming the existence of a tradition in which blood, frogs and lice (or swarms) appeared as mere displays.[73] As correctly observed by Gressmann,[74] the text of the Pentateuch enables us to reconstruct this tradition in the case of the plague of blood: at the burning bush, Moses was instructed "Take some water from the Nile and pour it on the dry ground, and it — the water that you take from the Nile — will turn to blood on the dry ground" (Exod 4:9). On this basis we may reconstruct a tradition that Moses (or Aaron) acted accordingly in Pharaoh's sight and that the magicians of Egypt repeated the same feat. Hebrew exegetes, it may be added, were sensitive to the close connection between the marvel entrusted to Moses at the burning bush and the subsequent plague of blood, which led them to attempt to explain the latter in the light of the former. Thus Abrabanel, in his commentary to Exod 7:14,[75] expounds:

> I have seen it suggested that when the actual plague [of blood] occurred, the water was not turned to blood immediately but rather its character turned blood-like and it became blood in potential only, but when it was poured out upon the dry ground it became actual blood. The proponent of this interpretation found support in the statement made earlier "Take some water from the Nile...and it will turn to blood on the dry ground".
> (Exod 4:9).

By analogy we are forced to imagine a scheme according to which the frogs and lice (or swarms) too were displays, conjured up in small quantities and not amounting to a plague that affected the country.

The competition motif is absent entirely from all of the didactic passages (with the exception of Jubilees which follows the Penta-

---

73 This observation does not, of course, apply to the later plague of boils, the description of which was influenced by those of the blood, frogs and lice. The question why the magicians should have aggravated the plagues afflicting their own countrymen is here less prominent, since they did not actually obtain any result. The purpose of formulating an additional plague was apparently to end the story of the magicians with their utter humiliation.

74 Gressmann, *op. cit.* (note 51, above), p. 90.

75 See above, note 35.

teuch),[76] as well as from the detailed accounts of Philo and Josephus. Artapanus limits his use of this motif to the plague of blood, which he accomplishes only by deviating from the plain sense of the text in order to avoid the perplexing problem of the magicians having aggravated the plague. According to Artapanus' account, after the episode of the crocodile, Moses struck the Nile with his rod, whereupon its water rose and inundated the whole of Egypt. Bodies of standing water stank; living creatures in the Nile perished and humans were at the point of death from thirst. In this desperate state of affairs Pharaoh promised to free the people for one month's time if Moses would restore the Nile to its former state. Moses struck the water again with his rod, bringing it back to its proper bed (an *actus contrarius*; cf. Exod 14:26), after which Pharaoh summoned the priests of Memphis and threatened to dismiss them and destroy their temple unless they could perform similarly. Accordingly, using spells and sorcery, they first conjured up a crocodile (to match Moses' serpent) and then imbued the Nile with color (to match Moses' second display). These magical feats improved Pharaoh's spirits, and instead of releasing the Hebrews he devised ways of tormenting them further.

The apparent difficulties in Artapanus arrangement of the events disappear when we observe that his account obviates both of the questions which can be posed regarding that of the Pentateuch, namely, why would the Egyptian magicians have aggravated the plague, and whence did they obtain the water needed in order to perform their miracle? In Artapanus' version, the magicians performed only a display — they changed the color of the water — which caused no harm, and they did so after the plague of blood had ended, at which time the waters of Egypt were again in their natural state. Clearly, in ironing out the difficulties in the Pentateuchal account, Artapanus has paid a heavy price: the loss of any relationship whatsoever between Moses' act and that of the magicians. Moses brought upon Egypt a flood involving the death of fish and general thirst; the magicians responded to this with theatrics — changing the color of the water. Artapanus' explanation cannot therefore be regarded as an indepen-

---

76 See below, p. 126.

dent tradition but only as a forced solution to a problem — and one which deviates too greatly from the plain sense of the text to have had any influence on the subsequent history of exegesis.

Nor does the attempt made by Tg. Jonathan to alleviate the difficulty in the Pentateuchal account, by proposing that the magicians' action turned to blood only the waters of the Goshen district (Tg. Jonathan at Exod 7:22), amount to any more than an idiosyncratic attempt. The flaw in this solution, which turns the action of the magicians into retaliation against the Israelites, is evident at Exod 8:3, where the text states clearly that the magicians "brought frogs upon the land of Egypt" and even Jonathan renders, perhaps reluctantly, in total accord with the Hebrew, *wĕʾassīqū yat ʿurdĕʿānayyā ʿal ʾarʿā dĕmiṣrāyīm*. A partial solution such as this, in which the magicians acted in totally different fashion in the two plagues, fails to resolve the difficulty.

More logical, and more in accord with the text, is the solution proposed by Jubilees. Here the magicians' action is guided by Prince Mastema, embodiment of evil. God permits them to peform an evil act but not to remedy it, in addition to which they are afflicted by boils (Jub 48:9-11). Here a note of derision can be detected: the magicians, as they are evil forces, are allowed to add to the woes of Egypt but not to cure them! This theme was revived by Abrabanel, who, unaware of the dualistic philosophy underlying the book of Jubilees, commented on Exod 8:14 as follows:

> The magicians, in order to preserve their own honor, strove to reproduce the plague [of lice] and to remove it thereafter at Pharaoh's command. In producing it they acted like Aaron: "*The magicians did the like with their spells*"; whereas when they attempted immediately afterwards "*to take the lice out*" [*lĕhōṣīʾ ʾet hakkinnīm*], i.e., of the earth, "*they could not*" — meaning they could not *remove* them.[77]

Abrabanel thus rewords the verse to read: "*The magicians did the like with their spells* (i.e. *produced* lice) *but could not* remove *the lice*"

77 See above, note 35.

(inverting the order of *lĕhōṣī² ²et hakkinnīm* and *wĕlō² yākōlū* and taking *lĕhōṣī²* to mean "remove from the earth" rather than "to produce"). Such an interpretation is most improbable;[78] Ibn Ezra's view is clearly to be preferred:

> "The magicians did the like": i.e., they struck the dust of the earth. "*lĕhōṣī² ²et hakkinnīm*": the meaning is "to produce them" from the earth, as Aaron had done — "but they could not".[79]

Abrabanel's interpretation is not only incompatible with the wording of the verse, it also ruins the structure of the rivalry narrative, since it raises the question why the magicians were content merely to increase the severity of the first two plagues without trying their hand at removing them, and why they have suddenly, in the third plague, become inspired to make such an attempt. We arrive at the same conclusion, namely, that the incorporation of the competition motif in the plague narrative can be explained only as a later stage in the history of tradition, and that this motif had originally constituted an independent narrative.

D. The "Rejected" Motifs — Summary

These, then, are the three motifs in the Pentateuchal narrative which are foreign to the didactic passages: the Israelite attempt to deceive Pharaoh; the battle between Israel's God and the gods of Egypt; the competition between the LORD's emissary and Pharaoh's magicians. They share in common a tendency to detract somewhat from the absolute supremacy and universal sovereignty of the LORD, whose power the didactic passages aim to describe as limitless. Upon this we have based our thesis that these Pentateuchal motifs are not to be regarded as developments or embellishments of motifs appearing in

---

78 Cassuto, *op. cit.* (note 36, above), pp. 105-106, has re-asserted Abrabanel's opinion, adding some further argumentation.

79 Abraham Ibn Ezra, Commentary on Pentateuch, ed. Y. L. Krinsky, repr. N. Y. [n.d.].

the didactic passages but rather as early traditions, possessing their own independent authority, which did not commend themselves to the authors of the didactic passages.

The only post-biblical source to mention the conflict between the LORD and the gods of Egypt is Jubilees, which reduces the judgments executed upon Egypt's gods to the mere burning of their images. This is also the only source which retains the motif of the competition between Moses and Aaron and the Egyptian magicians. It presents the latter as acting under the influence of the evil Prince Mastema, and distorts the sense of the Pentateuchal narrative by holding up the magicians to derision and mockery — though the beginnings of this trend can indeed be found in the biblical account of the plague of boils.

Among the post-biblical sources, the detailed narratives too tend to supplant these early motifs. The LORD's battle with the gods of Egypt is virtually absent in them, while the competition with the magicians is included in only a few plagues. The deception motif is present in Philo only, whereas Artapanus and Ezekiel reject it entirely and Josephus' uneasiness with it is all too obvious, leading to an illogical and inconsistent account.

IV. Other Details of the Plague Narrative

We shall now proceed to demonstrate that the Pentateuch has asserted its predominance over the later sources far less with regard to the precise details of the narrative than with regard to the actual plagues. Even Josephus, and, to a lesser extent, Philo, whose accounts of the actual plagues conform to the Pentateuch quite visibly (though not absolutely), are not constrained by the Pentateuchal account in many aspects which have no bearing upon the plagues themselves.

A. Who Produced the Plagues?

1. The Problem. First among the details of the plague narrative is the issue of whether the plagues are produced directly by God or through an intermediary. Discussion of this issue most logically begins with the observation that, both in the Bible and in later literature, divine acts are portrayed in three ways: as direct action on the part of the LORD Himself, as action performed on His behalf by a messenger or messengers of divine character ("angels"), or as action performed on His behalf by human agent or agents. Whenever celestial beings or earthly agents are employed, the text leaves no doubt that this is the case. However, sources which speak of God's own action are occasionally vague, so that the intent may either be to indicate that He acted directly or to leave the question of how He acted unanswered.

The presence of varying traditions on this matter is therefore not confined to the Exodus episode; rather, it is a fundamental tension characteristic of Israelite tradition as a whole, and cannot be dealt with here. Two examples, however, can be adduced for purposes of illustration: The first is the story of the death of Moses,[80] which is depicted in the later sources as having been brought about by the LORD, who then personally saw to His prophet's burial, while other sources assign some role in the episode to divine messengers. A more significant example is that of the traditions concerning Israel's ultimate redemption,[81] which divide into three types: those which predict that the LORD Himself will perform lasting deliverance, those which state that He will do so through the agency of an annointed king ("Messiah"), and those according to which He will act through a heavenly messenger.

The same type of diversity is present in the Exodus traditions, and in the plagues cycle in particular. And while there would be no point in enumerating either the many passages in which the LORD is said to have acted directly or those in which He acts through the agency of Moses (or Moses and Aaron), what does bear mention is the existence of traces of at least one tradition in which the LORD acts through an angel. The story of the parting of the sea includes the statement

---

80 See above, Chapter One, note 16.
81 Y. Yadin, "The Scrolls and the Epistle to the Hebrews", *Scripta Hierosolymitana*, 4 (1958), pp. 36-55; S. E. Loewenstamm, s.v. "*Mîkā᾿el*", *᾿Enṣîqlôpedîā Miqrā᾿ît*, IV, pp. 881-882.

that "the angel of God, who had been going ahead of the Israelite army, now moved and followed behind them; and the pillar of cloud shifted from in front of them and took up a place behind them" (Exod 14:19). The first half of the verse preserves the record of a tradition according to which an angel of the LORD performed the actions which in the main tradition, preserved in the second half of the verse, are attributed to the pillar of fire and the pillar of cloud — which symbolize the actual divine Presence. The former view is also preserved in the words spoken by Moses to the king of Edom: "We cried to the Lord and He heard our plea, and He sent a mal³āk who freed us from Egypt" (Num 20:16). And while, not surprisingly, some rabbinic authorities took the word mal³āk as referring to a human messenger, namely Moses,[82] the Targumim correctly render with mal³ākā (Tg. Onqelos; Tg. Jonathan more emphatically: ḥad mimmal³ākē šērūtā), which is reserved in the Targumic tradition for an angel, whereas a human messenger is always translated ³izgaddā.

An alternative to this tradition is the view that the LORD Himself guided His people from Egypt only as far as Mount Sinai, and that thenceforth this guidance was replaced by that of an angel. This divine decree is mentioned twice: once, without elaboration and unchallenged, in Exod 23:20-23, and once as a potential outcome of the Calf episode in Exod 33:2-6, annulled when God, at Moses' prayer, relented from His decree.

Traces of this view are preserved in the plague tradition as well. Psalm 78 speaks of the plague of pestilence as being produced by "a band of deadly messengers" (v. 49), and the slaying of the firstborn gave rise to a sharp controversy over whether the blow was delivered by God Himself, by a destroying angel, or by a band of such angels of destruction; we shall return to this topic presently.[83]

2. The Agent in the Pentateuchal Account. Two aspects of the ques-

---

82 See Yal. Šimʿoni on this verse: "Who freed us from Egypt — this means Moses, since we find that prophets are called mal³ākīm 'messengers', as it is said 'Bless the LORD, O His messengers (mal³ākāyw)' (Ps 103:20); so also 'But they mocked the messengers of God (mal³ākē ³ĕlōhīm)' (2 Chr 36:16); 'An angel of the LORD (mal³ak YHWH) came up from Gilgal' (Judg 2:1)"; see also Rashi.

83 Below, pp. 134-135.

tion of agency in the Pentateuchal account of the plagues require examination: that of the existing text, in its final redaction, and that of the text's historical analysis, in which various traditions must be distinguished within the description of a single plague. In the first case, that of the redacted text, no difficulties are encountered: the first three plagues were induced by Aaron, and, as noted earlier,[84] traditional Jewish exegesis accepts this redactional view at least with regard to the plague of blood. The fourth and fifth plagues were produced directly by God, the sixth by Moses assisted by Aaron, the seventh, eighth and ninth by Moses alone, and the tenth, once again, by God Himself.

More complex is the question of the extent to which various traditions can be discerned in the descriptions of some of the plagues. We agreed above[85] with the widely held opinion that it is possible to discern traces of a tradition according to which Moses, and not Aaron, called forth the plague of blood. Here we shall occupy ourselves with another issue: whether, in the accounts of plagues which, in the redacted Pentateuchal narrative, were brought about by one of God's agents, traces may be found of traditions according to which they were performed by God Himself.

In addressing this question it will be necessary to distinguish clearly between passages in which a plague is referred to either before or after it has come to pass, and passages which describe the actual process by which the plague was produced. To the former category belongs such a statement as "seven days had passed after the LORD struck the Nile" (Exod 7:25), and all those verses in which Moses proclaims to Pharaoh the imminent onset of a particular plague: frogs (7:27), hail (9:18), locusts (10:4) and — probably, despite special problems to be discussed below[86] — blood (7:17). The common opinion that these passages indicate varying traditions cannot be substantiated, since no real contradiction exists between the general statement that the LORD is about to inflict a plague and the particular narrative account of how

---

84 See above, pp. 89-90.
85 *Ibid.*
86 Below, p. 148.

He did so by some intermediary. This is amply exemplified by Psalm 105, in which the description of the plagues produced by God (vv. 28-36) is preceded by the general statement that Moses and Aaron performed His signs and wonders (vv. 26-27). The psalmist's procedure is unexceptionable; he felt no contradiction between his introductory words and the actual description of the plagues.

To the second category, descriptive verses appearing in the accounts of the plagues themselves, belongs the direct action of God mentioned in the plagues of hail and locusts (Exod 9:23 and 10:13); greater weight must be attached to the assertion that these may have been interpolated from a source which attributed these plagues to the LORD alone. Of special interest in this regard is the comparison between the account of the locusts, in which the LORD's action combines with that of Moses, and the account of the darkness, in which Moses alone appears. Compare:

The LORD said to Moses:	The LORD said to Moses
Hold out your arm	Hold out your arm
toward the sky	toward the sky
that there may be darkness	that hail may fall
upon the land of Egypt	upon all the land of Egypt
...	...
Moses held out his arm	Moses held out his rod
toward the sky	toward the sky
and thick darkness descended	and *The LORD sent thunder*
upon all the land of Egypt	*and hail, and fire streamed*
for three days.	*along the ground...*fire
	flashing in the midst of
	hail...
10:21-22	9:22-24

While the internal unity of the first passage is clear, the same cannot be said of the second. If the italicized words, which refer to the LORD's direct action, are deleted, the description of the hail is precisely parallel to that of the darkness. This lends some support to the common view that the plague of hail is a conflation of two sources, one of which saw the hail as a direct result of Moses' action while the other attributed it to the LORD alone and did not even recognize Moses' participation in the plague's onset. The argument is not decisive, however, since it can still be asserted that difference is one of formulation, and that the question of whether Moses' action in obedience to the divine command was followed by God's own action or whether Moses' action was the direct cause of the plague is immaterial, it being clear that the plague came about by the LORD's command and by His power.

Further, with regard to the plague of locusts, even assuming the existence of two such traditions, one that the LORD Himself inflicted the plague and the other that He did so through the agency of Moses, the question remains: is their fusion purely a redactional matter, or may we perhaps speak of a theological school which developed the idea of divine-prophetic cooperation? This theology is manifest in the sole biblical passage referring to Abraham by the title "prophet", thereby comparing him to Moses, i.e., God's words to Abimelech: "Therefore, restore the man's wife — since he is a prophet, he will intercede for you — to save your life" (Gen 20:7). Here too the logic of the narrative is complex; were it not, it would have recounted either that God told Abimelech that if he restored Abraham's wife to him he would be cured, without mentioning Abraham's intercession, or else that God was at first unwilling to cure Abimelech but finally acceded to Abraham's prayer. The text as it stands, in which God promises to save Abimelech *by virtue of* Abraham's prayer, elevates Abraham to the rank of partner in the execution of God's predetermined plan — which is apparently why he here merits the title of prophet. Now it is conceivable that the same theology determines the structure of the account of the locusts. The LORD resolved to inflict this plague upon Egypt, and it was indeed He who did so. But the execution of this divine resolve was preceded — by His consent — by the action of His prophet, an action which merges with His own.

The question of a tradition that God acted alone in the plague of blood will be taken up in the next section, and the joint action of God and Moses in the parting of the sea will be dealt with in Chapter Seven.[87]

3. The LORD *as Sole Producer of the Plagues.* Most of the extra-Pentateuchal evidence for the existence of a tradition that all of the plagues were brought about by God Himself is of doubtful validity. It should immediately be clear that no weight at all can be attached to the mention of the plagues with which the LORD smote Egypt contained in passages of praise and thanksgiving, such as Deut 11:3, Josh 24:5, Neh 9:10, 3 Macc 2:6 and Jdt 5:12. Similarly, no decisive proof can be adduced from Psalm 78, since the conquest of Canaan too is referred to in the words "He expelled nations before them" (v. 55), certainly without any intention of denying the part played by Israel in the conquest and of attributing it entirely to God. When the poet's purpose is to extol the mighty deeds of the LORD as part of a didactic history, he is not bound to record events in any detail at all; certainly he is not obliged to mention the agents of God who acted by His power.

The same, however, is not true of the didactic passage in Jubilees. While it evidently aims at assigning particular prominence to the role of Moses, its somewhat cryptic account does seem to have subsumed a tradition that the plagues were brought about by God alone. The passage begins by emphasizing that Moses executed all of the signs and wonders he was ordered to perform (48:4), goes on to state that the LORD avenged Israel by bringing the plagues (48:5), and concludes with the statement that all of the plagues were sent by Moses, who announced their onset to Pharaoh in advance (48:6-7). Thus the beginning of the passage creates the impression that Moses induced the plagues, whereas the latter part suggests that he merely announced them. A possible explanation for this obvious confusion is the amalgamation of two conflicting traditions. According to one, Moses brought about the plagues, just as he did in the accounts of Artapanus and Ezekiel.[88] In the other, Moses simply foretold the plagues, which accords with Josephus, whose narrative leaves no room for doubt on

87 Below, pp. 148, 270.
88 See pp. 135-136.

this point, especially since he accuses Pharaoh of having tried to cheat divine providence, as if Moses and not God were punishing Egypt on behalf of the Hebrews (Ant. II.xiv.3); Josephus is also unaware of the tradition that some of the plagues were removed at Moses' behest.

Now, the emphasis found in Josephus that God brought about all the plagues Himself is not present in the other Hellenistic sources, and it is difficult to assume that Josephus would have ventured upon such a bold innovation unless he had some support in early tradition. Along with the traces we have found in the Pentateuch of a tradition that it was God who brought about the plagues of hail and locusts, and the dual tradition evidenced in Jubilees, this aspect of Josephus' account inclines the scale in favor of the conclusion that there did exist a tradition that God Himself inflicted all the plagues.

To this ancient tradition and that reflected in the Pentateuchal account, a third may perhaps be added, namely, that the divine intervention occurred only in the last, decisive plague. In other words, according to this view, God sent all of the plagues through the agency of one of His messengers except for the last. The possibility that this tradition is reflected in the words "Moses and Aaron performed all these marvels before Pharaoh" (Exod 11:10), with which the ninth plague ends and which provide the transition to the direct action of the LORD, cannot be dismissed out of hand. If we take the wording of the verse quite literally, we would have here direct evidence of a tradition that Moses and Aaron were active even in the plagues of swarms and cattle pestilence.

4. Moses as Producer of the Plagues. Some evidence of a tradition that it was Moses who produced all of the plagues may be adduced from the divine command "And take with you this rod, with which you shall perform the signs" (Exod 4:17). It is at least certain that this is how the verse was understood by Ezekiel the Tragedian, who introduces his account of the plagues with the words "With this rod all these woes you shall effect" (l. 132), implying that Moses subsequently did just that. Artapanus' view, as noted above,[89] is the same; in fact, in Artapanus account (Eusebius IX:27, 21) God's role is con-

89 See pp. 102-103.

fined to commanding Moses to lead the Israelites out of Egypt, so that Moses, by producing the plagues, is simply implementing this general command, not complying with any specific directive to inflict one plague or another upon Egypt. It would appear that Ezekiel and Artapanus reflect an ancient tradition which, as we have noted, appears in Jubilees as well,[90] and according to which Moses brought about all of the plagues.

5. *The Role of Aaron.* On the other hand, there is no record of a tradition attributing all of the plagues to Aaron. Outside of the Pentateuch, Aaron's role is mentioned only in Psalm 105 and by Philo. The latter is unquestionably dependent on the Pentateuch in this matter and requires no further discussion. The question of agreement between Psalm 105 and the Pentateuch is not quite so clear. Since the psalm's compressed style leaves room for some doubt as to whether Moses and Aaron produced all of the plagues or only some of them, it is impossible to tell precisely how the psalmist envisaged the division of labor between them. What is clear is that he was far from assuming that the whole process was produced by Aaron.

The absence of any such tradition is even more obvious when Aaron's role is compared with those of the LORD and Moses. All traditions agree that it was the LORD who took Israel out of Egypt and smote the Egyptians with grievous plagues; differences of opinion are confined to the question of the extent to which He did so unassisted by His emissaries. Similarly, all of the narrative accounts affirm that in order to deliver the Israelites from Egypt God appeared to Moses and sent him to the Israelites and to Pharaoh. Even Josephus, who deprives Moses of any role in the production or removal of the plagues, fully admits that the LORD revealed Himself to Moses and

---

90 On the other hand, it is doubtful whether one can see in Stephen's address in Acts 7 any additional evidence for a tradition that Moses performed all of the plagues. Stephen says that Moses "led them out, having performed wonders and signs in Egypt and at the Red Sea, and in the wilderness for forty years" (Acts 7:36). These words do, of course, open up the possibility that in the speaker's opinion Moses performed all the signs and wonders, but in view of the general, non-detailed character of this historical survey, they may also be explained according to the Pentateuch, to mean that Moses performed only some of them.

entrusted him with this mission. Here too, then, the differences among the various traditions are restricted to the question of the extent of Moses' activity. Not a single tradition denies that Moses held a decisive role in this episode, an episode which, if his figure were to be eliminated, cannot even be imagined.

The situation with Aaron is completely different. As the accounts of Artapanus and Josephus demonstrate clearly, the entire Exodus could be recounted without Aaron. Before considering these late sources, however, we must clarify Aaron's role in the Pentateuchal Exodus narrative, and for this purpose we must necessarily go beyond the bounds of the plagues cycle.

A cursory examination suffices to indicate that Aaron's role in the Exodus story is entirely different from that of Moses. All of the sources affirm, in one form or another, that God commissioned Moses to lead the Israelites out of Egypt, and that Moses did indeed carry out this assignment. This basic pattern is a primary one, one which consistently recurs in every biblical account of divine delegation. Aaron's role, on the other hand, is unique, and is entirely a function of Moses' own conduct: it is because Moses, unlike all other divine emissaries in the Bible, maintains his initial refusal to convey the LORD's message to its destination that Aaron is first attached to him as a mouthpiece. Aaron thus becomes Moses' assistant retroactively, while initially Moses was to have discharged his mission alone.

The book of Exodus has preserved two accounts of this curious "annexation" of Aaron to his brother. The first (Exod 4:1-17) is an appendix to the theophany at the burning bush, in which Moses is told: "Come, therefore, I will send you to Pharaoh, and he will free My people, the Israelites, from Egypt" (3:10). Moses' mission, it is thus stated, is essentially to Pharaoh, and the fact that it will also require him to conduct negotiations with the Israelites themselves is only implied. The same may be inferred from Moses' refusal: "Who am I that I should go to Pharaoh and free the Israelites from Egypt?" (3:11); the problem he emphasizes is that of going to Pharaoh. To which God replies: "I will be with you; that shall be your sign that it was I who sent you. And when you have freed the people from Egypt, you shall worship God at this mountain" (3:12). With that, the discussion seems to conclude.

Yet it continues. Moses repeats his refusal, and this time the reason is his fear of serving as God's emissary to the Israelites. This familiar reluctance to undertake the prophetic mission, which is without a doubt an early motif, is reminiscent of the stories of Gideon (Judg 6:14-24) and Jeremiah (Jer 1:4-6). Nevertheless, Moses' vehemence far exceeds anything attested in similar accounts. What is more, all of the other emissaries of God eventually withdraw their refusal, deferring unconditionally to the divine will, while Moses is steadfast in his refusal until he is assured that his brother Aaron will come to meet him and speak on his behalf.

In the parallel account in Exod 6:2-7:2, analyzed convincingly by I. L. Seeligmann,[91] Moses' behavior differs. Here, he unhesitatingly obeys God's command to address the Israelites, but they refuse to listen to him. After noting this refusal, the narrative continues: "The LORD spoke to Moses, saying 'Go and tell Pharaoh king of Egypt to let the Israelites depart from his land'" (Exod 6:10). To this Moses demurs, pleading "The Israelites would not listen to me; how then should Pharaoh heed me, a man of impeded speech!" (6:12). The LORD's reply, which occurs only in 7:1-2, is "See, I place you in the role of God to Pharaoh, and your brother Aaron as your prophet. You shall repeat all that I command you, and your brother Aaron shall speak to Pharaoh".

This pericope is apparently a variant tradition of the commissioning of Moses in chapter 4. Yet here, intervening between Moses' argument and the LORD's reply, are three additional passages: (1) Exod 6:13, which indicates that the LORD spoke to Moses and Aaron, commanding both of them to go the Israelites and to Pharaoh; (2) Exod 6:14-27, a genealogy, apparently placed here because of its concluding verses "It is the same Aaron and Moses (thus — not "Moses and Aaron"!) to whom the LORD said, 'Bring forth the Israelites from the

---

91 Our analysis of Exod 6:10-7:2 is according to I. L. Seeligmann, "Hebräische Erzählung und biblische Geschichtsschreibung", *Theologische Zeitschrift*, 18 (1962), p. 322.

land of Egypt troop by troop.' It was they who spoke to Pharaoh king of Egypt to free the Israelites from the Egytpians, these are the same Moses and Aaron" (vv. 26-27); (3) Exod 6:28-30, a redactional passage recapitulating 6:10-12 in order to provide a transition back to the LORD's reply to Moses.

The fact that both narratives agree that the task of speaking to Pharaoh was essentially that of Moses, and both find it necessary to account for Aaron's role, indicates the secondary character of this motif. The common features shared by both narratives are evident. In the first, Moses pleads that he is "slow of speech and slow of tongue" (4:10), and in the second he repeats this argument, using the expression "impeded speech" (6:12). In both narratives the relationship between Moses and Aaron is likened to that of God and His prophet, though only in the second account is this stated explicitly (7:1), while in the first it simply follows from the fact that Aaron is Moses' mouthpiece (4:16).

What is more, the implications of the LORD's assurances in the two accounts are identical: (1) that Aaron is to speak on Moses' behalf on all occasions; (2) that Moses alone is to perform the signs (since there is not the slightest suggestion that he is incapable of doing so); and (3) that the LORD will speak only to Moses — not to Aaron. Despite this fact, all three of these implications are borne out only partially in the subsequent narrative: (1) Moses, and not Aaron, appears as the speaker, and not just at the beginning of the second account but elsewhere as well; (2) Aaron, and not Moses, performs many of the signs and wonders; (3) the LORD occasionally addresses Aaron directly. Thus, Aaron's status both falls below, on the one hand, and exceeds, on the other, what we are given to expect.

We now proceed to the precise examination of the narrative with regard to these three points.

Aaron, at the LORD's command, sets out to meet Moses, and eventually conveys the LORD's message, communicated to him by Moses, to the elders of Israel (4:27-30). This, of course, is according to plan. But during the course of their first interview with Pharaoh, both speak to him (5:1), and later Moses himself surprisingly affirms that it was he who had spoken to the king (5:23). Still this much could be explained by the fact that up to this point Moses has not yet been expressly told that Aaron is to act as his spokesman before Pharaoh — only that he is to do so before the elders of Israel. And even though at the beginning of the second account of Aaron's incorporation in Moses' mission, i.e. of chapter 6, it is Moses who speaks to the people, this too could be explained, as noted above, as necessitated by the logic of the story itself. Thereafter, however, when Moses has received from God an express assurance that Aaron will act as his "prophet" before Pharaoh (7:1-2), there is not a single passage stating that Aaron ever actually did as commanded. Most references to their appearances before Pharaoh say that Moses was the sole speaker (7:14-18, 26-29, 8:5-7, 16-18, 22-26; 9:1-5, 13-19; 10:25, 29; 11:4-8). The only exception is in the account of the locusts, where, as in the first meeting with Pharaoh, both brothers speak (10:3-6). Moreover, most references indicate that Moses alone appeared before Pharaoh to announce the plagues. Even in the case of the blood and frogs, it is Moses who acts as divine emissary, and Aaron, at least according to what we are later told, who performs the signs — though, to be sure, Aaron is never expressly said to accompany Moses prior to the plague of locusts, which is the only one in which both brothers are reported to have appeared before Pharaoh.

Now, among the occasions upon which Pharaoh pleaded for the removal of a plague, there are some instances of his summoning both Moses and Aaron (8:4; 9:27; 10:16; 12:31) or of both brothers' leaving Pharaoh's presence (8:8; 10:11) — though elsewhere only Moses' departure is mentioned (8:26; 9:33; 10:18). The actual requests to remove the plague are addressed to both brothers (8:4, 24; 9:28; 10:17), though only Moses prays to the LORD to this end (8:8, 25; 9:33; 10:18). When Pharaoh wishes to negotiate the terms of the Israelites' release, and not to beg for the removal of the plagues, he summons Moses only (10:24 — but LXX, Vg and Sam differ on this point from MT), and after the negotiations have broken down, it is Moses alone to whom Pharaoh says "Be gone from me!" (10:28). The extent of Aaron's role in the negotiations is thus a far lesser one than might have been expected, and is subject to frequent inconsistencies and variations in the accounts of the separate plagues.

No less remarkable than this lessening of Aaron's role is the manner in which it is sometimes enlarged. It is Aaron who performs the signs before the Israelites and the sign of the serpent before Pharaoh, as well as inducing the plagues of blood, frogs and lice, and participating in calling forth the boils. These acts of Aaron's are sometimes performed at Moses' own command, as suggested by the statement that "Moses told Aaron about all the things that the LORD had committed to him and all the signs about which He had instructed him...Aaron repeated all the words that the LORD had spoken to Moses, and he performed the signs in the sight of the people" (4:28, 30). Just as Moses put the words of the LORD in Aaron's mouth, he apparently placed the miracles of the LORD in Aaron's hands. As much is explicitly stated in the plagues of blood (7:19: "The LORD said to Moses: 'Say to Aaron...'"), frogs (8:1) and lice (8:12), whereas in advance of the plague of boils the LORD Himself addresses not Moses alone but Moses and Aaron (9:8). The same is true in the sign of the crocodile (7:8), though there the narrative subsequently reverts to the version according to which Aaron acted in obedience to Moses' instructions: "When Pharaoh speaks to you and says, 'Produce your marvel,' you shall say to Aaron, 'Take your rod...'" (7:9). Two traditions have been combined, one in which the LORD addresses only Moses, who then passes on the command to Aaron, and the other in which the LORD addresses them both.[92]

The great majority of the variants enumerated above cannot be

---

92 Varying traditions on the question of whether the LORD spoke to Moses alone, to Aaron, or to both are also observable in the book of Leviticus. The preference shown to Moses as the sole recipient of the divine speech and not merely a kind of *primus inter pares* appears prominently in the account of Aaron's investiture (Leviticus 8). So too we find that the divine command is generally addressed to Moses only (Lev 1:1; 4:1; 5:14,20; 6:1,17; 7:22,28; 8:1; 12:1; 14:1; 16:1; 17:1; 18:1; 19:1; 20:1; 22:1,17; 23:1,23,26,33; 24:1; 27:1). This view of the relation between Moses and Aaron finds expression in such verses as "The LORD spoke to Moses, saying: Command Aaron and his sons..." (Lev 6:1-2; compare 6:12-13,17-18; 8:36; 16:2; also 9:1,7,10,12). Note that the passages cited include the verses introducing laws of purity (12:1; 14:1) and laws specifically concerning the priests (6:1,12,17; 16:1; 21:1,16). Three laws of purity contain the introductory formula "The LORD spoke to Moses and Aaron" (11:1; 13:1; 15:1), and one is even introduced by "The LORD spoke to Aaron" (10:8).

explained harmonistically as functions of the inner logic of the narrative. One fact does bear mention: Aaron appears in every passage which mentions Pharaoh's magicians. This feature was noted by Abrabanel (Commentary to Exod 7:8):

> God was unwilling to have this miracle performed before Pharaoh with Moses' rod, lest the Egyptian magicians, by imitating Moses, should bring disgrace upon him; rather, He ordered Moses to tell Aaron to cast down his own rod, thus diminishing the effect of the miracle and thereby preserving the honor of Moses and his rod.[93]

Or, to put it otherwise, Moses is Pharaoh's equal: just as Pharaoh does not engage in sorcery, but rather issues orders to his magicians, so too Moses. This consideration, first formulated by B. Jacob,[94] may indeed have influenced the Pentateuchal account in its present form — even though it fails to account for the fact that Aaron also performs the signs in the sight of the Israelites, or for Moses' prominence in the plague of boils. The explanation for the former may be that once the tradition of Aaron's competition with the magicians had been established, he was naturally assigned the performance of all the miracles, including those performed for the Israelites — corresponding to the later rabbinic dictum that once one has begun to perform a virtuous deed, he should be the one to complete it. As for the latter, we have already had occasion to mention that the plague of boils possesses its own unique history and that no inference should be drawn from it about the history of the other plagues.

Whatever the reason for the inconsistency, the current view that the figure of Aaron is a secondary element in the plague narrative appears to be well-founded. Unlike Moses, Aaron has no distinct character of his own. He carries out tasks assigned to him by Moses or by God, nothing more. The motif which serves to incorporate Aaron in the narrative, i.e., Moses' refusal to execute his mission, is without parallel in the Bible. Aaron's rod seems to be no more than

93 See above, note 35.
94 Jacob, *op. cit.* (note 36, above), p. 271.

a variant of Moses' own rod, with which he was commanded to perform the signs. The conclusion is further corroborated by the analysis of the plague of blood presented above, and by the Midrash, which poses the question why certain plagues were produced by Aaron and not by Moses[95] but never asks the converse.

We may thus accept the view that the figure of Aaron is a secondary element in the plague narrative, but with the following two reservations. If the Priestly account of the plagues is defined as an account which assigns to Aaron the performance of all the plagues,[96] no trace of the Priestly source can be found in the plagues narrative, since, as we have argued in detail, those texts which mention Aaron do not follow a consistent line but rather depict his role in a truly bewildering number of variant traditions, attesting to numerous partial redactions but not to any final, systematic redaction embracing the entire narrative. Thus, not even the analysis of the Pentateuchal account as it stands allows for the assumption that there existed an independent tradition, which has not survived, which attributed the performance of all of the plagues to Aaron.

The second reservation refers to the origin of the Aaronic tradition. Modern critics, of course, have long been aware of the lack of uniformity with regard to the portrayal of Aaron.[97] Without entering into the scholarly controversy, we may note that the account of Aaron's performance of the signs before the people is generally assigned to the

---

95 See for instance Mišnat R. Eliezer 19: "Said R. Tanhum: 'The Holy One, blessed be He, told Moses: It is not right for the water which preserved you when you were thrown into the sea and the dust which protected you when you killed the Egyptian to be smitten by you.' Therefore they were smitten by Aaron." Compare Midr. HaGadol Wāʾērāʾ 7:19, and similarly Tg. Jonathan to Exod 8:2: "But Moses did not strike the water or the earth or the frogs because they had saved him when his mother cast him into the river"; again at 8:12: "It is impossible for you to strike the earth, since when you killed the Egyptian it saved you by receiving his body".

96 On this question see Pedersen, *op. cit.* (note 72, above), who denies the existence of a P account and asserts that the text has undergone only partial redactions; for an opposing view see S. Mowinckel, "Die vermeintliche 'Passahlegende' Ex. 1–15 in Bezug auf die Frage Literarkritik und Traditionskritik", *Studia Theologica*, 5 (1951), pp. 76ff.

97 See for example the source-division in B. Baentsch, *Exodus, Leviticus, Numeri*, Göttingen 1903; G. Beer, *Exodus*, Tübingen 1939, and compare Wellhausen, *op. cit.* (Chapter Two, note 32), pp. 62, 71f.

Elohist, while the remainder of the traditions concerning Aaron are assigned to P or to one of the redactors. Though this approach is not without some validity, it cannot be adopted as stated. The statement "He shall speak for you to the people; thus he shall serve as your spokesman, with you playing the role of God to him" (Exod 4:16), which likens a human being to God, indeed does not give the impression of originating in the relatively late Priestly source and most probably derives from an earlier, prophetic theology. But the same can be said for the statement "See, I place you in the role of God to Pharaoh, with your brother Aaron as your prophet" (7:1), which implies that Moses will be his prophet Aaron's "God" as well.[98] In light of this it seems probable that a secondary tradition, prophetic in nature, assigned to Aaron the role of "prophet" for Moses, and it is this tradition which underlies the role of Aaron in the plague narrative, where it has been partially rejected in favor of the mainstream tradition, that Moses was the only spokesman. At the same time, the assertion that Aaron too performed signs, at Moses' behest, becomes more plausible, even though there is no mention of this possibility in all the dialogues between the LORD and Moses which precede his first mission to the Israelites and to Pharaoh. It may in fact be the case that the desire to spare the honor of Moses (and not necessarily a Priestly tendency to maximize the participation of the High Priest) has had an effect on the development of this motif. Against the background of these traditions there finally emerged the unmistakably Priestly claim that the LORD spoke directly to Aaron — in contradiction of the original idea that Aaron was to be Moses' "prophet", which can be discerned in the accounts of signs performed by Aaron at Moses' command.

The same uncertainty reflected in the Pentateuch with regard to Aaron's status may be seen in the Hellenistic literature as well, where each writer depicts Aaron in his own fashion. Closest to the Penta-

---

98 Evidence for a similar early tradition can apparently be found also in Mic 6:4: "In fact, I brought you up from the land of Egypt, I redeemed you from the house of bondage, and I sent before you Moses, Aaron, and Miriam". The very prominence given to the figure of Miriam is decisive, since only a few passages regarding her have been preserved in the Pentateuch.

teuch is Philo, who, as noted, attributes to Aaron the sign of the serpent and all of the plagues which he performs in the Pentateuchal account. It might indeed be said that Philo goes a bit beyond the Pentateuch in the account of the blood, omitting all mention of Moses' own action. This, however, is clearly an attempt to solve the difficulties in the Pentateuchal story. However, insofar as Aaron's role in the story prior to the onset of the plagues is concerned, Philo does deviate from the Pentateuch, sometimes to a greater, sometimes a lesser extent. In his concern for Moses' honor, he revises the account of the burning bush, according to which, in the Pentateuch, Moses is not satisfied by God's promise to instruct him and continues to resist, thus angering the LORD, until eventually he secures the promise that Aaron will be his mouthpiece. Philo, combining the two speeches of God, omits all mention of Moses' recalcitrance, so that God begins by promising Moses that He will teach him what to say and immediately proceeds to add that Aaron may speak on his behalf whenever necessary (VM I.xiv, p. 94). At their first meeting with the Israelites both speak (xv, p.94), but the performance of signs before the people is delayed until after Pharaoh increases their burden; what is more important, it is Moses, not Aaron, who performs them (xv, p. 95).

Ezekiel the Tragedian relates that Moses did not resist the task of addressing the Israelites, and that his claim, uttered at the burning bush, that he was "slow of speech", was only in regard to the mission to Pharaoh (ll. 110-115). To this God replies, as in the Pentateuch, that Aaron will speak to the king in his stead (ll. 116-119). The divine promise appended to this in the Pentateuchal account, that Aaron will speak to the people, is of course transformed here into an assurance that Aaron will speak on Moses' behalf to Pharaoh. This reformulation amounts to a conflation of the two Pentateuchal accounts of Aaron's incorporation in Moses' mission, Exodus 3 and Exodus 6, a conflation which succeeds in doing away with the incongruity between the two. What emerges is that on the first occasion Moses was reluctant to appear before the Israelites, and on the second he addressed the Israelites unhesitatingly but refused to appear before Pharaoh. The plagues themselves, as noted above, were all brought about, according to Ezekiel, by Moses' rod.

Aaron's role is still more limited in the account of Artapanus, where Aaron appears only once and then only incidentally. After God has commanded Moses to return to Egypt and to free the Hebrews, Moses resolves to go to war against Egypt, and before doing so to go to his brother Aaron (Eusebius IX:27, 22). Nowhere does Artapanus give a reason for this, since in the main body of the narrative Aaron plays no role whatsoever. Of the Aaronic tradition, nothing remains here but a relic, devoid of all function.

This same overall evaluation also applies to the detailed narrative in Josephus. Here, too, all mention of Aaron is absent from the burning bush episode, yet when Moses sets out to return to Egypt, Aaron, at God's command, comes to meet him, and Moses relates to him all that has happened and tells him of God's instructions. As they continue on their journey together, they are greeted by the elders of Israel, who have heard of Moses' impending arrival. Though Moses attempts to gain their support, he does not succeed in convincing them until he performs before their eyes the signs which the LORD has entrusted to him (Ant. II.xiii.1). Only by inference can it even be concluded that Aaron is present, and with this Aaron's part in the narrative ends. Josephus is thus closer to the Pentateuch than Artapanus, since he does speak of Aaron's meeting Moses and accompanying him to Egypt, where he participates in the first meeting with the elders. Yet in both of these late sources, Aaron figures only in the account of Moses' return to Egypt, and has no active role to play. To the question of what purpose is served by having God send Aaron to meet Moses there is no answer in either narrative.

6. The Theological Implications. With this we conclude the survey of the variant traditions on the question of who produced the plagues. These variants are of considerable significance from the theological standpoint. The tradition that Moses, with his own rod, performed divine feats beyond the power of mere mortals elevates Moses, the servant of the LORD, to the rank of God's partner, suggesting even some blurring of the distinction between the divine and human spheres of action. The other view, that the plagues were inflicted by God acting alone, is a direct contrast. The first view tends to attribute superhuman powers to the greatest of the prophets, while the second affirms that Moses, despite his greatness, does not differ essentially from ordinary humanity. Thus, beyond the variant traditions themselves lies a fundamental issue in Israelite thought, one which also appears in the accounts of Moses' death, which according to one approach was an ascent to God and according to the other was the passing of an ordinary mortal.[99] The tension is less pronounced in those passages where Aaron acts alongside Moses and at his command; the fact that Moses is interposed between the LORD and Aaron serves somewhat to detach God from the agent who carries out His word but acts at the bidding of mere flesh and blood.

B. How the Plagues Were Inflicted: The Divine Rod

In the Pentateuch, reference to the LORD's direct action in inflicting the plagues is confined to two vague references to the hand of God: "I will stretch out my hand and smite Egypt" (Exod 3:20), and, in the account of the pestilence, "the hand of the LORD will strike your livestock" (9:3).

The actions of Moses and Aaron, on the other hand, are described in great detail. We may begin by noting that in all but one plague (the boils, here too differing from the remainder of the plague account), both Moses and Aaron act by means of the rod held in their hands which, in most instances, is referred to explicitly. Only in the plague of darkness does the narrative neglect to mention the rod, stating simply that Moses held out his arm toward the sky (10:21-22). However, it can be deduced from the comparison of several parallel statements that this is an elliptical way of saying that he held out his rod: compare the command "Say to Aaron: Hold out your arm with the rod" to its

---

99 S. E. Loewenstamm, *op. cit.* (note 80, above), pp. 148ff. The difficulty in distinguishing between Moses' rod and that of Aaron is felt especially in the words "Take with you the rod that turned into a serpent" (Exod 9:15). According to the plain sense of the text the reference is, of course, to the changing of Moses' rod into a serpent at the burning bush. But it is difficult to escape the impression that the passage originally referred to the transformation of the rod into a crocodile, in the sight of Pharaoh, immediately before the plague of blood. Tg. Jonathan was already aware of this connection, deviating from the plain sense by translating "Take with you Aaron's rod, which was turned into a serpent"; see also Ibn Ezra to Exod 7:15.

execution: "Aaron held out his arm" (8:1-2); similarly "Hold out your arm towards the sky" and "Moses held out his rod toward the sky" (9:22-23; the LXX has "hand" in v. 23); and again "Then the LORD said to Moses: Hold out your arm" and "So Moses held out his rod" (10:12-13).

The importance of Moses' rod is enunciated in the account of the vision of the burning bush, which concludes with the divine command "Take with you this rod, with which you shall peform the signs" (Exod 4:17). In accord with this, the report of Moses' return to Egypt ends by relating that "Moses took the rod of God in his hands" (4:20). Later the rod's importance is confirmed, not only in the account of the plagues but also through its prominence in the parting of the sea, the splitting of the rocks in the wilderness, and the war with Amalek. In contrast, Aaron's rod is used only in the Exodus itself, and even here it is obviously nothing more than a variant of Moses' rod.

The original character of Moses' rod is alluded to in Exod 7:17. In this difficult passage, God tells Moses to say to Pharaoh: "Thus says the LORD: By this you shall know that I am the LORD. See, I shall strike the water in the Nile with the rod that is in my hand, and it will be turned to blood". Now, if Moses is to say in God's name "I shall strike", the literal meaning of the verse can only be that it is God who will strike the Nile with His rod! Only in light of the text immediately preceding, which makes it clear that Moses is to speak these words to Pharaoh while holding in his hand the rod which he had earlier turned into a serpent (7:15), can another interpretation be offered, namely, that the reference is to Moses' own rod — but this is not the plain sense of the verse. Critics searching for an escape from this impasse suggest in desperation that the words "with the rod that is in my hand" have been interpolated from E (in which all of the plagues were induced by Moses) into the J account (which ascribes all of the plagues to God alone). If the verse is taken as it is, however, we are forced to admit, with Cassuto, that "the boundaries between the Sender and the messenger are, as it were, somewhat blurred".[100] Such a situation can be explained only by the assumption that the rod

---

100 Cassuto, *op. cit.* (note 36, above), p. 97.

in Moses' hand and the rod of God are one and the same, and that it is held not only by Moses but simultaneously by God Himself.

A clear reference to this image is to be found in Isa 63:12: "Who made His glorious arm march at the right hand of Moses, who divided the waters before them to make Himself a name for all time". The verse depicts the parting of the sea by means of God's rod, which Moses held in his hand, alongside of which marched the arm of God. And what is conveyed figuratively in these expressions is pictured concretely in the seals of the Hittite kings Muwatalli and Tudhaliyah IV, which depict the storm-god and the king side by side, the latter holding a staff precisely identical to those held by the god himself in other depictions. In the seals, the god's hand actually takes hold of the king's right hand which grasps the divine staff.[101]

To elucidate the concept it will be helpful to recall that the ancient Near Eastern peoples generally depicted their gods as holding staffs. In Enuma Eliš (IV.130), Marduk crushes the head of Tiamat *ina meṭišu* "with his rod"; In the Ugaritic epic of Anath the goddess' staff is mentioned as the weapon with which she strikes her human enemies.[102] The "pairs" of rods with which Baal defeated the Prince of the Sea and the Judge of the River belong to this category as well.[103] According to Eusebius (I:9, 29), citing a work entitled παραδόξου ἱστορίας which he attributes to Philo of Byblos, the Phoenicians kept the staffs of their gods in their temples; there is good evidence that the same practice was maintained in Egypt, where kings occasionally also took these rods along with them on military campaigns.[104]

Traces of these mythological views of divine staffs can also be found in biblical poetry, though biblical poets were occasionally less explicit in referring to the LORD's own rod. Thus the psalmist says simply "He split rocks in the wilderness" (Ps 78:15); Isaiah speaks of the rod which the LORD will lift up against Assyria (Isa 10:24,26),

101 S. E. Loewenstamm, in *IEJ*, 8 (1958), p. 138.
102 Gordon, *op. cit.* (note 30, above), p. 187 (Anath II, l. 15; *ANET*[2], p. 136).
103 *Ibid.*, p. 150 (Text 68).
104 H. Bonnet, *Reallexikon der Aegyptischen Religionsgeschichte*, Berlin 1952, pp. 254ff.

and another of Isaiah's oracles concerning Assyria has apparently been influenced by the same association of ideas:

> For the LORD will make His majestic voice heard
> And display the sweep of His arm
> In raging wrath,
> In a devouring blaze of fire,
> In tempest, and rainstorm, and hailstones.
> Truly, Assyria shall be cowed by the voice of the LORD,
> who beats with the rod.
>
> (Isa 30:30-31)

Though some render the last verse differently, taking Assyria, rather than the LORD, as the subject of "beats" ("Assyria, who beats with the rod, shall be cowed..."), it is more likely that the "rod" is an alternative metaphorical representation of the "blaze of fire", and that both refer to the bolts of lightning with which God is expected to smite Assyria. Consideration should also be given here to the suggestion[105] that allusion is made to divine staffs in a passage in Habakkuk:

> All bared and ready is your bow;
> Sworn (?) are the rods of the word (?)...
>
> (Hab 3:9)

Here too, despite the fact that no commentator has satisfactorily interpreted the verse in all its details,[106] there is no disputing that the

---

105 U. Cassuto, "Chapter iii of Habakkuk and the Ras Shamra Texts", in: *Biblical and Oriental Studies*, II, trans. by I. Abrahams, Jerusalem 1975, pp. 11-12 (= "Il Capitolo 3 di Habaquq e i Testi di Ras Shamra", *Annario di Studi Ebraici 1935-1937*, Roma 1938, p. 18).

106 On the proposed emendations, the commentaries on Habakkuk may be consulted, in addition to which see W. F. Albright, "The Psalm of Habakkuk", in H.H. Rowley (ed.), *Studies in Old Testament Prophecy*, Edinburgh 1950, pp. 11-12; 15-16. Albright reads *šbʿt mṭw tʾmr*, explaining *mṭw* on the basis of Southern Arabic to mean war, campaign, and suggests rendering "(Thou art) sated by the fight which Thou hast decreed". The only scholar to retain MT is S. Mowinckel, "Zum Psalm des Habakkuk", *Theologische Zeitschrift*, 9 (1953), pp. 15f., who renders "His arrows are decisive, sworn (*šbʿt*) with a word (ʾmr) of powerful effect". Mowinckel goes on to admit that the meaning "arrow" for *mṭh* is unattested, but is, he argues, semasiologically speaking, highly probable, and required by the parallelism. This entire approach, however, is clearly forced.

passage is a mythological depiction of the LORD's battles of old, and that the "rods" are parallel to the LORD's "bow". Cassuto has also noted the striking similarity between *ʾmr* ("word"?) in the verse and the Ugaritic *ʾaymr* which denotes one of Baal's rods.[107]

The notion that Moses' own rod has its origins in the "rod of God" mentioned in Exod 4:20 and 17:9 is echoed in the universal rabbinic affirmation of the rod's antiquity. It is said to have been used by God to create the world,[108] or at least to have been created at twilight on the eve of the first Sabbath.[109] The midrashic tradition that the rod was placed in Moses' hands by God Himself, a tradition which assumed various forms, accords well with the rabbinic view of the rod's antiquity. In some passages God is said to have bequeathed the rod to Adam, from whom it was passed on successively until eventually it was handed over to Moses by Jethro;[110] elsewhere God is described as handing His sceptre directly to Moses.[111] Below, in connection with the parting of the sea, we shall have occasion to mention the midrash which likens Moses' rod to a ring sold by a merchant to a purchaser.[112] Against this background one can easily understand the midrashic statement that the divine name was engraved on the staff,[113] and the theory advanced by the rabbis that Moses' staff, Aaron's staff and God's staff are all one and the same rod, in each passage referred to in accord with whoever wielded it.[114]

It may thus be concluded that Moses' rod was originally God's own staff, an instrument endowed with superhuman smiting power, which God bestowed upon His servant Moses, who then used it to act on God's behalf and at His command. The original character of the rod, however, has not been preserved everywhere in the Bible in its pristine form. Its depiction has been influenced by the motif of a magic wand, and no less by an anti-mythological tendency to represent it as

---

107 Cassuto, *loc. cit.* (note 105, above).
108 Midr. Pĕṭīrat Mōše, B (ed. A. Jellinek in *Bet HaMidraš*, I, Leipzig 1853), p. 112.
109 M. ʾAbot 5:6 and parallels.
110 Pirqe R. El. 41ff.; Tg. Jonathan to Exod 2:21; etc.
111 Exod. Rab. Wāʾērāʾ 8:1.
112 Mekilta deRabbi Šimᶜon bar Yoḥai Bĕšallaḥ 14:21; see below p. 281.
113 Num. Rab. Koraḥ 18:23.
114 Exod. Rab. Bešallaḥ 27:9.

a simple shepherd's staff. The latter tendency is clearly visible in the Pentateuchal passage in which the rod is first introduced, i.e., the account of how it was changed into a serpent (Exod 4:1-5). God's question "What is that in your hand?" and Moses' reply "A rod" have the effect of representing the rod as a shepherd's staff (just as the story of the Garden of Eden represents the mythological serpent simply as one of the animals of the field in Gen 3:1). Further, in this narrative the rod does not actually do anything; it is simply the recipient of a miraculous act. And though Moses is the one who casts it to the ground, there is no room for any doubt that it is God who transforms it into a serpent; Moses acts at His command and is ignorant of what the result of his action will be. An anti-mythological statement is thus made: even where it might be supposed that some superhuman, miraculous power inheres in the rod, the sole active force is God Himself.

The mythological nature of the rod is further suppressed, in most of the narrative accounts, by the fact that Moses wields it at God's command, implying that the execution of the divine word is the decisive factor. Combined with this is the fact that the rod's action is not always that of a crushing weapon; often it is made out to be the magical effect of a sorcerer's wand. Still, even in the plague narrative, the original character of the rod is unmistakable. It is most prominent in the first and seventh plagues, the plagues which begin the first and third triads. Rather than being a coincidence, this may mean that the rod's power is carried over from these to the other two plagues in each triad. Surely it is no coincidence that in the first triad the rod is invariably Aaron's (at least in the final, redacted version, in which Aaron's rod induces even the blood), whereas in the third triad it is the rod of Moses which is employed. The earlier tradition of Moses' striking the Nile with his rod (Exod 7:17-20; 17:5) and turning its waters into blood must necessarily have evoked the memory of battles fought by the God of Heaven against the rivers which He smote with His staff; indeed the very word "blood" conjures up the image of a wounded enemy. The later version, however, in which Aaron's rod, and not Moses', transforms all the waters of Egypt into blood, replaces the mythological act of striking with the divine rod with the magical act of waving a wand. To be sure, this magical view of the rod is even more apparent in the second and third plagues, in which the action of the rod in no way resembles that of a weapon. Aaron conjures up the frogs in the same way that he turned the waters of Egypt into blood: by a wave of his wand. This, though, is clearly a symbolic striking (Exod 8:12), and the same is true of the lice: Aaron produces them by striking the ground with his rod (8:13).[115] Thus the rod which appears as a crushing weapon in the first plague is carried over, at least secondarily, to the second and third plagues of the first triad. In

---

115 Some similarities may be noted between Aaron's actions in the above-mentioned plagues and the widely attested act of striking with a rod called a *Lebensrute* ("life-rod") in order to promote the power of fertility (see W. Mannhardt, *Wald- und Feldkulte*, I, Berlin 1904, pp. 251-303; W. R. Roscher, *Ausführliches Lexikon der griechischen und römischen Mythologie*, VI, Leipzig-Berlin 1937, p. 547; F. J. de Waele, s.v. "Stab", Pauly-Wissowa, *Realencyclopädie der classischen Altertumswissenschaft*, II Reihe, 6 Bd., col. 1911). At any rate it should be noted that Artapanus already refers to such an explanation. After describing all the creatures conjured up by Moses with his rods ("swarms of insects, frogs, locusts and lice"), he remarks: "On this account the Egyptians dedicate the rod in every Temple...to Isis, since the earth is Isis, and when it was struck with the rod, it released the marvels" (Eusebius IX:27, 32). In this statement, which shows Artapanus' well-known propensity to look among the Hebrews for the source of Egyptian customs, he associates with Moses' action the practice of striking the ground, which is identified with Isis, the goddess of the earth and of fertility. The act causes the earth to bring forth her fruits. Apparently Artapanus' words are based upon the identification of the Egyptian goddess Isis with the Greek Demeter, goddess of the earth and the earth's produce, to which Herodotus already attests (II:59): "Isis is Demeter in the Greek language". To this we may compare the words of Pausanias (VII.xv.3), who adds to his description of the πέτρωμα at Heleusis: "Above it is a circular chamber in which is to be found Demeter's veil, which is called κίτρια. This same veil is worn by the priest on the festival which is called the Great Feast, and according to a traditional custom he strikes the gods of the underworld" (i.e. the ground).

We have elaborated here on Artapanus at some length because one cannot dismiss the possibility that the *Lebensrute* motif may yield some clue to the explanation of the Pentateuch. At the same time, we cannot ignore the uncertainties. We have not been able to find in the literature of the Ancient Near East any clear evidence to support the assumption that there was a practice of awakening fertility by means of a rod (see, however, m. Sukk. 4:6). Moreover, the rod which calls up life in the folklore of other peoples invariably brings blessing, whereas in the Pentateuch the rod has the effect of a curse. We are therefore compelled, however reluctantly, to leave unsolved the question of a connection between the Pentateuchal accounts of the frogs and lice and the folkloristic motif of the life-awakening rod.

the seventh plague the rod is associated with thunder and lightning (Exod 9:23-24; Ps 105:32); here it suffices, quite understandably, for Moses to hold out his rod toward heaven, from which God hurls down the plague itself. The force of the rod is of course carried over to the eighth and ninth plagues: locusts (Exod 10:12-13) and darkness (10:21-22).

C. How the Plagues were Terminated; Pharaoh's Reactions

The duration of each plague and how it was terminated is of lesser importance than the actual occurrence of the plague itself, and is secondary from a tradition-history standpoint as well. Hence these aspects are dealt with only in the detailed narrative accounts of the plagues and are absent entirely from the didactic passages. Even in the Pentateuch, reference to the duration of the plagues is limited to the explicit statement "thick darkness descended upon all the land of Egypt for three days" (Exod 10:22), which makes use of an obviously typological number, and the passage with which the account of the blood ends and that of the frogs begins: "Seven days had passed after the LORD had struck the Nile" (7:25). Philo transforms this oblique reference to a clear statement of the actual length of the plague of blood (VM I.xvii, p. 96), and it goes without saying that seven too is a typological number. The duration of the remaining plagues is not even indirectly suggested in the Pentateuch or anywhere else, which makes it impossible to determine whether or not the two existing references, pertaining to the blood, frogs and darkness, are the remnant of what was once a tradition of the plagues' overall chronology.

In the Pentateuch, the manner in which each plague ends depends upon the reaction of Pharaoh to it. Pharaoh's reactions, however, belong to the secondary stratum of tradition, except, of course, his reaction to the last plague, whereupon, according to all forms of the tradition, Pharaoh allowed the Israelites to depart. His reactions to the remaining plagues are described in various ways and require detailed analysis.

According to one version, Pharaoh did not react to the plagues at all. The plague's disappearance thus poses no particular problem, and is not referred to explicitly. This is the version adopted by the book of Exodus in the first (Exod 7:23), third (8:15), fifth (9:7) and sixth (9:12) plagues. According to a second, more elaborately developed view, during each plague Pharaoh implored Moses (and Aaron) to beseech the LORD on his behalf to remove the plague, promising to free the Israelites when the plague disappeared, but when, in response to Moses' prayer, the plague was removed, Pharaoh failed to keep his promise. Such a promise is explicitly given in the second (8:4-11) and fourth (8:21-27) plagues, as well as in the seventh (9:27-30) where it is accompanied by Pharaoh's admission "I stand guilty this time". At the end of the eighth plague (10:16-20) the existence of a promise is merely implied in Pharaoh's admission of guilt, but this difference is no more than a stylistic feature of the text.

Two aspects of the latter view are of some traditio-historical importance. The first is the matter of the reason for Moses' prayer. On the most elementary level, Moses complied with Pharaoh's request because he believed, or at least hoped, that the king would keep his promise. This reason, which is quite obviously the original one, is suggested in the account of the fourth plague, when Moses warns Pharaoh, "But let not Pharaoh again act deceitfully, not letting the people go to sacrifice to the LORD" (8:25). However, we find as early as the description of the second plague that this idea has been combined with a further consideration: the desire to ensure that the might of the LORD be exhibited in the removal of the plague just as it was displayed in the plague's arrival. This thought is evidenced in Moses' reply to Pharaoh: "As you say — that you may know that there is none like the LORD our God; the frogs shall retreat from you" (8:6-7). In the seventh plague Moses goes even further, telling Pharaoh that he will intercede for him "so that you may know that the earth is the LORD's; but I know that you and your courtiers do not yet fear the LORD" (9:29-30). Moses thus prays to the LORD, fully aware that Pharaoh will not keep his promise, only in order that the greater glory of God might be manifest in Pharaoh's sight. Likewise in the plague of locusts, even though here the actual reason for Moses' prayer is not expressed (10:18): God's announcement to Moses that He has hardened Pharaoh's heart and that Pharaoh will not free the Israelites, with which the plague of locusts opens, as well as the general progression of the story, make clear that Moses was here impelled by the same consideration as at the time of the seventh plague.

In the second, seventh and eighth plagues, Pharaoh gives his promise to allow the Israelites to depart without delay and without reservation. This is not the case in the fourth plague; here he first offers a compromise, the Israelites may sacrifice to their God in Egypt, and at Moses' refusal, Pharaoh goes a step further, offering to allow them to leave, begging them "Plead for me", and entreating them not to go too far (8:21-24). Not only the tradition-history of this passage requires discussion; the plain meaning too calls for comment. Pharaoh's warning that the Israelites must not travel too far is certainly no real limitation on their movement. "Do not go far" is a flexible demand, and one open to interpretation. If Pharaoh's intent is to deny the Israelites permission to journey a distance of three days in the desert, why does he not define his limitation precisely? This point is confirmed by Moses' reaction to Pharaoh's words, which are in accord with the story as a whole: he cannot possibly agree to any partial concessions.

From the tradition-history standpoint, however, another question remains: what is the reason for these negotiations, the likes of which are not to be found in the parallel accounts of the second, seventh and eighth plagues? Though we shall return to the matter below, we may point out here that these inexplicable negotiations suggest a third approach to the question of Pharaoh's reaction to the plagues, which appears in the accounts of the eighth and ninth plagues and according to which Pharaoh made partial concessions to Moses' demands. Only before the onset of the eighth plague does Pharaoh (at his courtiers' urgent entreaty) react immediately to the announcement of the plague by giving permission for the menfolk alone to leave, and Moses is not satisfied by the offer (10:7-11). These negotiations resume after the ninth plague (10:24-29), after which Pharaoh makes another concession and agrees to free the Israelites, stipulating only that they leave behind their livestock — whereupon the negotiations break down once again. The unqualified permission given after the tenth and final plague is thus also the last of a series of three concessions. The gradual character of this sequence is expressed in Pharaoh's own words: "Take also your herds, your flocks *as well*, as you have demanded, and begone!" (12:32); such an ascending series, whereby Pharaoh's concessions are progressively extended until he completely and decisively capitulates, is entirely understandable. Here, then, a clear logic in the structure of the narrative can be perceived. In the remainder of the account, however, Pharaoh's reactions seem to vary haphazardly, and their rationale cannot be determined by any evident principle of narrative progression.

The most intriguing attempt to clarify the tradition-history of this element of the plagues narrative is that of Gressmann,[116] who believes the absence of any reaction on Pharaoh's part to be the earliest tradition but is unable to attribute it to any of the accepted Pentateuchal sources. Gressmann despairs of any attempt to re-create the P and E accounts, but offers a complete reconstruction of J, which, according to the accepted view, included seven plagues: blood, frogs, swarms, pestilence, hail, locusts and the slaying of the firstborn. According to Gressmann's reconstruction of J, Pharaoh did not react at all to the plague of blood. At the plague of frogs Pharaoh promised to let Israel depart, but revoked his promise when, at Moses' prayer, the plague had passed. When the swarms had receded he agreed that the Israelites might sacrifice to the LORD in Egypt; when the pestilence had ended he was willing to permit them to sacrifice on the outskirts of the wilderness ("but do not go far", Exod 8:24); by the time the hail had ceased he agreed to the departure of the men only, and when the plague of locusts had passed he was prepared to allow all of the people to depart as long as they left their livestock behind.

While Gressmann's theory that the earliest tradition is that Pharaoh paid no heed at all to the plagues makes good sense, the reconstruction he offers, consisting of a seven-staged series of concessions, is without foundation. First, Gressmann does not even attempt to explain how the received account evolved from the version he postulates. Second, his own ascending progression is not properly constructed. After the third and fourth plagues, Pharaoh makes his

116 *Op. cit.* (note 51, above), pp. 70ff.

agreement contingent upon the Israelites' destination, whereas in in the fifth and sixth he stipulates conditions with respect to the categories of persons to be released. Yet the relation between these two types of restrictions ought to be one of parallelism and not of degree. It may therefore be assumed that two alternative traditions were current in Israel, each comprising a three-tiered ascending series. According to one version, Pharaoh at first allowed the men to depart, later all the people, and finally the livestock as well. In the other, parallel tradition, Pharaoh first gave permission to offer sacrifices in Egypt, then on the outskirts of the wilderness, and ultimately in the wilderness — at a distance of three days' journey.

We are now in a position to offer our own hypothesis of the evolution of the Pentateuchal account. We believe that this account was preceded by three separate versions of the plagues episode:

A. According to the earliest version, the plagues had no effect at all on Pharaoh, and they disappeared of their own accord. This version has left its mark on the narrative in the passages mentioned above, and requires no further comment.

B. A second version related that Pharaoh asked Moses (and Aaron) to remove each plague and promised to release the Israelites when the plague was over. This version too is plainly discernible in the text.

C. In the third version, Pharaoh offered gradual and partial concessions comprising a three-tiered ascending series, beginning with the eighth and ninth plagues and culminating in his complete capitulation after the last plague.

The third tradition could easily have been combined with either of the two earlier ones. It appeared in two formulations: one describing Pharaoh's concessions as restricted in terms of who was to be permitted to depart, and the other describing them as limited in terms of place. The former is discernible in the existing accounts of the eighth and ninth plagues, but even here close scrutiny reveals some variation. In the eighth plague, Pharaoh is prepared to allow the men to depart *before* the onset of the plague, whereas *during* the plague his behavior is described in accord with version B above. In the ninth plague, his concession appears after the plague had passed. Two recensions of the eighth plague must have been current: one of which

— corresponding with the existing Pentateuchal text — recounted the events of the plague according to version B, while the other stated that Pharaoh made his concession when the plague had ended. The clash between the two led to the latter's having been transferred from its original place after the account of the eighth plague to its present location, before the plague's arrival. But this slight change did not impair the essential integrity of the tradition of concessions limited with respect to persons, necessitating the virtual rejection of the alternative tradition of concessions limited with respect to destination. The redactor, unable to preserve both and preferring the former, did not dare to pass over the latter in total silence, choosing instead to insert some mention of it into the account of the fourth plague, a course of action which is somewhat forced but entirely understandable given the impossibility of preserving the two alternative versions together in their authentic form.

This analysis, of course, cannot go beyond the realm of conjecture. What is clear is that various secondary traditions have been combined and even fused together in the received text, and this process persisted in the Hellenistic literature, each representative of which has described the plagues in his own fashion. And yet in one feature all the Hellenistic authors agree: they omit all reference to the tradition of Pharaoh's concessions limited with respect to destination, a tradition which the Pentateuch itself has relegated to an inconspicuous position. Here, the Hellenistic sources have simply continued along the line of development begun in the Pentateuch.

Artapanus proceeds in general according to version A, having no recourse to version B except in the plague of blood — where the Pentateuch actually adheres to version A. Version C makes no appearance in Artapanus.

In Philo, version A appears in the plagues of lice (third plague in the Pentateuch as well as in Philo), hail (fourth in Philo, seventh in the Pentateuch), swarms (eighth, fourth in the Pentateuch) and pestilence (ninth, fifth in the Pentateuch). He thus agrees with the Pentateuch in the lice and pestilence and differs in hail and swarms. Philo follows version B in the the plagues of frogs (his, as well as the Pentateuch's, second plague) and locusts (his fifth, the Pentateuch's eighth), as does the Pentateuch. Pharaoh's promise to free the Israelites when the plague ends, given during the plague of locusts in the Pentateuch, is attributed by Philo to the urgent entreaties of Pharaoh's courtiers, which in the Pentateuch lead to a partial concession on Pharaoh's part before the onset of the plague. Philo does not mention why Moses acceded to Pharaoh's request. A trace of version A can be perceived in Philo's account of the blood (first plague in Philo as in the Pentateuch), differing from the Pentateuch but resembling Artapanus, and boils (his seventh, the Pentateuch's sixth) — contrary to the Pentateuch. In Philo the blood disappears after a plea that Moses pray to the LORD — but the plea is made by the Egyptians, not by Pharaoh, and is not accompanied by any promise to free the Israelites; in the plagues of darkness and boils no such plea is mentioned. Philo's whole account is comprehensible only in light of his tendency to accentuate, in the plague narrative as elsewhere, both the divine mercy ("He, whose nature is to show mercy, changed the blood into water fit for drinking"; VM I.xvii, p. 96) and the mercy of Moses ("until Moses again took pity and besought God"; VM I.xxi, p. 100) — a tendency unattested in the Pentateuch.

Despite the elaborate detail which characterizes Philo's account, version C is nowhere represented in it. Philo was apparently troubled by the idea of Pharaoh's partial concessions, since it might have implied approval of the king's behavior.

Proceeding to Josephus, we recall that his narrative has transformed the cattle pestilence into a few obscure references to a disease affecting man, and that these references are incorporated into the account of the swarms to form a single episode. Version A determines Josephus' description of the sixth, seventh, and ninth plagues (the latter two against the Pentateuch). Version B has left its mark upon the first plague (against the Pentateuch but in agreement with Artapanus and Philo) and the second. There is no mention of Moses' prayer to remove the plagues; rather we are told simply that Pharaoh, perplexed by the miracle and fearing for his people's fate, agreed to permit the Hebrews to depart while the plague was in progress, but that once it was gone he recovered and revoked his consent (Ant. II.xiv.1-2). Of course, God's removal of the plague in response to

Moses' prayer is necessarily omitted; instead these plagues, as do all the others in Josephus' account, simply disappear on their own. Josephus therefore seems to have rejected the motif, so dear to Philo, whereby it was Moses' prayer that ended the plagues. Josephus' reason for denying any role to Moses in bringing about or removing the plagues has been discussed above.[117]

In his account of the third plague, Josephus moves from version B to C. During the course of the plague, he speaks of Pharaoh as promising unconditionally to allow the Israelites to depart, but when the plague ends Josephus has Pharaoh qualify his permission, allowing only the men to go and demanding that the women and children remain behind as hostages (Ant. II.xiv.3). This combination of versions B and C is unparalleled in any of the other sources, but it is easily understood. After the fifth plague, which, in Josephus, is a disease affecting humans which comes in the wake of the swarms, Pharaoh permits the women to leave, demanding only that the children remain behind (xiv.4), and at the conclusion of the seventh plague he lifts this restriction, insisting only that the livestock be left (xiv.5). Thus, in striking contrast to Philo, who makes no reference to Pharaoh's partial concessions, Josephus develops this feature of the narrative well beyond the Pentateuchal account. It should not be inferred, however, that Josephus did not share the dilemma faced by Philo; only that he solved it in another manner — by presenting the partial concessions in a negative light rather than in a positive one. This idea has no precedent in the Pentateuch, where Pharaoh's concessions are a matter of simple progression by which the king gradually weakens and eventually breaks down. Josephus has transformed the concessions into Pharaoh's gravest sin: the first is an attempt to circumvent divine Providence, as if it were not God but Moses who was afflicting the Egyptians; the effect is to increase God's anger. Similarly, the third concession, Josephus relates, was Pharaoh's attempt to enter into a contest with God, a deliberate traitor to the Omnipotent One (or perhaps "the Good Thing"? Gr. τοῦ κρείττονος).

---

117 Above, p. 135.

D. The Hardening of Pharaoh's Heart

In contrast to the paradoxical theology of Josephus, which views Pharaoh's concessions as indications of his obstinacy, God's hardening of Pharaoh's heart is everywhere associated with Pharaoh's absolute refusal to set the Israelites free. It serves as a *Leitmotiv*, running not only through the plague narrative but throughout the entire story of the Exodus. The crocodile sign is preceded by God's proclamation:

> But I will harden Pharaoh's heart, that I may multiply My signs and marvels in the land of Egypt. When Pharaoh does not heed you, I will lay My hand upon Egypt and deliver My ranks, My people the Israelites, from the land of Egypt with extraordinary chastisements. And the Egyptians shall know that I am the LORD, when I stretch out My hand over Egypt and bring out the Israelites from their midst.
>
> (Exod 7:3-5)

This theme recurs over and over again in the text. After the crocodile sign, "Pharaoh's heart stiffened, and he did not heed them, as the LORD had spoken" (7:13). The plague of blood is introduced with the words "The LORD said to Moses: Pharaoh is stubborn; he refuses to let the people go" (7:14), and the account of this plague ends with the repeated statement that "Pharaoh's heart stiffened, and he did not heed them, as the LORD had spoken" (7:22). After the plague of frogs, when Pharaoh breaks his promise to free the Israelites, the formulation is changed: "But when Pharaoh saw that there was relief, he became stubborn and would not heed them, as the LORD had spoken" (8:10). The plague of lice is followed by the third repetition of the formula "Pharaoh's heart stiffened, and he did not heed them, as the LORD had spoken" (8:15). From this point on, the wording of the formula varies continually. After the swarms: "But Pharaoh became stubborn this time also, and would not let the people go" (8:28); after the pestilence: "But the LORD stiffened the heart of Pharaoh, and he would not heed them, just as the LORD had told Moses" (9:12). After the plague of hail we actually find two alternative formulae combined thus: "But when Pharaoh saw that the rain and the hail and the thunder had ceased, he reverted to his guilty ways, as did his courtiers. So Pharaoh's heart stiffened and he would not let the Israelites go, just as the LORD had foretold through Moses" (9:34-35).[118] The same motif is developed in a curious fashion in the plague of locusts: only here is the onset of the plague preceded by God's pronouncement, reminiscent of the advance notice given before the crocodile sign:

> Go to Pharaoh. For I have hardened his heart and the hearts of his courtiers, in order that I may display My signs among them, and that you may recount in the hearing of your sons and of your sons' sons how I made a mockery of the Egyptians and how I displayed My signs among them — in order that you may know that I am the LORD.
>
> (Exod 10:1-2)

Corresponding with this opening passage, the same plague concludes with "But the LORD stiffened Pharaoh's heart, and he would not let the Israelites go" (10:20). Similarly the plague of darkness ends with "But the LORD stiffened Pharaoh's heart and he would not consent to let them go" (10:27).

This motif is the connective between the plague narrative and the account of the parting of the sea, which opens by relating that the LORD said to Moses, "Then I will stiffen Pharaoh's heart and he will pursue them, that I may gain glory through Pharaoh and all his host; and the Egyptians shall know that I am the LORD" (14:4; cf. 14:8).

Most puzzling of all the occurrences is the solemn pronouncement made by the LORD before the onset of the locusts (see above) — without any apparent reason, since its content can easily be deduced from the narrative as a whole. Recalling that the plague of locusts is the penultimate plague in Psalm 105, we may conjecture that this unique introductory proclamation originates in a version of the narrative in which this plague occupied a position of prominence which could

---

118 "As the LORD had foretold through Moses (*bĕyad Mōše*)" here obviously recalls v. 12 "as the LORD had told Moses (*ʾel Mōše*)"; indeed, the LXX reading is identical in both passages. MT, however, is supported by v. 30.

justify such a preamble.[119] The thrice-repeated simple formula "Pharaoh's heart stiffened, and he did not heed them, as the LORD had spoken", in contrast to the varied formulations occurring throughout the remainder of the narrative, may perhaps indicate a textual tradition in which these words served as a refrain, concluding the accounts of all the plagues.

It is immediately noticeable that in both introductory speeches the LORD announces that He will harden Pharaoh's heart and that this announcement accords with the concluding verses of the sixth, eighth and ninth plagues: "The LORD stiffened Pharaoh's heart", whereas in the remaining plagues the concluding formula states that Pharaoh's heart stiffened, or that he himself hardened it. The most straightforward reading of the text as it stands is that those verses which state that "Pharaoh's heart stiffened...just as the LORD had spoken" are designed to echo 7:3 in which God says that He will harden Pharaoh's heart — the simple explanation being that Pharaoh's heart has become hard because God has hardened it. But this reading becomes problematic when verses which state that Pharaoh hardened his own heart are taken into consideration, and only with difficulty can it be reconciled with the statement in Exod 3:19 ("Yet I know that the king of Egypt will not let you go except by force"). Perhaps here too the tradition has evolved, and the tradition that the LORD Himself hardened Pharaoh's heart was preceded by an earlier view, that the LORD merely knew in advance that Pharaoh would harden his heart. The development of the later motif would thus be a result of the idea that God's glory manifested itself, in the sight of the Egyptians and of Israel, in the large number of miraculous deeds He performed. It is even possible that the later motif was designed in order to alleviate all possible doubt as to the LORD's power and His ability to humble Pharaoh in a single stroke.

Needless to say, the monotheistic tendency of the text finds its most

---

119 The perplexing character of Exod 10:1-2 has been discussed by H. Eising, "Die aegyptischen Plagen", *Lex Tua Veritas — Festschrift H. Junker*, Trier 1961, p. 78. Eising does not, however, offer any explanation for the difficulty, observing only that "this is a unique motif, of interest for the character of the plague of locusts". See also Excursus II, below.

extreme and consistent expression here, just as it does in Psalm 105, which goes so far as to explain the enslavement itself according to the same principle: "He changed their heart to hate His people, to plot against His servants" (v. 25). The frequently asked question of the moral justification for the LORD's punishing Pharaoh for a crime He himself had made him commit belongs to the history of theology, both Jewish and Christian,[120] but is of no interest for the exegesis of the text. The text is entirely untroubled by the matter: it is simply taken as axiomatic that this wicked Pharaoh deserved every form of punishment conceivable. Later, of course, the Hellenistic sources did find fault with the idea that God hardened Pharaoh's heart in order to enhance the miraculous character of His plagues. Yet they found no solution, as evidenced by the fact that not a single one of the Hellenistic authors so much as mentions the topic. The silence of the later sources on this question is surely the intentional suppression of an insoluble problem.

E. The Israelites' Immunity to the Plagues

Actual differences in tradition must be distinguished from mere variations in formulation, which do not necessarily indicate opposing views of the sequence of events or differing theologies. To the latter category belongs the expression of the idea that the Israelites were unharmed by the plagues. Such preferential treatment, to be sure, is an inevitable function of the narrative, yet there is no fixed, formulaic way of expressing it. The Pentateuch mentions explicitly that Israel was unharmed by the swarms (Exod 8:18), pestilence (9:4), hail (9:28), darkness (10:23) and the slaying of the firstborn (11:7), but is silent on this point in connection with the other plagues. Yet there can be no doubt that the Mishnaic statement "Ten miracles were wrought for our ancestors in Egypt" ('Abot 5:5), as explained by the medieval commentator whose words are preserved in Midr. HaGadol Wāʾērāʾ 7:25 — "this means that they were delivered from ten plagues, as Scripture states explicitly in some of the plagues and as

120 See Jacob, *op. cit.* (note 36, above), pp. 202-211.

may be deduced concerning all the others" — is an accurate reading of the intent of the text. Josephus' account is analogous: he mentions that the Israelites were untouched by the plague of blood (Ant. II.xiv.1) but does not return to this motif thereafter. The only source which treats the topic systematically is Philo, who appends to the account of the plagues a separate chapter relating how Israel was delivered from each of the ten plagues (VM I.xxvi, pp. 103-104). Most probably, however, Philo's innovation is entirely a matter of providing the systematic formulation of an idea shared by all of the sources.

V. Summary

The comprehensive comparison of all of the accounts of the plagues immediately reveals the overriding importance of the narrative in the book of Exodus, which is the only source to include all of the motifs attested in the other sources. There is no motif present in the extra-Pentateuchal sources which is not attested in the Pentateuchal narrative, while there are many motifs present in the latter that are lacking in the external sources. This does not of course imply that all motifs assume the same form in the later sources that they have in the Pentateuch. For instance, in the Pentateuch, the signs that are transmitted to Moses in the vision at the bush are performed by Aaron, in the presence of the elders, *before* the first interview with Pharaoh; according to Philo it is Moses who performs these signs, to the people, *after* the interview. The Pentateuch apparently contains a somewhat obscure allusion to the idea that the signs were actually to be performed by Moses, before Pharaoh; this tradition, though later rejected in the Pentateuch,[121] is affirmed by Josephus, who describes how Moses did indeed perform the signs before Pharaoh.[122] Similarly, the Pentateuch opposes the tradition that the Egyptians were themselves stricken by the pestilence, while Psalm 105 and Ezekiel the Tragedian affirm it. Nevertheless, these and other such variations in no

121 See above, p. 119.
122 *Ibid.*

way detract from the basic rule that the Pentateuch is careful not to erase the record of a single one of the traditional motifs.

This incontrovertible fact admits of two mutually exclusive explanations. Either the accounts existing outside of the Pentateuch may be explained as abridged versions of the Pentateuchal narrative, containing one modification or another, or else the Pentateuch may be explained as having collected, as thoroughly as possible, all available traditions on the plagues, accepting, rejecting and adapting them to each other. In the preceding study we have established at length the correctness of the latter explanation. In this regard there is thus a prominent feature common to our view and that held by conventional source-critical analysis, namely, that the Pentateuch is the result of the combination of several traditions; the difference between the two views is confined to the area of method.

The accepted critical view divides the Pentateuchal account into three narrative sources, most often adhering to the rule that according to J the plagues were brought about directly by the LORD, according to E by Moses and according to P by Aaron. The fallacy in this approach is that it assumes from the outset what in fact it seeks to prove: that the various traditions underlying the Pentateuchal narrative deprive it of all unity, and that the variations of tradition observable in the Pentateuch are of minor importance compared to the main question of who induced the plagues. These two preconceived notions obstruct the path of free inquiry. We, on the other hand, through harmonistic exegesis, have established what must be obvious to any unprejudiced eye: that the ten plagues of the Pentateuch divide into three groups of three, to which the tenth and decisive plague is added.

Our examination of the plethora of various traditions has been carried out without assuming *a priori* that all the variations are the result of differing views on the question of who induced the plagues. This means that in our view the Pentateuchal account is on the one hand a unified whole, but on the other hand contains a vast number of different traditions on many issues, of which the question of who produced the plagues is only one. Our internal analysis of the text of the Pentateuch is thus liberated from the bonds of rigid dogma.

We have also broken down the artificial barrier which had been erected around the Pentateuch so as to separate it from the other available sources. By showing that the two didactic passages in the Psalms, each of which enumerates a series of seven plagues — coinciding in the main and differing only on minor points — are of earlier date than the ten-plague account in the Pentateuch, we have revealed two of the traditions upon which the Pentateuchal tradition is based.

The comparative analysis has been conducted in conjunction with the internal study of the Pentateuchal account. Thus, for instance, we have stressed that only one of the ten plagues mentioned in the Pentateuch, that of boils, is not contained in the Psalms, which in turn has enabled us to see the unique position of this plague in the overall plague tradition. The plague of boils is the only one in which Moses acts with Aaron's assistance, the only one in which the two act without the rod, and the only one in which the LORD addresses Aaron directly. Moreover we have noted that this plague seems to have been added to the graduated series of three episodes which ends with Aaron's victory over the Egyptian magicians in the plague of lice. Hence, and on the strength of the varying traditions regarding the plague of pestilence, we have concluded that the episode of the boils is the latest element in the plagues tradition, having originally served as an alternative to the pestilence. Conventional source criticism, by simply assigning the boils to P, actually obscures the uniquely problematic nature of this plague, instead of elucidating it.

The analysis of the Pentateuchal text, in turn, has been conducted in conjunction with the study of the later sources, even with regard to the repeatedly raised issue of who produced the plagues. Thus we have seen that while there are late sources according to which the LORD inflicted all the plagues directly, and others which say He did so only through the agency of Moses, not one states that He did so through the agency of Aaron. This accords with the internal traditio-historical analysis of the Pentateuch, which has ruled out the possibility that a tradition attributing the performance of all of the plagues to Aaron ever existed, and has suggested quite the opposite — that the Pentateuch was actually preceded by traditions assigning all of the plagues either to the LORD's direct action or the agency of Moses.

Not confining ourselves to what is stated explicitly in the later sources, we have also taken into account the motifs which these sources pass over in silence. Such silence, we are now convinced, can also be instructive. In particular we have noted the process by which those early motifs which the Pentateuch itself has already relegated to positions of secondary importance, incorporating them into the main body of the narrative only with some difficulty, have been omitted from the later sources. Thus, for example, in the Pentateuchal account of the fourth plague we have discovered traces of a rejected tradition that the limitations upon Pharaoh's concessions pertained to the destination of the journey. The goal of preserving some record of this rejected tradition has confused the narrative to such an extent that the uninitiated reader, unaware of the tradition-history of the text, would find it incomprehensible. No wonder that this motif has disappeared entirely from the tradition as contained in the later sources.

We have observed a similar process with regard to the tradition of the competition with Pharaoh's magicians in the first three plagues. In the Pentateuch, these plagues are, first and foremost, real plagues. At the same time the narrative has preserved the earlier tradition which saw them merely as displays of God's power. Here too, the desire to conserve impairs the clear logic of the narrative. As we have seen, the later sources have gone to even greater lengths to supplant this motif. Almost all of them have in effect silenced it, and the two sources in which it does appear, Artapanus and Jubilees, have re-interpreted it in their own way. Once again, the later sources, by their silence, cast additional, indirect light upon on the contending traditions which are manifest in the Pentateuch.

In view of the abundance of varying traditions observable in the Pentateuch, which are reliable evidence of the long and complicated pre-history of the received text, the antiquity of the plague tradition may safely be posited from the outset. We have endeavored further to substantiate this general assumption on the grounds that Psalm 78, which contains one of the two psalmodic accounts of the plagues, and which dates from the period of Solomon, opens with the following exordium:

I will expound a theme,
hold forth on the lessons of the past,
things we have heard and known,
that our fathers have told us.

(Ps 78:2-3)

Since the psalmist regards the seven-plagues tradition as an ancient one, there would seem to be good reason to conclude that this tradition belongs to the very origins of the corpus of Hebrew tradition as a whole. Yet our analysis has led us to the suggestion that even though the Pentateuch is later than the psalm, included among its underlying elements is a most ancient tradition which saw in the first three plagues mere spectacles. If this theory is correct, it would imply that in the earliest tradition, at least in one of its forms, these three acts were followed directly by the slaying of the firstborn.

This critical conjecture, for which decisive proof cannot be adduced from any available source, in no way calls into question the antiquity of the tradition concerning the slaying of the firstborn. There is no reasonable ground for assigning this tradition to a date later than that of the tradition regarding the parting of the sea. The contention of critical scholarship, that the logical connection between the two motifs appears to be secondary, fails to convince. First, it may well be that two ancient traditions developed independently and were later combined by a secondary process. Second, the critics' view of the loose connection of the two traditions is greatly exaggerated. From a certain standpoint, to be sure, the story of the plagues and the account of the drowning of the Egyptians in the sea may perhaps be viewed as contradictory. And as aptly noted by A. Reichert,[123] the didactic Psalm 105 omits the sea episode entirely, implying the reason for the omission in the words "Egypt rejoiced when they left, for dread of them had fallen upon them" (Ps 105:38). But the logic of the narrative in Exodus as it stands is also quite intelligible. Pharaoh's reasons for pursuing the Israelites (Exod 14:3-4) are a reflex of two motifs which characterize the entire plagues cycle: (1) that the Israel-

---

123 Private communication.

ites had deceived Pharaoh, never revealing to him that their real intent was to leave Egypt for good, and that the plagues succeeded only in securing Pharaoh's permission to depart on a three-day journey, and (2) that here, too as throughout the plagues cycle, the LORD stiffened Pharaoh's heart, once again out of a desire to make His signs and wonders ever more numerous.

We have thus refuted the interpretation offered by some recent critics who, in their attempt to supplement the documentary hypothesis with an examination of the antecedent traditions, arrive at a denial of the antiquity of the plague tradition and ultimately of the role of Moses in the story of the Exodus. If this nihilistic exegesis has any basis at all other than mere scepticism, it is in the half-truth that the Pentateuchal narratives essentially enlarge and embellish the traditions reflected in the didactic passages, which celebrate the power of God without mentioning Moses. But half-truths, here as everywhere, can be more dangerous than outright falsehoods. From the words of a declaration of belief, glorifying the LORD's power and mercy while omitting details of the historical process, one simply cannot arrive at the conclusion that the ancient traditions were ignorant of these details, even of so basic a fact as the identity of the man who organized and executed the Exodus from Egypt. Rather, as emerges quite obviously from our analysis of the sources, Israelite tradition contained various views on the precise division of labor between God and His emissaries.

Our judgment of the source-critical method holds true for the question of the relationship between the detailed narratives and the didactic passages in the psalms. There is no single, simple rule which can be used mechanically to solve the problems surrounding the history of tradition. Only meticulous study of each separate issue can enable the historical study of the tradition to come close to achieving any real results.

EXCURSUS II

RECENT CRITICAL ANALYSES OF THE PLAGUE
NARRATIVE*

I. The Two-Source Proposal

The extremely complex structure exhibited by the lengthy plague narrative in Exodus poses a difficult problem for the scholar attempting
to analyze it with the scalpel of source criticism. Indeed, so immense
are the problems he is likely to encounter in the attempt that they may
even raise doubts as to the very possibility of solving this enigmatic
passage by means of classical higher critical methods. And in fact, we
have already arrived at the conclusion that no such possibility exists,
and that scholarly effort should be re-directed to the traditio-
historical study of the passage.[1]

Our scepticism has been questioned by M. Greenberg, in his
"Narrative and Redactional Art in the Plague Pericope (Exodus
7-11)".[2] Not finding it necessary to refute in detail my reservations
about conventional criticism, Greenberg seeks to overturn them on

---

* This Excursus originally appeared under the title "^{c}Al haṣṣā^{c}ōt hādāšōt lēnittū^{a}h
  pārāšat hammakkōt", in SHNATON: An Annual for Biblical and Ancient Near Eastern Studies, 1 (1975), pp. 183-188. See also the author's "An Observation on Source-
  Criticism of the Plague-Pericope", VT, 24 (1974), pp. 374-378.
1 Above, pp. 167-169.
2 This study of Greenberg's appeared (in Hebrew) in B. Uffenheimer (ed.), Bible and
  Jewish History — Studies in Bible and Jewish History Dedicated to the Memory of
  Jacob Liver, Tel Aviv 1971, pp. 65-75. An English study of the topic, somewhat different in emphasis, is M. Greenberg, "The Redaction of the Plague Narrative in Exodus" in H. Goedicke (ed.), Near Eastern Studies in Honor of William Foxwell
  Albright, Baltimore and London 1971, pp. 243-252. See also M. Greenberg, Understanding Exodus, New York 1969, pp. 151-192.

the strength of his overall analysis of the pericope, an analysis which is merely an attempt to improve upon the accepted view.

Like his predecessors, Greenberg asserts that one narrative source included the seven plagues of (1) blood, (2) frogs, (3) swarms, (4) pestilence, (5) hail, (6) locusts and (7) the slaying of the firstborn. This reconstructed narrative, which is generally regarded as belonging to J, is called "B" by Greenberg. What is new in Greenberg's analysis is his extension of the P narrative, which he calls "A", to also include seven plagues, adding to the five plagues recognized as belonging to the Priestly source (blood, frogs, lice, boils and the slaying of the firstborn) also the accreditation sign of the crocodile and the plague of darkness, thereby arriving at (1) crocodile-sign, (2) blood, (3) frogs, (4) lice, (5) boils, (6) darkness, and (7) the slaying of the firstborn. According to this suggestion, therefore, both sources contained seven-part climactic series, and both of them ended with the decisive plague, the slaying of the firstborn.

The captivating simplicity of this solution cannot be denied, nor can the fact that Greenberg does not claim that the general lines of his proposal are capable of solving all of the critical problems of the passage. Three plagues are common to both sources: blood, frogs and the slaying of the firstborn, yet only with regard to the first two do critics agree that it is possible to isolate the P strand, while in the plague of the firstborn, where no such consensus exists, even Greenberg does not suggest a source division. Further, Greenberg is also forced to assume that "B" has undergone secondary expansion, consisting of the reference to human pestilence (Exod 9:13-16) and the description of the hail as having smitten man and beast (9:19-20, 22, 25). He has also attributed to the redactor the dominant role in creating literary unity, without entering into a detailed discussion of his method.

Greenberg has also grouped together aspects of the text which are not consistent with each other. For instance, he treats Moses' sixfold repetition of the words "Let My people go, that they may serve Me" along with the emphasis laid upon the theme "that the Egyptians may know that I am the LORD when I stretch out My hand over Egypt and bring out the Israelites from their midst" (7:5), which recurs, with slight reformulation, in the plagues of blood (7:17), frogs (8:6), swarms (8:18) and hail (9:16, 29). Structurally these phenomena are quite dissimilar. The repetition of "Let My people go" is a verbal one, and the fact that it recurs precisely six times can easily be accounted for, since precisely six times Moses warns Pharaoh. This in turn is simply the result of the redactional pattern, recognized long ago by Samuel ben Meir and Abrabanel in their comments on Exod 7:26, according to which Moses confronts Pharaoh with an ultimatum in the first two of each of the three triads of plagues preceding the slaying of the firstborn.[3] Moreover, the redactional unity is evident even in such a detail as the fact that the longer formulation, "Let My people go that they may worship Me in the wilderness. But you have paid no heed until now" etc., is reserved for the first occurrence of the pattern (7:16), whereas in the following occurrences (7:26; 8:16; 9:1, 3; 10:13) the reader is spared and shorter versions appear.   .

Such an aspect of the narrative is no doubt evidence of systematic and internally consistent redaction. The repeated theme "that the Egyptians may know" etc., on the other hand, is certainly not. The repetition is not verbal, and even the most casual glance is enough to raise the question of why this theme has been attached only to the plagues of blood, frogs, swarms and hail, and no others. What is more, the only one of these plagues which actually serves as proof that the LORD is Master of the whole earth is the blood. In the accounts of the frogs and the hail this theme is introduced as the result of the plague's disappearance, whereas in the plague of swarms it is deduced from the fact that the Israelites were immune to the plague's effect, a motif which itself is totally inconsistent. The reference to human pestilence in Exod 9:16 is another matter entirely; its purpose is to explain why the Egyptians were not smitten by such a pestilence. No system or uniformity can be detected in the use of these motifs.

---

3 See above, p. 87.

II. Difficulties in the Two-Source Analysis

A. Source "B"

We proceed to the the source-critical analysis, which is the main point at issue. Greenberg assigns seven plagues to "B": blood, frogs, swarms, pestilence, hail, locusts and the slaying of the firstborn. In further support of the accepted view that in this source the locusts immediately preceded the slaying of the firstborn, Greenberg argues that Pharaoh's plea, spoken to Moses during the first of the two plagues, "Forgive my offense, just this once..." (Exod 10:17), implies that this is to be the penultimate plague. The intervening plague of darkness, he concludes, must therefore have been interpolated from source "A" by the redactor.

Now Greenberg's decision to regard Exod 10:17 as evidence that the locusts are to be followed by only one more plague is probably correct, and was in fact preceded by our own contention that the extreme solemnity of Exod 10:1-2, with which the account of the locusts begins, can have no other reason than that, just as in Ps 105:34-35, this is the penultimate plague.[4]

Indeed, the uniqueness of the plague of locusts can be defined even more precisely when consideration is given to the fact that Moses, as is well known, is told to warn Pharaoh of the onset of six plagues — the first, second, fourth, fifth, seventh and eighth — and that the sixth occurrence of this warning, preceding the eighth plague, differs from the first five. In the first five, the LORD's command to Moses contains two elements: the demand that Pharaoh release the Israelites, and the threat of the specific plague to follow. The narrative then immediately proceeds — again, in each of the first five cases — to the arrival of the plague, omitting Moses' actual appearance before Pharaoh.

4 See above, p. 163.

The pattern in all five cases is elliptical.[5] Only in the sixth occurrence of the pattern, in the introduction to the plague of locusts, does this pattern vary. Here, the LORD's solemn address to Moses (Exod 10:1-2) lacks the two fundamental characteristics found hitherto: it contains no mention of the plague which is to follow or of the demand to "Let My people go". Instead, however, the narrative includes, in vv. 3-6, an account of Moses and Aaron's joint speech to Pharaoh, which includes the two elements which were missing from vv. 1-2: the demand for the Israelites to be released, and the threat of the plague which will be inflicted if they are not. To be sure, this too is elliptical. But the introductory passage is more highly developed, and this is not so much the result of the greater solemnity of the LORD's charge to Moses but rather of the added account of Moses' and Aaron's speech, which is without parallel in the five preceding cases.

There are, then, several considerations supporting the claim that the plague of locusts is depicted as the penultimate plague. This finding, however, in no way proves that the redactor interpolated the plague of darkness from some other source. The alternative possibility, that he has re-arranged the sequence of plagues within one source, remains equally valid, and becomes even more likely in light of Psalm 105, where the locusts are positioned sixth (v. 34), that is, in the most prominent position among the plagues preceding the slaying of the firstborn, whereas the darkness is the first plague. Further corrobora-

---

5 To be sure, the elliptical style of composition is not equally striking in all cases. It is particularly remarkable in the accounts of blood, frogs and hail, each of which is introduced with the words "The LORD said to Moses" (Exod 7:19; 8:1; 9:22). In these cases, two separate divine addresses occur in immediate succession without any indication of what has intervened. The omission is less noticeable in the accounts of the swarms and the pestilence, which the LORD Himself produces immediately after His initial address to Moses, thereby simply carrying out His own words. The arrival of the swarms is thus expressed in the words "And the LORD did so" (8:20). The account of the pestilence makes the connection even more explicit. Moses is told to conclude his opening speech to Pharaoh with the words "The LORD has fixed the time: *tomorrow the LORD will do this thing* in the land" (9:5), and the immediately following report of the plague's arrival opens with "So *the LORD did this thing on the morrow*" (9:6). This allows us to speculate that the elliptical pattern has its origin in the accounts of those plagues which were brought about by God Himself.

tion may be found in the comparison with Psalm 78, which assigns to the locusts the inconspicuous third place and does not mention the plague of darkness at all. The most logical conclusion is that the redactor took over the plagues of locusts and darkness from one and the same source, later transferring the plague of darkness, which in Psalm 105 begins the series, to the penultimate place, in order to leave open the first position for the plague of blood, which is first in Psalm 78. It was impossible for him to do justice to all the traditions which served as the basis for his compilation without altering the sequence of events in any of them. Any analysis in which the locusts and darkness are assigned to separate sources is thereby refuted.

A further problem in Greenberg's reconstructed source "B" is the unrelieved tension between the fourth plague, a pestilence affecting livestock which is so great that its severity approaches that of a pestilence affecting humans, and the sixth plague, that of locusts, which is far less severe.[6] Neither the series of plagues in Ps 78:44-51 nor that in Ps 105:28-36 displays this incongruity: in Psalm 105, the absence of the pestilence prevents the locusts from being preceded by a more severe plague, and in Psalm 78 the pestilence, first affecting livestock, then humans,[7] immediately precedes the slaying of the firstborn.

It follows that to assume the existence of source "B" is to assume that it has absorbed elements from both traditions, that reflected in Psalm 78 and that reflected in Psalm 105. The influence of the latter would be perceptible in the sequence hail-locusts, which stems from the view that the locusts immediately preceded the slaying of the firstborn, as opposed to the former, where the sequence is locusts-hail and the locusts are not in a particularly prominent position. The influence of the former would be perceptible in the verses dealing with the pestilence, primarily the account of the cattle pestilence (Exod 9:1-7), but also the threat of a pestilence to afflict humans (13-15).

---

6 True, in the Pentateuchal account the hail smote not only the vegetation but also livestock and even humans, but this, as seen correctly by Greenberg, is a secondary expansion.

7 Ps. 78:48a, when emended, speaks of a pestilence affecting humans; as does the MT of 48b. For the evidence, see above pp. 80-82.

Here, however, the redactor has detracted somewhat from the pestilence tradition, obscuring it in no fewer than three ways: (1) He has transferred the plague to an earlier stage in the narrative; (2) he has interpolated the boils (Exod 9:8-12) between the pestilence and the ensuing announcement of a plague affecting humans; (3) he has omitted the actual arrival of a pestilence affecting humans, instead attributing to Moses a speech in which the threat of such a plague is withdrawn (9:16). Even so, Exod 9:13-15 remains decisive for the evaluation of the pre-existing sources, and the importance of this passage is not negated by the widely held theory that it is a secondary expansion of source "B". The theory arises from the fact that the verses in question do nothing to advance the narrative as it now stands, but it cannot explain why a redactor would have added a section not only devoid of function but also in opposition to the structural principle which obtains throughout the plague narrative, namely, that the announcement of the imminent arrival of a plague is the literary introduction to its onset.

The passage can be understood only if it is assumed that it originated in a source which included a pestilence affecting humans. The purpose of v. 16 is to minimize this plague, by stating that even though Moses had threatened the Egyptians themselves with pestilence, they were not actually stricken since he immediatley retracted his threat. Such an assumption, which is corroborated by Psalm 78, also provides an explanation for the uniqueness of the passage: since the pestilence among humans is the only tradition which the redactor rejected, the passage which mentions it is unparalleled in the plague narrative.

Let us now review our criticism of the source "B" hypothesis: (1) the locusts and the darkness seem to have originated in one and the same source, and (2) even if we ignore this probability, it would still remain that source "B" has drawn on at least two separate traditions, one placing the locusts immediately before the slaying of the firstborn and not mentioning pestilence, and the other placing pestilence before the slaying of the firstborn. This being the case, the hypothetical source "B" is so far from being uniform that its very existence as an independent narrative cannot reasonably be assumed.

It is more probable, then, that in his attempt to do justice to a variety of traditions, the redactor was simply at an impasse. The difficulty he faced in combining the two traditions is similar to that which he encountered when he was forced to place the plague of locusts before that of darkness. Groping in the dark, however, is not an appropriate method for reconstructing literary sources; this should only be done in the light of the visible sources, namely, Psalms 78 and 105, each of which contains a complete and simple account.

B. Source "A"

Turning now to the proposed source "A", which, it is suggested, contained (1) the crocodile-sign, (2) blood, (3) frogs, (4) lice, (5) boils, (6) darkness and (7) the slaying of the firstborn, we begin by noting that the presumed existence of such a version is of course in direct opposition to what we have just concluded, namely, that locusts and darkness originate in the same source. Aside from this there are other difficulties, since the slaying of the firstborn would be preceded here by five accreditation signs and only one actual plague — that of darkness. And whereas the players appearing on the stage in the five "signs" are Aaron and the magicians, they are absent in the plague of darkness, thus creating the distinct impression that the darkness and the five plagues preceding it are not all of a piece.

Furthermore, the five "signs" show no indication of being a continuous story. Now, Greenberg is of the opinion that the crocodile-sign is an appropriate prologue to the other four, since, unlike what followed, it was not harmful and therefore did not exacerbate the conflict between the sides, and it was indecisive, since Aaron's act became worthless the moment the magicians duplicated it. Taking up these two considerations in reverse order, we recall that the crocodile episode includes the statement that "Aaron's rod swallowed up their rods" (7:12), which means that although the magicians initially matched Aaron's performance, they were then outdone, and the match did not end in a draw but in a victory for Aaron. The similarity between this one-act competition and the three-act competition which follows in the story of the blood, frogs and lice cannot be ignored. The magicians initially matched Aaron's performance (blood, frogs) and were then defeated (lice). The same two stages which appear in the crocodile-sign — first a draw; then Aaron's victory — appear here as well, the only difference being that the crocodile-sign compresses the two stages into one episode, while in the following narrative it extends over three plagues. The logical conclusion is that these are two parallel traditions, rather than one continuous account.

Turning to Greenberg's contention that the progression from the crocodile-sign to the acts which followed it in "A" is a movement from a sign serving only for accreditation to signs which were also annoyances, we must consider briefly the nature of these "signs". Whereas the crocodile-sign displays a clear logic and has doubtless survived in its original form, the same cannot be said of the blood, frogs and lice. Here the reader cannot help but wonder why the magicians should have performed acts which intensified the sufferings of their countrymen, and where they obtained water to turn into blood once Aaron had bloodied all the waters of Egypt. These problems, visible even to the most naive of readers, can only be solved if we assume that the present account was preceded by one in which Aaron produced blood, frogs and lice in minute quantities, causing no widespread suffering (see Exod 4:9). This earlier account was redacted to harmonize with the other tradition, in which the blood, frogs and lice were actual plagues and not mere signs. Since there are no grounds for attributing this redactional stage to one of the Pentateuchal sources, it should be ascribed to the final redactor, whose aim was to do justice to as many differing traditions concerning the events leading up to Israel's liberation as possible. Thus the contention that in source "A" the crocodile-sign alone was purely a sign and not a plague is untenable.

Most probably then, there existed two versions of the contest tradition: the story of the crocodile-sign and the three-part story of the blood, frogs and lice. The former has survived in its original form, while the latter has been reworked by the redactor of the plague narrative, who aimed at finding a compromise between this tradition and another in which blood, frogs and lice were actual plagues. The combined weight of the evidence leads us to conclude that the crocodile-sign and the story of the blood, frogs and lice do not belong to the same literary source.

We have so far omitted the plague of boils from the discussion, and shall touch upon it only briefly since it has received full treatment above, and our contention that it diverges in several respects from the remainder of the plagues, and that it should be regarded as the latest element in the plague narrative, has been outlined in detail.[8] Here we shall merely point out that the plague of boils is not only absent in Psalm 78, but also in Psalm 105, which includes the plague of darkness — indicating that the boils and the darkness cannot be assigned to the same source. We must reiterate then, that the series of "signs" cannot be grouped together as a continuous narrative.

C. The Underlying Traditions

The background against which these stories developed is another matter entirely. Their most ancient form has probably been preserved in Exod 4:21-23, which seems to imply that after Moses had displayed the "signs" which were imparted to him at the burning bush (Exod 4:1-9), the LORD struck Egypt with one plague only: the slaying of the firstborn. Support for this may be found in Ps 135:8, where this is the only plague mentioned. In a more developed form of this tradition, the "signs" were transformed into a sort of contest between Aaron and Pharaoh's magicians. Though the intermediate stages between the early tradition of Exod 4:21-23 and the contest narratives cannot be discerned with any certainty, we might at least suggest the possible existence of a tradition in which the slaying of the firstborn was preceded by the contest comprised of blood, frogs and lice, in the third phase of which Aaron is triumphant. If this conjecture is correct, the three "signs" were grouped together with the slaying of the firstborn, constituting a four-part series with a double climax, occurring in the third and fourth members. This structure would resemble that of the account of God's appearance to Samuel

8 See above, pp. 95, 122, 168.

(1 Sam 3:1-14). But there is no decisive proof for such a hypothesis, and the only thing which seems certain is that one cannot speak of five successive plagues occurring in one continuous source which preceded the present text.

IV. The Psalm-Tradition Proposal

Another proposal, suggested by G. Kravitz in a master's thesis entitled "Word Interchange in the Command-Fulfillment Pattern in the Pentateuch and in Ugaritic Epic",[9] appears to be nearer the mark. Kravitz distinguishes between the J narrative, which contained seven plagues — blood, frogs, swarms, cattle pestilence, hail, locusts and the slaying of the firstborn, and the P narrative, which contained eight: blood, frogs, and lice produced by Aaron's rod; boils produced by Aaron and Moses jointly; hail, locusts and darkness produced by Moses' rod, and the slaying of the firstborn, performed by the LORD. The boils, he contends, are the latest element to have been included in the P narrative, and the more ancient stage of the P version is reflected by Psalm 105 — the only difference being that in P the darkness precedes the slaying of the firstborn while in the Psalm it stands at the head of the series. Similarly, Kravitz maintains, the J source is a later version of the tradition reflected in Psalm 78. J rejected the human pestilence, and in order to preserve the completeness suggested by the number seven, turned the swarms-frogs, which are one plague in Psalm 78 (v. 45), into two distinct plagues.

Though this proposal is most impressive, it may have underestimated the work of the final redactor, who is responsible for the ten-plague pattern and was compelled to re-organize the ancient traditions. Presumably, this is the same redactor who minimized the pestilence tradition, and it would seem to be simpler to attribute to him the plague of boils as well, since it was he who sought to arrive at the number ten, than to assume that the Priestly author added an eighth plague to an existing seven-plague series. This view of the

9 M.A. Thesis (unpublished), Hebrew University, Jerusalem 1971.

redactor's activity enables us to explain, as we have above, why the darkness has been placed in the ninth position in the Pentateuchal account, in contrast to Psalm 105 where it occurs first.

V. Summary

We may now review our conclusions and posit what we believe may be said of the sources used by the redactor who created the pattern of three triads of plagues culminating in a tenth plague. This redactor was evidently aware of two series of seven plagues each, and these are none other than the two series exhibited in Psalms 78 and 105. He was also aware of, or perhaps invented, a late tradition of boils, apparently a variant of the pestilence tradition, and was further acquainted with an early tradition which regarded blood, frogs and lice purely as accreditation signs without any of the features of actual plagues.

THE NUMBER OF PLAGUES IN PSALM 105*

It has long been observed that the plague tradition of the late Psalm 105 is closer to the Pentateuch than that of the earlier Psalm 78. The exact definition of the relation between the plague traditions in Psalm 105 and the book of Exodus, however, remains a matter of debate. In response to the above attempt to demonstrate that a certain similarity between the two traditions does not impair the unique character of the psalmist's report,[1] B. Margulis has recently expounded the opposite thesis, arguing that the Pentateuchal account should be regarded as the source of the psalm.[2]

In accordance with his view, Margulis counts the swarms and lice in v. 31 as two plagues, and dismisses our view that they are a single plague as "a forced contamination of the traditional third and fourth plagues into one". The absence of cattle pestilence is due, in his opinion, to a homoioteleuton in the MT. He finds support for this assumption in the fragment of Psalm 105 preserved in 11QPs[a], which enables us to reconstruct the full text of the psalm. This text related the total destruction of livestock by pestilence. Margulis concludes his investigation with the remark that it was for this reason that the psalmist exempted the livestock from the plague of hail and omitted the plague of boils completely.

---

* This Excursus appeared in *Biblica*, 52 (1971), pp. 34-38. For reasons of clarity and uniformity, stylistic changes have been made in the version presented here, on the basis of the author's Hebrew version, which may be found in the Hebrew edition of the present volume, pp. 161-163.

1 Above, pp. 82-102, 166-167.

2 B. Margulis, "The Plagues Tradition in Psalm 105", *Biblica*, 50 (1969), pp. 491-496.

Margulis thus ascribes to the poet a critical attitude toward the Pentateuch, i.e., he supposes that the psalmist excluded the livestock from the plagues of hail and boils because it no longer existed. But if this is so, then why did he exclude men from these plagues as well, restricting the plague of hail to plants and omitting the plague of boils altogether? This omission of a plague is a drastic deviation from the Pentateuch, and could easily have been avoided, as illustrated by Ezekiel the Tragedian (l. 137),[3] Artapanus (Eusebius, IX:27, 31)[4] and Josephus (Ant. II.xiv.4),[5] all of whom restrict the plague of boils to men. Still more astonishing is Margulis' tacit assumption that a writer relying on the Pentateuch could take the liberty of transferring the plague of darkness from its "traditional" place as the penultimate plague to the beginning of the pericope, though no logical reason whatsoever may be adduced for this far-reaching alteration. The inevitable conclusion is that the author was not concerned with a faithful reproduction of his allegedly authoritative source, the account of the plagues in Exodus.

These methodological objections to Margulis, however, are only of minor importance. The crucial questions are whether the psalmist counted swarms and lice as two plagues or one, and whether he assumed the livestock to have been smitten or not. We shall begin with v. 31: "Swarms came at His command; lice, throughout their country". It may readily be admitted that to interpret this verse in the light of the Pentateuch would result in the enumeration of two plagues. But this interpretation fails to do justice to the technique employed by the psalmist in presenting the plagues. It should be noted that he has dealt with each of the other plagues in at least two parallel hemistichs. Applying this rule to v. 31, we arrive at the correct interpretation: the verse describes a single plague. This view is decisively corroborated by comparing v. 31 to v. 34: "Locusts came at His command; grasshoppers without number". Though the structure of the latter is clearly similar to that of the verse in question, none would distinguish two plagues in v. 34, locusts and grasshoppers! The struc-

---

3 See above, Chapter Four, note 3.
4 See above, Chapter Four, note 1.
5 See above, Chapter Four, note 1.

tural analysis of v. 31 therefore proves that the poet regarded swarms and lice as one plague only.

The resulting difference between Psalm 105 and the book of Exodus may easily be explained. In all three biblical accounts of the plagues — Exodus, Psalm 78 and Psalm 105 — the first plague, blood, is followed by the assault of annoying small creatures. But there are three variants in the description of this assault. Ps 78:45 restricts it to *one* plague,[6] consisting of "swarms" and frogs (in that order!); Ps 105:30-31 relates that *two* plagues occurred at this stage, namely, (1) frogs and (2) swarms/lice; and the narrative in Exodus speaks of *three* distinct plagues: (1) frogs, (2) lice, (3) swarms. In this respect, then, Psalm 105 occupies an intermediate position between Psalm 78 and the book of Exodus.

We turn now to the proposed reconstruction of v. 29. Margulis begins with the correct observation that the lacunae in 11QPsᵃ ll. 4-5 indicate the existence of a version of v. 29 whose length exceeds that of the MT, and adds that the letters preserved at the end of l. 4 are not in accordance with the MT. These and other similar considerations lead him to a reconstruction of v. 29 in which direct reference is made to cattle pestilence. The proposed text would read:

4 [hpk ᵓt mymyhm l]dm .   śm
5 [yᵓwrm lbᵓwš wyk bdbr mqnm wymt ᵓt dgtm š]ršh ᵓršm

([...He turned their waters into] blood,
made [their waters fetid;
He smote their livestock with pestilence
and killed their fish. Their] land teemed with...)

From this version, allegedly, the MT originated ("via homoioteleuton, cp. ...mq[nm]...dm śm....") But no group of letters which could possibly have caused such a copyist's error as that suggested by Margulis can be perceived here.

---

6 Of course, a "traditional" interpretation would assume that the verse refers to two plagues. The parallel pair swarms/frogs, however, should be compared with grubs/locusts in v. 46, hail/frost in v. 47, pestilence (reading *dbr*; see above, pp. 80-81)/lightning bolts in v. 48 and slaying/pestilence in v. 50.

As for the reconstructed reading itself, it consists of four hemistichs, the first, second and fourth (see Exod 7:21) of which deal with the plague of blood. Only the third speaks of cattle pestilence, which is to say, the very plague under discussion is inserted, in this proposed reading, within the account of the plague of blood. Not only is no such "sandwiching" attested anywhere in any other account of the plagues, but it should be recalled that in all three sources, in the MT, the arrival of small creatures is directly subsequent to the plague of blood. In Margulis' reconstruction of Psalm 105, in contrast to this well-attested tradition, the cattle pestilence would follow the blood, thus preceding the frogs. For these reasons, the proposal is not convincing.

In all probability, the longer text in 11QPs^a is simply the result of an expanded description of the plague of blood in this late version of the psalm. The lack of cattle pestilence in the late plague tradition of Psalm 105 is not surprising when we recall its conspicuous absence from the post-biblical writings of Ezekiel the Tragedian (ll. 132-147), Artapanus (Eusebius IX:27, 28-31), Wisdom of Solomon (11:2-14; 16:1-15; 17:1-18, 21; 18:5-19; see also 19:1-27) and even Josephus (Ant. II.xiv, esp. para. 3).[7] All these late sources are evidence that the cattle pestilence does not belong to the nucleus of the plague tradition, and was certainly not a part of its later development. In addition, they make it clear that the canonization of the Pentateuch did not put an end to the development of the plague tradition, which remained fluid well into Second Temple times.

To conclude, Psalm 105 confronts us with an unique form of the plague tradition. It is hardly coincidental that it enumerates seven plagues, because seven is the stereotype number signifying wholeness. And although the number seven alternates in this function with the number ten, we have shown above that seven, not ten, is preferred when speaking of a climactic series,[8] and the plague tradition, culmi-

---

7   Like Psalm 105, Artapanus and Wisdom of Solomon, Josephus did not record any plague afflicting livestock, omitting even the death of the fish from his description of the plague of blood. But see also Ant. II.xiv.5, where it is stated that the Egyptians' livestock had perished (see above, p. 110), and Midr. HaGadol Wā ᵓērā ᵓ (to Exod 9:10), which questions the justice of inflicting punishment upon animals.

8   Above, pp. 82-86.

nating in the last plague, the slaying of the firstborn, clearly belongs to this genre. In light of these typological considerations we should expect the similar, but not identical, plague traditions to crystallize in series of seven plagues, which is what has happened in Psalms 78[9] and 105. The Pentateuchal account resulted from the amalgamation of all variants of the plague traditions, including, for instance, the extension of the hail from a plague which struck plants to one which affected livestock and humans, and the introduction of the plague of boils, a late alternative to the pestilence. The only ancient tradition rejected by the Pentateuch is that of the pestilence affecting humans, and even this, as we have seen, is not passed over in silence (Exod 9:14-16).[10] The process of collecting the different traditions resulted in the sum of ten plagues, ten also being a typological number — if not a climactic one, at least one expressing completeness. This stage of the plague tradition was preceded by separate variants, each of which included seven plagues, and two of which have been preserved in Psalms 78 and 105. We cannot be certain whether Psalm 78 is actually later than the Pentateuch or not, but it certainly represents a poetic tradition which precedes the Pentateuch.

9 Counting swarms and frogs as one plague (see above, note 6); the cattle pestilence (!) in v. 48 and that afflicting humans (vv. 49-50) as two. On the latter as a separate plague in its own right, and on the meaning of the word *ḥayyātām* in v. 50b, see above, pp. 81-82. To the references there, add Pss 26:9 and 74:19.

10 For a detailed discussion, see Lauha, *op. cit.* (Chapter One, note 14), pp. 52f., see also above, pp. 94-96.

CHAPTER FIVE

THE PASCHAL SACRIFICE

I. The Absence of the Paschal Sacrifice in the Didactic Psalms

Though the plagues, as we have already had occasion to note,[1] did not affect the Israelites, it was not deemed necessary in the Pentateuchal account to state this fact explicitly in each and every plague. Only occasionally does the Pentateuch mention this favored treatment that Israel received, and the same is true of the other detailed narratives, all of which refer only here and there, but not consistently, to Israel's immunity to the plagues. Philo's systematic account of the plagues is the only exception. We have also mentioned[2] that this theme is missing entirely from the didactic passages extolling the LORD for having smitten the Egyptians and delivering His people: no particular attention is paid to the fact that when the LORD struck Egypt in order to rescue Israel, He made certain to refrain from smiting Israel too in the process.

In light of this general tendency we may also account for the absence of all mention of the paschal sacrifice in the didactic passages. Viewed purely from the perspective of the plague narrative, the sole significance of the paschal sacrifice lies in the fact that, when the Egyptian firstborn were all slain, no harm came to the firstborn of Israel. It should be clear from the outset that so obvious a fact would hardly be mentioned in pragmatic historiography, in which the basic lines of the story are sufficient and all detail is omitted.

1 Above, pp. 165-166.
2 *Ibid.*

II. The Paschal Sacrifice and the Plague Narrative

The above considerations do not, however, detract from the important role assigned to the paschal sacrifice in the Pentateuch. Not only does Moses, appearing before Pharaoh to announce the slaying of the firstborn, solemnly proclaim, "Not a dog shall snarl at any of the Israelites, at man or beast — in order that you may know that the LORD makes a distinction between Egypt and Israel" (Exod 11:7); the narrative goes on to relate the divine commands given to Moses concerning the precisely detailed ceremony to be performed by the Israelites in order to be saved (12:1-13), even recording the exact words in which Moses conveys these orders to the people (12:21-28). If the paschal sacrifice is nothing more than an episode in the story of the plagues, the lengthy treatment it receives is somewhat surprising — which is why scholars who have begun by postulating such an assumption have been forced to conclude that the detailed account of the Pesah is a later expansion of the original plague narrative, and that the latter alone recounts the essential course of events.

This prevailing view of the paschal sacrifice rests entirely upon Wellhausen's analysis of the Pesah tradition. In the *Prolegomena*,[3] the sacrifice is not even mentioned — as befits a secondary element. In *Die Composition des Hexateuchs*,[4] Wellhausen elaborates, claiming in essence that Israel's early tradition was concerned solely with the fatal plague inflicted by the LORD upon Egypt, and that the sparing of the Israelites was simply self-evident. Followers of Wellhausen, among them Gressmann,[5] have continued to maintain that the early saga saw no reason to dwell upon a fact so obvious as that the Israelites were unaffected by the slaying of the firstborn — just as they had been unaffected by the preceding plagues.

However, as we shall now proceed to argue, the very assumption that the account of the Pesah is merely a late expansion of the plague tradition is questionable on two grounds.

---

3 J. Wellhausen, *Prolegomena to the History of Ancient Israel*, trans. by Menzies-Black, 1885 (repr. N.Y. 1957), pp. 83-89.
4 Berlin 1899, p. 72.
5 *Op. cit.* (Chapter Two, note 2), pp. 102ff.

III. The Slaying of the Firstborn and the Pesah

A. The Sequence of the Narrative

If the account of the Pesah had in fact evolved from that of the plagues, we would surely expect the two narratives to cohere. It would be logical to expect the text to contain some clear expression of the idea that the LORD spared the firstborn of the Israelites when He smote those of the Egyptians. And yet no explicit statement of this kind is ever made, not even in the one passage which connects the slaying of the firstborn with the Pesah — namely Moses' declaration to Pharaoh (quoted above) that the slaying of the firstborn will not affect the Israelites. Even this declaration refrains from stating openly that the LORD will not smite the Israelite firstborn, preferring the non-specific formulation "Not a dog shall snarl" etc.

The difficulty becomes even greater when we consider that the Pesah story itself states simply that the LORD "saved our houses" (Exod 12:27) — not "our firstborn". Nor is this mere hair-splitting, since the implication of the injunction "None of you shall go outside the door of his house" on the night of the Pesah is that whoever does so — and not just the firstborn — will be slain by the destructive power which is afoot. Another discrepancy, no less essential, is that the LORD Himself slays the firstborn of Egypt, while the lives of the Israelites were in danger of being cut down by a malevolent angel whom the text calls "the Destroyer" (12:23).

The inconsistency, problematic in itself, is a function of varying theological stances. The biblical account states that the LORD will "pass over" (*psh*) the houses of the Israelites when He sees the blood (12:13), to which R. Ishmael, not without good reason, objected:

> Is not all revealed to Him of whom it is said "He knows what is in the darkness, and light dwells with Him" (Dan 2:22), and also "Darkness is not too dark for You" (Ps 139:12)? What then is the meaning of "when I see the blood"? That in reward for the one commandment you perform, I will appear to you and spare you, as it is said *"ūpāsahtī ʿălēkem"*, and *psh* means "spare."
>
> (Yal. Šimʿoni 200)

The issue raised here is also the origin of the midrashic view that the blood was placed *inside* the doorways of the houses,[6] as put succinctly by Rashi (commentary to Exod 12:13):

> "[The blood] shall be a sign for you" — a sign for you, and not a sign for others. Hence we conclude that the blood was placed inside [the entrance of the house]. "And when I see the blood" — though everything is revealed to Him, the Holy One, blessed be He, said: I shall take notice of whether you are engaged in the performance of My commands.

Such interpretations shed clear light on the difficulties encountered by later theology in its attempt to elucidate the Pesah narrative. As contained in the Pentateuch, however, the account of the slaying of the firstborn is aware of no such theological problem. The Pentateuchal account is wholly mysterious, which is what makes the absolute sovereignty of the LORD, slaying at midnight all the Egyptian firstborn at one fell stroke, so remarkable. The story does not tell how He acted, and it is precisely this silence that enhances the sense that His power is infinite and cannot be measured in earthly terms.

B. The Legal Connection

The view that the Pesah story is an expansion of the plague of the firstborn is also questionable from the standpoint of biblical law. The explicit rationale given for the legislation concerning the firstborn of Israel (Exod 13:11-16; Num 3:11-13; 8:16-17) is that they were saved from the slaying of the firstborn in Egypt. By confiscating the firstborn of Egypt, the LORD tangibly revealed His claim that all firstborn are His. In fact, Wellhausen concluded from this that the real origin of the Pesah story is to be sought in the legislation concerning Israel's firstborn.[7] Many scholars regard the express mention of

---

6 Mek. Bōᵓ 6; see also S. Lieberman in *Tarbiz*, 6 (1935), p. 235 (Hebrew).

7 *Op. cit.* (above, note 3), p. 88: "The only view sanctioned by the nature of the case is that the Israelite custom of offering the firstlings gave rise to the narrative of the slaying of the first-born of Egypt; unless the custom be pre-supposed the story is inexplicable, and the peculiar selection of its victims by the plague is left without a motive".

the slaying of the firstborn of Egypt within the context of the legislation concerning the firstborn of Israel as an allusion to all that occurred on the night of the Exodus, including the sparing of Israel's firstborn, and have proposed that some connection exists between the two.

But this exegetical approach ought not to be confused with the explicit content of the biblical account, and in no sense is it admissible to employ those biblical passages which juxtapose the law of the firstborn with the Feast of Massot without first determining the nature of the juxtaposition.[8] Just as there is no connection between the rationale given for the law of the firstborn and that given for the Pesah sacrifice, so there is, as Nikolsky has shown,[9] no real similarity in their content. The law of the firstborn consists of the command to offer the firstborn of the flock and the herd and the stipulation that firstborn asses and humans are to be redeemed. The law of the Pesah, in contrast, mentions only a yearling male lamb, and not specifically the firstborn. A firstborn of the flock or herd remains seven days with its mother and is offered to the LORD on the eighth (Exod 22:29); the paschal lamb was to be separated from the flock on the tenth day of the first month and sacrificed on the fourteenth at twilight (12:3,6). The Priestly code contains the regulation that the firstborn were to be eaten exclusively by the priests (Num 18:17,18, as distinct from D, Deut 15:20), whereas at the paschal sacrifice celebrated in Egypt the priests play no role at all. Moreover numerous additional stipulations, such as the command to roast the Pesah in fire (Exod 12:8), long recognized by scholars as being quite archaic (the Mishnah even preserves the ancient practice of using a spit of pomegranate wood; see m. Pesah. 7:1), the command to eat the Pesah at night (Exod 12:8), "your loins girded, your sandals on your feet and your staff in your hand" (12:11), indoors, the blood placed on the lintel and the doorposts (12:22), and the instructions regarding who may partake of the sacrifice (12:3-4, 44-45) are unique to the paschal sacrifice and unparalleled in the law of the firstborn.

---

8 Exod 13:2; 34:19-20. The juxtaposition would appear to be merely associative.
9 N. M. Nikolsky, "Pascha im Kulte des jerusalemischen Tempels", *ZAW*, 45 (1927), pp. 171-190; 241-253.

C. Attempts at Restoring the Ancient Cohesion

We must conclude therefore that the narrative cohesion between the slaying of the firstborn and the paschal sacrifice is extremely tenuous, and that the legal cohesion is even more so, the laws of the Pesaḥ and those of the firstborn differing in every aspect. Scholars who believe the account of the paschal sacrifice to be merely an expansion of the story of the last plague are therefore forced to theorize, albeit reluctantly, that there originally existed a closer connection between the two, and those critics who maintain that the literary juxtaposition of the two is the original one must of course make the same hypothesis.

This hypothesis has been expressed in various forms. Wellhausen,[10] seizing upon references to the Israelites' request for a leave of absence in order to sacrifice in the wilderness, proposed that their actual intent was to offer the firstborn of their livestock to the LORD. According to this hypothetical tradition, Pharaoh's punishment for refusing to permit the Israelites to sacrifice the firstborn of their livestock was the slaying of the firstborn of Egypt. Wellhausen was followed by E. Meyer,[11] who added to the original thesis the idea that the Israelites had also intended to perform the ritual of redeeming human fisrtborn. This proposal was fully developed by Gressmann,[12] who asserted that in the original form of the tradition Pharaoh was punished for not permitting the Israelites to sacrifice the firstborn of their cattle and of mankind, and that this tradition was later marred, when a reworking of the Pesaḥ festival transferred it from Mount Sinai to Egypt.

The theory advanced by Pedersen is a more modest one. Accepting that the original Pesaḥ did in fact take place in Egypt, he writes:

> The interest centres entirely around the first-born who are slain, that is, among the Egyptians; and the first-born who are saved, that is, among the Israelites. They hold the interest to such a degree that...the ordinance concerning the Paschal lamb

10 *Op. cit.* (above, note 3), p. 87.
11 E. Meyer, *Die Israeliten und ihre Nachbarstämme*, Halle 1906, p. 40.
12 *Loc. cit.* (above, note 5).

entirely disregards the command that it is to be a first-born animal which is sacrificed, though this must necessarily be the starting-point of the whole idea. It is not mentioned in this main legend, and has disappeared entirely from the laws....[13]

Others have attempted to account for the eventual abolition of a law requiring the sacrifice of human firstborn by more logical considerations. Thus Frazer[14] maintained that the Israelites originally sacrificed their firstborn children on the night of the Pesah and that this sacrifice was ultimately replaced by the offering of a lamb, the blood of which, placed on the entrance, misled the Angel of Death and saved the firstborn son. Dalman,[15] after citing Frazer, translates his theory from the language of folklore to that of biblical theology, suggesting that the LORD renounced the sacrifice of human firstborn and consented to the substitution of a lamb — just as related in the story of the binding of Isaac.

A unique version of this theory is that proposed by Brock-Utne, according to whom the Pesah-night was originally a shepherds' feast, celebrated on the night before setting out for summer pasturing, and performed with staff in hand and with girded loins.[16] According to the theory, on this night the LORD became suspicious that the shepherds were about to herd away from His domain the firstborn of man and beast, thus depriving Him of what was His. He therefore traversed the earth to take possession of them — i.e., to kill them. Only the Israelites were immune to this danger, since they had a pact with their God not to slay their firstborn. This pact was re-affirmed annu-

---

13 J. Pedersen, *Israel, its Life and Culture*, London-Copenhagen 1926-1940, Vol. III-IV, p. 402.

14 J. G. Frazer, *The Golden Bough*[3], Pt. III, *The Dying God*, London 1930, pp. 174-178.

15 G. Dalman, *Arbeit und Sitte in Palästina*, I,2, Gütersloh 1928, p. 447.

16 A. Brock-Utne, "Eine Religionsgeschichtliche Studie zu dem ursprünglichen Passahopfer", *Archiv für Religionswissenschaft*, 31 (1934), pp. 272-278. Brock-Utne claims to have found this idea in W. J. Moulton, *A Dictionary of the Bible*, III, p. 688, a book which I am unable to obtain, and mentions also a certain Redslob, Hamburger Gymnasialprogramm, 1856. More recently the theory has been advanced by L. Rost, "Weidewechsel und altisraelitischer Festkalender", *Zeitschrift des deutschen Palästina-Vereins*, 66 (1943), pp. 205-216, without any reference to his predecessors.

ally in a solemn rite, the paschal sacrifice. Brock-Utne's theory, like that of Dalman, holds that God renounced His claim upon the firstborn of Israel.

Now, all theories which suggest that the paschal sacrifice was originally connected with the slaying of the firstborn must necessarily involve some arbitrary auxiliary assumption. The Wellhausen school, in all its forms, denies the authenticity of the tradition that Israel's intent was to offer sacrifices from their livestock in the wilderness — as they told Pharaoh (Exod 8:22-23), never once referring to the sacrifice of their firstborn. But this tradition itself is in no way suspect.[17] Further, all those who have followed Wellhausen in assuming that in the earliest tradition Pharaoh was punished "measure for measure" in the plague of the firstborn have failed to explain why this assumed original version of the story was rejected in favor of the present one, in which a series of apotropaic measures are taken, directed against the "Destroyer" and quite unconnected to any command concerning the firstborn.

The awesome dread of the "Destroyer", however, which is correctly recognized as the true background of the Pesah story, cannot by any means be considered a later invention which has displaced an earlier, perfectly rational tradition easily intelligible according to the "measure-for-measure" principle. It is incomprehensible how an original connection between the Pesah regulations and the slaying of the firstborn could have become so tenuous if the Pentateuch itself states that the firstborn were smitten on the very same night as the paschal sacrifice was eaten by the Israelites. Pedersen's theory is thus negated, while Frazer's view, that it was originally the human firstborn that were sacrificed, must be rejected on the simple grounds that no one can offer up his firstborn child repeatedly year after year. The same objection applies to Dalman's view; there is simply no way of performing an annual redemption of human firstborn by means of a lamb. Indeed, the biblical text contains no mention of any such rite; the Pesah narrative differs completely from the story of the binding

---

17 It may even perhaps be echoed in the words of Hosea "...they will go with their sheep and cattle to seek the LORD, but they will not find Him" (5:6).

of Isaac. Brock-Utne's assertion that God's covenant released the Israelites from having to carry out some command relating to their firstborn is no less questionable: Israel, according to Pentateuchal tradition, was never given any dispensation from such requirements. To put the matter briefly, all attempts to reconstruct, by transferring the laws of the firstborn to the paschal sacrifice, an earlier stage in the evolution of the Pesah — a stage in which the connection between the sacrifice and the plague of the firstborn is more explicit than that in the existing text — are unfounded.

IV. The Original Character of the Paschal Sacrifice

We have now arrived, on a somewhat broader basis, at the same conclusion as that reached by Nikolsky[18] solely on the basis of a comparison of the Pesah laws with those of the firstborn: the paschal sacrifice has its own roots, and it has been secondarily integrated into the account of the Exodus and the slaying of the firstborn. It follows that in order to determine the original character of the Pesah, we must consider it without reference to its present context in the book of Exodus.

A: The Religious Character of the Pesah

We shall begin by discussing the central term associated with the topic, namely, the noun *pesah*. Though the biblical text derives it from the verb *pāsah*, the meaning of this verb is obscure. In this discussion we shall draw special attention to the important studies of Riedel,[19] Glasson[20] and Kopf.[21]

Beginning with the earliest exegesis, dating from the Second Temple period, and right down to the present, two basic interpretations

---

18 See above, p. 193.
19 W. Riedel, "Miscellen", *ZAW*, 20 (1900), pp. 319-329.
20 T. F. Glasson, "The 'Passover', a Misnomer", *JThS*, NS, 10 (1959), pp. 79-84.
21 L. Kopf, "Arabische Etymologien und Parallelen zum Bibelwörterbuch", *VT*, 8 (1958), pp. 194f.

of the verb *pāsaḥ* may be observed: (1) "to shield, to protect"; (2) "to pass over". The antiquity of the former is assured by Scripture itself. As has been pointed out frequently, only with difficulty can the meaning "pass over" be employed in Exod 12:27 "because He *pāsaḥ* over the houses of the Israelites in Egypt when he smote the Egyptians, but saved our houses". One in danger is not "saved" by "passing over" him; he requires active protection. The meaning "protect" also emerges from Isa 31:5: *gānōn wĕhiṣṣīl pāsōᵃḥ wĕhimlīṭ* ("shielding and saving, protecting and rescuing"). Just as the parallel and synonymous verbs *gānōn* and *pāsōᵃḥ* indicate the result of *hiṣṣīl* and *himlīṭ*, so does the verb *hiṣṣīl* in Exod 12:27 indicate the result of the action denoted by *pāsaḥ* in the same verse.[22] "Protect" is thus the only interpretation which accords with the text itself, and it should be accepted — notwithstanding any reservations we may have concerning Kopf's suggestion that Hebrew *psḥ* is connected with Arabic فَسَح "to widen", believing that it appears in Exodus 12 in the sense of "save" (compare Arabic فَسَح, Hebrew *hōšīaᶜ*) and that the Hebrew sense of "protect" evolved from this.

The meaning "shield, protect" is also supported by a large number of earlier interpreters. The LXX translates *psḥ* in Exod 12:13, 27 with σκεπάζω "shield", while Symmachus in Exod 12:11 renders the noun *pesaḥ* by ὑπερμάχησις "defense". The same interpretation is given in Rabbinic literature without source, and this very anonymity suggests antiquity: "The Holy One, blessed be He, protected (*hēgēn ᵓal*) the houses of his children in Egypt so that they might not be smitten, as it is said (Exod 12:13) 'And the LORD will *psḥ* over the entrance" (Mek. Bĕšallaḥ, proem). Another midrash formulates the same idea in a bolder depiction of the same scene: "'He will see the blood' (Exod

---

22 Riedel (above, note 19) views *pāsōᵃḥ* in Isa 31:5 as a denominative verb, derived from a root *psḥ* meaning "to hold a Pesah", and interprets the verse to mean that the LORD will repeat the actions performed at the Exodus, smiting the Egyptians and delivering Israel. But Egypt is not Israel's enemy in this passage, rather her ally, and her fate is of no interest to the prophet. The prophet is expressing an entirely different idea: that if Israel relies on the help of Egypt, then "the helper shall trip and the helped one shall fall" (v. 3), whereas if Israel trusts God alone, He will protect and deliver His people.

12:23) — it is as if He stood by the entrance and prevented the Destroyer from smiting Israel" (Exod. Rab., Bōᵓ 18:7).

Elsewhere the midrashic tradition refrains from so daring a portrayal, replacing the verb *hgn* "protect" with *ḥws* "spare" which always — both in Aramaic and Hebrew — indicates not actual protection but only refraining from causing harm, the result of feelings of compassion.[23] Thus Mek. Bōᵓ 11 states that "*psḥ* means *ḥys*,[24] as in 'Like the birds that fly, so the LORD of hosts shall shield Jerusalem, shielding and saving, protecting and rescuing'(Isa 31:5)". The same root (*ḥws/ḥys*) is employed throughout Tg. Onqelos for *psḥ*, and by Tg. Jonathan in most cases (though not all; see Exod 12:23, where Tg. Jonathan reads "The word of the LORD will *protect* [*ygyn*] the entrance"; this is followed by Tg. Neofiti, which reads *wᵓpsḥ wᵓgn*, adding *ᵓḥws* in the margin; so too in v. 27). The underlying theology implicit in the translation *ḥws* "spare" becomes clearer in light of the Targum to Zech 9:15, where "The LORD of Hosts will shield them"

---

23 S. Lieberman, *Hellenism in Jewish Palestine*, New York 1950, pp. 50ff, and Glasson, *loc. cit.* (above, note 20) explain the verb *ḥws* in these texts to mean "protect", a conclusion at which they have apparently arrived on the basis of the many midrashic and Targumic passages relating to Pesah in which *hgn* "protect" and *ḥws* "spare" are interchanged. The Aramaic verb *ḥws* (usually Qal, occasionally Paᶜel), however, is never used in the Targumim for Hebrew *gnn* in either Qal or Hiphᶜil. The use of the Aramaic verb becomes clear from the following survey: (1) Aramaic *ḥws* is invariably used to translate Hebrew *ḥws*; (2) it is usually employed to translate Hebrew *ḥml*, the exceptions being those passages in which *ḥws* and *ḥml* occur together, where, in order to avoid repetition, the Targum generally renders *ḥml* by *rḥm* (Deut 13:9; Ezek 5:11; 7:4,9; 8:18; 9:5,10; 16:5), though if, in addition to Hebrew *ḥws* and *ḥml*, Hebrew *rḥm* is also present, it will be translated by *rḥm* in Aramaic, and Hebrew *ḥml* will be remain *ḥml* in Aramaic as well (Jer 13:14; 21:7); (3) Aramaic *ḥws* is used occasionally as the equivalent of Hebrew *ḥnn*. This is the case throughout the Psalter, as well as Tg. Yer. II to Exod 33:19; Num 6:25; Deut 28:50 (though never in Tg. Onqelos) and in Tg. Jonathan to 2 Kgs 13:23; Isa 30:18; Lam 4:16; (4) Aramaic *ḥws* appears occasionally in the Targumim as a free or midrashic rendering, for instance, *himmālēṭ ᶜal napšekā* in Gen 19:17, which the Targumim render *ḥūs ᶜal napšāk*, or the totally free translation of 2 Sam 23:6, which the Targum paraphrases "But the wicked, who do evil, are like thorns; when they first appear they are soft enough to be plucked, but if one spares them (*wĕkad ᵓĕnāš ḥayyēs ᶜălēhōn*) and leaves them they grow strong". This survey proves conclusively what would in any case have been apparent: that the Aramaic verb *ḥws* is equivalent to the cognate verb in Hebrew.

24 Other vss. *ḥswt;* so Yalqut.

(*yāgēn ʿălēhem*) is translated *yĕraḥēm ʿălēhōn* "will have mercy on them". Evidently the rationale is that while a man who wishes to save his children from an enemy must shield them, God need not do so — His compassion is sufficient to deliver them from danger.

The evolution of the interpretation "spare", therefore, as a derivative of "shield, protect", is essentially straightforward. The same cannot be said regarding the origin of the interpretation "pass over", though, to be sure, the connection of "spare" and "pass over" cannot be denied; to "spare" someone is to "pass over" him, to refrain from harming him. The translation "pass over" appears for the first time in the LXX to Exod 12:23, where the verb *psḥ* is rendered παρέρχομαι — unlike vss. 13 and 27 where the LXX have σκεπάζω. The presence of two such diametrically opposed translations of one Hebrew verb in the same chapter is indeed surprising, which is why Glasson[25] resorted to the conjecture that παρελεύσεται in v. 23 was inadvertently caused by attraction of the second verb in the verse to the first — *ʿbr* (of which παρελεύσεται is a standard rendering). Whether Glasson is right, or whether perhaps two lines of exegesis have become confused, is difficult to determine; in any case the interpretation "pass over" is attested as early as Second Temple times.

Further evidence of the antiquity of this interpretation is furnished by the book of Jubilees, which relates that the LORD sent all the forces of Mastema to slay the firstborn of Egypt but ordered them to "pass over" the houses of the Israelites (Jub 49:2-4). This depiction can be understood only if we assume it to have been preceded by an exegetical tradition according to which God Himself passed over the houses of Israel.

The same basic notion can be found in Philo's account, though it diverges from the Bible more widely than does Jubilees. Philo states that it was Israel who "passed over", i.e. departed, from Egypt, which, he says, is why they offer a paschal, i.e. "passing-over", sacrifice (Leg. All. III.xxx, p. 106 and elsewhere).[26] The interpretation "pass over" is expressly associated with the biblical text in Josephus, who relates

---

25 *Op. cit.* (note 20, above).
26 And see below, pp. 210-211; for references see note 42.

that God passed over the Israelites when He brought the plague of the firstborn upon Egypt (Ant. II.xiv.6), and the same line is followed by Jerome, who in the Vulgate invariably translates *psḥ* with *transire* (except for some mss. which render "*transcendet*" at Exod 12:23).

The Midrash too is aware of this interpretation. Here it appears as a minority opinion in the form of a linguistic *derashah:* "R. Yoshia says: Read not *ūpāsaḥtī* but *ūpāsaʿtī*[27] ("I will step over"), since the Holy One, blessed be He, leaped over the houses of His children in Egypt" (Mek. Bōʾ 7). Some of the medievals adopted this view; Rashi's comment to Exod 12:13 begins with the view of the Targum (*"ūpāsaḥtī"* means *wĕhāmaltī"*) but immediately adds "I, however, interpret all occurrences of the root *psḥ* to mean 'leaping and jumping'". Kimhi[28] claimed that this understanding is supported by Isa 35:6 "Then the lame shall leap (*yĕdallēg*) like a deer".

Among the modern scholars are some who suggest that the verb *psḥ* originally denoted the movements of a *pisseᵃḥ* ("lame man"), and later evolved to denote the act of limping, skipping, or, followed by the preposition *ʿal*, "skipping over". Hence it has been asserted that the Pesaḥ festival was originally accompanied by limping dances.[29] However, the words "Then shall the lame leap (*yĕdallēg*) like a deer, and the tongue of the dumb shall shout aloud" (Isa 35:6) prove the contrary, since the assumption of the passage is that as a rule ("now", as opposed to "then") the lame do not leap, just as the dumb do not sing! The Hebrew root *dlg* does not denote the contorted movements of a cripple, but rather the agile, and perfectly normal, running of a deer, or of a youth in all his strength who, like a deer, comes "leaping (*mĕdallēg*) over mountains, bounding over hills" (Cant 2:8). There

---

27 See below, Excursus IV. This interpretation is the result of the weakening of the laryngeals and pharyngeals in late Hebrew; see E. Y. Kutscher, *The Language and Linguistic Background of the Isaiah Scroll (1QIsᵃ)*, Leiden 1974, pp. 505-511. Note especially the interchange at Isa 37:30 between MT *šḥys* and 1QIsa *šʿys* and the opposite phenomenon in 54:11, MT *sʿrh;* Q *shrh*.

28 R. David Kimhi, *Sēfer HaŠorāšīm*, Berlin 1847, p. 296.

29 Riedel, *loc. cit.* (note 19, above) briefly mentions this opinion, quoting Schwally but without reference. More recently it has been proposed by M. Buber, *Moses*, Oxford 1947, p. 71: "It may be assumed that at the old nomad feast a hopping dance had been presented, possibly by boys masked as he-goats."

is therefore no proof for a semantic development from "lame" to "skip, pass over". It appears certain, despite the many interpretations of *psh* in ancient exegesis, that the only one that can be substantiated, and the only one that fits the plain sense of the biblical text, is "shield, protect".

To this we may add the overriding consideration that only according to this understanding can we appreciate the logic of the Pesah-narrative as a whole. As long recognized by scholars, the Pesah story preserves a clear echo of the widespread Near Eastern idea that blood, placed on the entrance of a house, on animals, even on human beings, has apotropaic power.[30] As seen long ago by Dalman,[31] this idea, that the blood itself protects, is not far removed from the notion that God, by virtue of the blood placed by His command on the entrance, protects the inhabitants of a house, particularly in view of the ancient Near Eastern practice of appealing to the gods for protection from malefic demons.[32]

If, as we have now concluded, the noun *pesah* denotes protection against the "Destroyer" who threatens the lives of the Israelites on a certain night, it is logical to expect an apotropaic tendency to be perceptible in at least some of the remaining aspects of the Pesah ritual. We are now in a position to explain why the Pesah legislation makes such a point of the stipulation that no uncircumcised person may partake of the sacrifice (Exod 12:48), since circumcision, like the paschal sacrifice itself, has a distinctly apotropaic significance. For even though in the Bible this has been obscured by the theological idea that circumcision is the sign of the Covenant, the theological import has not evolved in opposition to the original meaning of the rite; rather, its essence is that by virtue of the Covenant act — circumcision — God agrees to protect him to whom He has granted His covenant. The

---

30 Extensive bibliography is cited by P. Heinisch, *Das Buch Exodus*, Bonn 1934, pp. 97f.
31 *Op. cit.* (above, note 15), pp. 446ff.
32 In Akkadian, see e.g. Šurpu (above, Chapter Four, note 28), Tab. 4, esp. ll. 45-54, 100; Tab. 7; Tab. 9, ll. 70-87; in Canaanite compare the adjuration from Arslan Tash; see N. H. Tur-Sinai, *HaLāšōn WēhaSēfer, HaLāšōn*, Jerusalem 1954, pp. 53-65.

ancient significance of circumcision is contained in the narrative of the Bloody Bridegroom (Exod 4:24-26), the antiquity of which is not disputed. While scholars may differ on the interpretation of some of the details of the story, it is universally agreed that the purpose of circumcision in the narrative is to protect against some mortal danger. To this we may add the account of Philo of Byblos, who relates that Kronos, faced by pestilence and calamity, offered up his only son as a sacrifice to his father Uranus, circumcised himself and compelled his allies to do likewise (Eusebius I:10, 33). To these two decisive indications of the apotropaic character of circumcision, a third should be added, namely, the stipulation now under discussion: that the paschal sacrifice, since it protects human life, may be eaten only by those who have already undergone the apotropaic rite of circumcision.

Though this relationship between the paschal sacrifice and circumcision has not yet received the attention of scholars, it was perceived, and characteristically expressed, by the Midrash. The most complete formulation is that of the Mekilta:

> "You shall keep watch over it" (Exod 12:6): Why did Scripture require the purchase of the paschal lamb to take place four days before its slaughter? R. Matia b. Heresh used to say: Scripture says 'I passed by you, and saw that your time for love had arrived' (Ezek 16:8), which means that the time had arrived for fulfilling the oath which the Holy One, blessed be He, had sworn to Abraham, to deliver his children. However, they had as yet no commandments to perform by which to merit redemption, as Scripture says further, 'Though your breasts were firm and your hair had sprouted, you were naked and bare' (*ibid.*) — bare of commandments. Therefore the Holy One, blessed be He, gave them two commandments, the Pesah and circumcision, which they were to perform in order to be worthy of being redeemed, as Scripture says: 'When I passed by you and saw you wallowing in your blood' etc. (Ezek 16:6), and further: 'You, because of the blood of your covenant I have released your prisoners out of the waterless pit' (Zech 9:11). For this reason Scripture required that the purchase of the paschal lamb take place

four days before its slaughter, for one cannot obtain reward other than through deeds".

(Mek. Bōʾ 5)

The source of this complex midrash is illuminated by Tg. Jonathan, which glosses the repetitious "And I said to you: In your blood live! And I said to you: In your blood live!", with which the verse cited by the Mekilta (Ezek 16:6) concludes, with the words "And I said to you: For the sake of the *circumcision blood* will I spare you; And I said to you: for the sake of the *paschal blood* will I redeem you". Thus, the Midrash infers from the repetition that two kinds of blood are referred to in the text — that of circumcision and that of the paschal sacrifice — and is immediately reminded of the promise made to Abraham that his descendants would depart from Egypt. In addition to the homiletical motif, however, we can clearly perceive an awareness that the function of the blood in the two rituals is closely allied. This same awareness is reflected in Tg. Jonathan to Exod 12:13: "And the blood of the slaughtered offering and of the severed foreskin shall be a pledge to you by making it a sign upon the houses in which you dwell...", which means that not only the blood of the sacrifice but the circumcision blood as well was to be placed in the entrances of the houses! The relationship between Pesah and circumcision may be present in the account of the paschal sacrifice held at Gilgal (Josh 5:10-11), which follows immediately upon the report of the circumcision of the Israelites born in the wilderness (vv.2-9), implying that the circumcision is what qualified the new generation of Israelites to perform the paschal sacrifice.

Nor is this all. The prohibition of breaking a bone of the paschal lamb (Exod 12:46; Num 9:12) would also appear to be in keeping with the same general picture, at least in the view of Jubilees, which states "They shall roast it in fire without breaking any of its bones, for no bone of the children of Israel will be broken" (49:13).[33] This

---

33 The Latin version ("Non erit turbulatio filiis Israel in die hac", i.e. "There will be no trouble for the children of Israel on that day"), which weakens the sympathetic character of the ritual but does not completely eradicate it, is evidently the result of deliberate obfuscation.

"sympathetic" interpretation would seem to be the plain meaning of the text, and even Henninger,[34] who disagrees, admits that this is the explanation for the prohibition of breaking a bone given today among certain peoples including the Arabs. While Henninger maintains that this is a secondary interpretation, and that the original belief underlying the prohibition was that the intact condition of the animal's bones was an assurance that it would be resurrected, his contention is by no means decisive for the exegesis of the text at hand. For whatever may have been the most ancient and primitive belief among other peoples concerning the prohibition of breaking a bone of a sacrificial animal, no proof exists that this is the belief reflected in the Pentateuch, and the possibility that some other belief lies at the root of the Pentateuchal legislation should not be discounted. Nowhere in the Bible is the idea that a slaughtered beast would later be brought back to life mentioned, neither in general nor with reference to the paschal sacrifice. Rather, since the whole of the Pesah ritual is designed to protect the lives and physical integrity of its participants, the testimony of the book of Jubilees should be taken as reliable and authentic.[35]

This apotropaic aspect of the paschal sacrifice was also recognized by the Rabbis, as aptly stated by R. Jose the Galilean: "The enemies of Israel [a euphemism for Israel] deserved to be extirpated in Egypt, until the last of them had completed the paschal sacrifice, as Scripture states (Exod 12:27): 'You shall say: It is a paschal sacrifice to the LORD' etc." (Mek. Bo᾿ 12).

It is impossible to determine whether or not the Pentateuch attaches apotropaic power to the correct performance of the paschal sacrifice throughout the entire year, as does the book of Jubilees, which concludes its treatment of the topic with the statement "And the plague will not come to kill or to smite during that year when they

---

34 J. Henninger, "Zum Verbot des Knochenzerbrechens bei den Semiten", *Studi Orientali in onore di Giorgio Levi della Vida*, I, Roma 1956, pp. 448-458; A. Scheiber, "Ihr sollt kein Bein dran zerbrechen", *VT*, 13 (1963), pp. 95-97.

35 On the later development of the prohibition of breaking a bone in Rabbinic literature, where it was restricted in order to avoid widespread infraction (which is apparently the view held by Jubilees as well), see J. Lauterbach in *HaṢōfe lěḤokmat Yiśrā᾿ēl*, 9 (1925), pp. 235-241.

have observed the paschal offering in its appointed time in all respects according to His command" (Jub 49:15). However, even if we attribute to later generations the development of the idea that the annually recurring Pesah ritual was apotropaic, it is still the case that this belief evolved from the apotropaic character attributed by the Pentateuch itself to the original Pesah performed in Egypt.

B. The Social Aspect of the Pesah

In determining the social character of the paschal sacrifice we may safely follow the path already taken by scholars in the nineteenth century, who maintained that the Pesah was originally a pastoral rite. It is likely that the original Pesah-rite was performed, as suggested above,[36] before setting out for the summer pasture. Only at a later stage was the ritual connected with the Exodus from Egypt; however, this later integration with the Exodus-story was an extremely thorough one, unlike the much looser connection with the plague of the firstborn.[37]

Though we agree in general with Nikolsky in dissociating the Pesah from the slaying of the firstborn, the inference he derives from Exod 12:21 "Pick out lambs *lĕmišpĕḥōtēkem*", namely, that the the entire extended family — he takes *mišpāḥā* here in the wider, technical sense, that is, tribal sub-division or clan — shared together in the paschal sacrifice,[38] should be called into question. Nikolsky regards the command given in Exodus that the sacrifice is to be eaten by a limited circle of participants to be the result of the deterioration of the wider, tribal organization, but apparently has not taken into account the implications of this assumption. For to adopt it would mean to admit further that the paschal offering would have to be eaten out of doors — since a small shepherd's hut could not accommodate a party consisting of an entire clan. And this in turn would require assigning a late date to the prescribed daubing of blood upon the lintels and the

---

36 Above, p. 195.
37 In addition to the works cited in note 16, see R. Schaefer, *Das Passah-Mazzoth-Fest*, Gütersloh 1900, where literature from the nineteenth century is included.
38 *Loc. cit.* (above, note 9).

doorposts, as well as to the prohibition of setting foot out of the house during the Pesah-night. But in so doing we would be denying the originally apotropaic character of the Pesah, which was actually its primary and essential feature!

The most natural sense of the text is thus to be preferred: the paschal sacrifice was consumed by a party consisting of the smallest social unit, the existence of which, even during the period of tribal organization, cannot be denied. This being the case, the word *mišpāḥā* here is not used in the technical sense of "clan" but rather in the more general meaning of related members of one "family", i.e., a man, his wife, his children, and his slaves.[39]

V. Why the the Pesah was Incorporated into the Plague of the Firstborn

Our view that the paschal sacrifice was not initially connected with the Exodus from Egypt in general and the slaying of the firstborn in particular demands, of course, some explanation of why these originally independent motifs came to be interconnected. The probable explanation, which is derived in large measure from the scholarly hypothesis that the Pesah originated in a ritual performed before the shepherds' *departure* for summer pasture, is that this *departure* eventually came to be identified with the *departure* from Egypt. The matter of the firstborn may be understood along the same lines. Since, as Nikolsky has stressed,[40] the spring was the lambing season, and since, as we may add, the Pesah ritual itself included the belief that the night on which it was performed was a night of danger to human life, there must have evolved from this the notion that the LORD smote the firstborn of Egypt on the very same danger-fraught night. Thus historical significance was attached to an existing "night of terror" tradition, bringing out the contrast between the fate of the Egyptians and that of the Israelites at this decisive turning-point in Israel's national history.

39 BDB, s.v. *mišpāḥā*, 1a (p. 1046).
40 *Loc. cit.* (above, note 9).

VI. The Pesah and the Plague of the Firstborn
in the Bible and in Extra-biblical Sources

In the Bible, the primary connection of the paschal sacrifice and the plague of the firstborn is chronological: the paschal sacrifice was offered on the same night on which the LORD smote the firstborn of Egypt. Nevertheless, as we have seen, the original independence of these two motifs can still be discerned. The Pesah in fact served to protect all the Israelites, not only their firstborn; further, the "Destroyer" from whom the LORD shielded Israel is nowhere said to have smitten the Egyptian firstborn: this was done by God Himself.

Israelite tradition solved these problems in various ways. One was by obscuring the original apotropaic character of the Pesah and transforming it into a mere reminder of the Exodus. We first encounter this tendency in the Pentateuch itself, where the Pesah motif is combined with that of the Exodus, since the very process of historicization already involves a diminishing of the apotropaic element. Once the Exodus from Egypt and the slaying of the firstborn have been placed in the past, the implication is that the same is true of the danger threatening Israel on Pesah-night. Thus, ancient customs rooted in a belief in a "Destroyer" are displaced from the demonology in which they originally grew and transplanted into the soil of Israel's religious-historical consciousness which determined her uniqueness.

It should not be surprising, therefore, that the book of Exodus itself has already defined the Pesah as a *reminder* of the Exodus: "And when your children ask you, 'What do you mean by this rite?' you shall say, 'It is the paschal sacrifice to the LORD, because He protected the houses of the Israelites in Egypt when He smote the Egyptians, but saved our houses'" (Exod 12:26-27). To be sure, the emphasis is still on the LORD's protection of Israel, and the smiting of the Egyptians is relegated to a temporal clause. Still, the sacrifice has become a commemoration of events long past, which is all that is needed to insert the ancient tradition of the paschal offering into the historiographical framework.

This process continued to develop in Deuteronomy, where the

Pesah has been removed from its original, domestic setting and transferred to the central Sanctuary: "You are not permitted to slaughter the Pesah in any of the settlements...but at the place which the LORD your God will choose to establish His name, there alone shall you slaughter the Pesah" (Deut 16:5-6). This enactment is accompanied by the omission of the apotropaic ritual of placing the blood on the lintel and doorposts; indeed the entire apotropaic character of the Pesah is eradicated in the words "Observe the month of Abib and offer a paschal sacrifice to the LORD your God, for it was in the month of Abib, at night, that the LORD your God freed you from Egypt. You shall slaughter the paschal sacrifice for the LORD your God, from the flock *and the herd"* (vss. 1-2) — no mention of the danger of a "Destroyer", from whose threat God saved Israel on Pesah-night; the slaughtered sheep (or cattle!) are merely a reminder of the Exodus and no more.[41]

This view of the *annual* Pesah was bound to have an influence on the manner in which the first Pesah was depicted in later literature. Wisdom of Solomon omits the motif of the "Destroyer" who endangered the Israelites, and relates as follows:

> ... that night was known beforehand to our fathers, that knowing surely on what oaths they trusted they might be cheered. By Your people was expected preservation of the righteous and destruction of their enemies; for wherein You did punish the

41 Many scholars find a similar obfuscation of the Pesah's unique character in Deut 16:7, taking the word *ubiššaltā* "you shall cook" to mean that the paschal sacrifice is to be boiled, as was the normal practice with sacrificial flesh. This would abolish the more ancient prescription that it was to be roasted (Exod 12:8); the innovation, however, was rejected by Jewish tradition; see m. Pesah. 7:1-2. According to this view, the Chronicler found it necessary to re-interpret the Deuteronomic passage, relating that the Levites "cooked (*wayyĕbaššĕlû*) the paschal sacrifice *in fire*" (2 Chr 35:13) and thereby implying that the law in Deuteronomy, like that in Exodus, actually referred to roasting. This critical approach is somewhat doubtful, however; it may be the case that the verb *bšl* originally denoted any preparation of food by means of heat, thus including from the outset the process of roasting. On the unique character of the paschal sacrifice in Deuteronomy, see further M. Weinfeld, "The Change in the Conception of Religion in Deuteronomy", *Tarbiz*, 31 (1962), p. 5, who regards the Deuteronomic approach to the Pesah as an expression of D's general tendency to eliminate mythological and magical elements from Israel's religion.

adversaries, therein calling us to You did You glorify us. For in secret did the pious children of good men sacrifice, and with one accord arranged the law of divinity, that the saints should share alike in the same blessings and dangers, already chanting the praises of the fathers. But there sounded back a discordant cry of the enemies...

(18:6-10)

The phrase "wherein You did punish the adversaries", etc. is not entirely clear, but the succeeding words indicate that the reference is to two contrasting but simultaneously occurring events, namely, the death of the Egyptian firstborn and the paschal sacrifice offered by the Israelites (which, in the unique view of the Wisdom of Solomon, was tantamount to accepting the yoke of divine legislation). And while it is still possible that "expected preservation of the righteous" refers indirectly to some danger from which Israel was saved, such an interpretation is forced, and the view that the deliverance referred to is simply the redemption from Egyptian bondage is to be preferred.

Philo's account of the Exodus follows the example of the didactic psalms, omitting all reference to the paschal sacrifice.[42] Elsewhere in his writings, however, he does mention the Pesah, for instance when speaking of the first and second Pesah, explaining the sacrifice allegorically: "Moses...awards special praise among the sacrificers of the Passover to those who sacrificed the first time, because when they had separated themselves from the passions of Egypt by crossing the Sea they kept to that crossing and no more hankered after them" (Leg. All. III.xxx, p. 106). Allegorically speaking, this means that the Israelites, by performing the paschal rite, "passed" from the domain of impure lust symbolized by Egypt; simply speaking, it refers to their "passing" over the border, out of Egyptian territory. This provides an explanation for Philo's translation of *pesah* as διαβατήριον, a cultic term

---

42 Here too Philo's works are cited according to the Loeb edition (trans. by F. A. Colson and G. H. Whitaker, London 1937), Vol. I, p. 365 and Vol. VII, pp. 395-397. On the question whether Philo's description corresponds to Second Temple halakhic practice, see I. Heinemann, *Philons griechische und jüdische Bildung*, Breslau 1932, p. 33 *vs.* S. Belkin, *Philo and the Oral Law*, Cambridge, MA 1940, pp. 61-66.

denoting a sacrifice offered by persons embarking on a journey, about to cross a border, a river, or the like, and for his description of the festival celebration (Spec. Leg. II.xxvii, p. 292). No wonder that Philo also omits from this context all mention of the slaying of the firstborn, and makes no reference to the apotropaic character of the paschal sacrifice and of the act of placing blood in the doorway. He says of the paschal sacrifice that "the festival is a reminder and thank-offering for that great migration...so exceedingly joyful were they that in their vast enthusiasm and impatient eagerness, they naturally enough sacrificed without waiting for their priest" *(ibid.).* This practice, he continues, was fixed for all time, an exception to the rule applying to all other sacrifices which must be offered only by priests. Thus, in Philo's description, even the Pesah celebrated in Egypt was essentially no more than a specialized thank-offering, and there is practically no need to pose the two questions which present themselves in the Pentateuch — why the sacrifice protected all the Israelites and not merely the firstborn, and what was the relation between God's protection of the Israelites from the "Destroyer" and the slaying of Egypt's firstborn which He executed Himself.

However, even these radical re-interpretations have not succeeded in completely eliminating the two questions inherent in the Pentateuchal account. Although the first question is never actually addressed in the later sources, it may be that the customary Fast of the Firstborn, observed on the eve of Passover, and which is apparently already alluded to in y. Pesaḥ. 10:1; 37a, is a sort of compromise interpretation, namely, that the blood of the paschal sacrifice "particularly"[43] protected the firstborn.

The second question, that of the discrepancy between the statement that the LORD protected the Israelites from a "Destroyer" and the claim that the LORD Himself smote the Egyptian firstborn, is treated extensively by the later sources, and every possible attempt is made to eliminate the inconsistency.

A full and eminently logical solution is that contained in Jubilees, which states that the forces of Mastema were sent by God to slay the

---

43 Buber, *op. cit.* (above, note 29), p. 70.

firstborn of Egypt and commanded to pass over the houses of the Israelites which had the sign of the blood upon their doors. The evil forces did as they were commanded, while the Israelites partook of the paschal lamb, drinking wine and singing hymns of praise and thanksgiving to God (Jub 49:2-7), meaning presumably the *hallel*-psalms. This account is internally consistent, since it relates that the LORD Himself did not go forth at all on the night of the Exodus but rather sent out the powers of Mastema. Since He commanded them to pass over the Israelite houses, no other form of protection was needed; further, it was not the LORD who did the "passing over" but the evil forces. The theology implied in this account is a very moderate dualism, since it denies that the LORD, who is a God of goodness, directly performed any act of slaughter, attributing this function instead to the forces of Mastema, while at the same time indicating that the latter acted at the command of their master.

The brief allusions in the writings of Ezekiel the Tragedian are not sufficient to allow for detailed analysis, but his statement that the blood was placed on the two doorposts in order that death might turn away from the Hebrews (l. 187) recalls the description in Jubilees of the powers of Mastema passing over the Israelites and slaying the firstborn of Egypt.

Another source in which the "Destroyer" is held to have smote the firstborn of Egypt is Theodoret, *Quaestiones in Exodum*, XXIV. Here we learn that the blood was placed upon the entrance "that the Destroyer might see the blood and pass over the houses of the Hebrews when he entered to smite the firstborn". The author of this text elaborates at great length, claiming to have relied upon a text taken from the Bible but which in fact is no more than a paraphrase of an otherwise unknown midrashic interpretation of Exod 12:26-27 in light of 13:14 and Deut 6:20-21 (perhaps also 16:1): "The Lawgiver thus said: When your son asks you, 'What is this Pesah?' you shall tell him, 'It is because on this day God brought our forefathers out of Egypt and delivered our firstborn when the Destroyer smote the firstborn of the Egyptians'".[44] The Pesah is primarily a reminder

---

44 Theodoret, *Quaestiones in Exodum*, Migne, *Patrologia Graeca*, 80, Paris 1864, pp. 226–298.

of the Exodus, but the earlier motifs are still discernible, unified for obviously harmonistic reasons. The slaying of the firstborn and the paschal sacrifice are combined to form a single motif: while the "Destroyer" was smiting the firstborn of Egypt, the LORD rescued the *firstborn* of Israel from him. The complete harmonization, implied in the stress laid on the firstborn of Israel, is found only here. The apotropaic element, expressed in the word "rescue", is more pronounced than in Jubilees.

The picture which emerges from Tg. Jonathan to Exod 12:12-13 is more complex:

> I shall reveal Myself, in My glorious presence, on that night in the land of Egypt, and together with Me ninety thousand myriads of destroying angels, and I shall slay every firstborn in the land of Egypt...and I will see the merit of the blood and I will spare you, so that the Angel of Death, who has been given permission to destroy when I deal out death in the land of Egypt, will have no power over you.

We should begin by observing that the "Destroyer" in v. 13 of the biblical text has here become the Angel of Death, recalling the word θάνατος in Ezekiel the Tragedian's account. However, in the Targum's paraphrastic supplement to v. 12, this Angel of Death has been transformed into ninety thousand myriads of destroying angels, recalling "all the powers of Mastema" in Jubilees. Disregarding this inconsistency, however, the image we obtain is one of the LORD setting out, attended by the "Destroyer", who by His permission slays the firstborn of the Egyptians but not the Israelites — whom the LORD has spared. Here too, the LORD does not kill the Egyptian firstborn Himself, but the difficulty in resolving the problem created by the biblical text is considerably more acute here than in Jubilees, since the Targum does not venture to depart quite so radically from the text. The Targum does indeed indicate that the Angel of Death has been given God's permission to slay, apparently because this is, in the Targum's view, the plain meaning of the verse: that the LORD slew the firstborn of Egypt *by the agency of* this angel. But in what follows, instead of stating simply that the "Destroyer" was not given similar permission to act against the Israelites, the Targum says that *the* LORD spared Israel — recalling the active protection which He gave them in the Pentateuchal account. The Targum maintains the Pentateuch's own formulation, that the LORD smote the firstborn of Egypt, even though the clear implication of the Targum's depiction of the scene is that He did not do so in person.

Common to all the solutions we have cited so far is that they all attribute the slaying of the firstborn to a "Destroyer" or a number of destroyers, thereby both avoiding the idea that God could have done evil and at the same time holding fast to the connection between the plague of the firstborn and the Pesah. An entirely different approach is taken by the Wisdom of Solomon, where only the former element is found. Here, as we have seen,[45] no mention is made of any threat to Israelite lives by the "Destroyer", yet nevertheless it is the Word of the LORD, in the form of a destructive angel, that smites the Egyptian firstborn:

> For while peaceful silence enveloped all things, and night in her own swift course was at midway, Your all-powerful word from heaven, from the royal throne, a stern warrior, leapt into the midst of the doomed land, bearing as a sharp sword Your irrevocable commandment. and standing filled all things with death, and touched the heaven yet trod upon the earth.
>
> (18:14-16)

Scholars have rightly compared this with 1 Chr 21:16 "David looked up and saw the angel of the LORD standing between heaven and earth, with a drawn sword in his hand directed against Jerusalem". Even though this substitution of the Word of the LORD, appearing in the likeness of a warrior, for the LORD Himself is not particularly designed for the purpose of strengthening the connection between the slaying of the firstborn and the paschal sacrifice, the effect is still to allay any suspicion that evil could have come from God. We may also sense here a literary intent, namely, to portray as vividly and as shockingly as possible the act of slaughter itself.

45 Above, p. 209.

The transfer of the slaying of the firstborn from God to some emissary was not universally accepted. The Midrash negates it explicitly. For instance, the Mekilta (Bōᵓ 7) comments on Exod 12:12. "'And I shall strike down every firstborn in the land of Egypt' — I might have thought the meaning is, by means of an angel or an emissary; therefore the text says further (v. 29) 'The LORD struck down all the firstborn the land of Egypt', indicating that it was not by means of an angel or an emissary". The Mekilta repeats the same midrash in its comment on Exod 12:29 (Bōᵓ 13); similarly the Yerushalmi: "When the All-Merciful came to deliver Israel, He did not send an emissary or an angel, but He came Himself, as it is written (Exod 12:12) 'I will pass through the land of Egypt'" (y. Sanh. 2:1, 20a; Hor. 3:1, 47a). This same thought receives its most emphatic expression in the Passover Haggadah:

> And the LORD freed us from Egypt (Deut 26:8): Not by means of an angel, nor by means of a seraph, nor by means of an emissary, but the Holy One, blessed be He, Himself. As it is said (Exod 12:12): "For that night I will go through the land of Egypt, and I will strike down every firstborn in the land of Egypt, both man and beast, and I will mete out punishments to all the gods of Egypt, I am the LORD". "For I will go through the land of Egypt" — I Myself, and not an angel; "and I will strike down every firstborn" — I Myself and not a seraph; "and I will mete out punishments to all the gods of Egypt" — I Myself and not an emissary; "I am the LORD" — I am He, and none other.[46]

---

46 Goldschmidt, *op. cit.* (above, Chapter Two, note 28), pp. 35; 44-45, denies that this midrash reflects a theological dispute, claiming instead that its sole purpose is to explain the superfluous mention of the Tetragrammaton in Deut 26:8. The superfluity, however, is not in Deuteronomy at all but in Exod 12:12, and the formulation of the Haggadah's interpretation is clear evidence of its polemical character — especially in view of the fact that the theology rejected by the Hagaddah is well attested in the writings of its proponents. Nor can Goldschmidt's assertion that the Rabbis interpreted the statement "He sent a messenger who freed us from Egypt" (Num 20:16) to refer to something other than an angel be accepted; here too, rabbinic opinion was divided.

No wonder that the Haggadah, in explaining the rationale for the paschal sacrifice, omits all reference to the "Destroyer", confining itself to the citation of Exod 12:27: "You shall say, 'It is the paschal sacrifice to the LORD, because He protected the houses of the Israelites in Egypt when he smote the Egyptians, but saved our houses'".

An intermediate position is taken by Josephus. Though he does mention the Pesah ritual in his account of the Exodus (Ant. II.xiv.6), he transforms the placing of the blood on the entrance to the house into a purification of the house by sprinkling blood with a bunch of hyssop, and he interprets *pesah* to mean "passing over", since God "passed over our people when He smote the Egyptians with plague". Like the Midrash, Josephus does not recognize the action of a destroying angel, only the act of God. In inflicting the plagues, the LORD had no need of the assistance of His servant Moses, much less did He need the help of a destroying angel. In this spirit of uncompromising monotheism, Josephus sees no reason to refrain even from attributing to God the direct infliction of evil. However, in place of the rejected mythological motif of the destroying angel, Josephus introduces the more rationalistic notion of "plague", i.e., a pestilence, which was apparently intended to make the abstract concept of God acting alone more intelligible to the Hellenistic reader. Scholars have already noted that the expression "launch a plague upon" (ἐπανέσκηψε τὴν νόσον) is taken from Thucydides (II.47).[47]

In diametric opposition to Philo, Josephus retains a reference to the apotropaic character of the paschal sacrifice. This is to be found in his notion of the blood with which the Israelites "purified" their houses. But the motif is greatly attenuated; no mention is made of God's seeing the sign of the blood. Along with the "Destroyer", of course, all discussion of divine protection of the Israelites from this malefic demon is omitted.

---

47 See the margin of the Loeb edition (Vol. IV, p. 301).

VII. Summary

Let us now recapitulate our theory of the nature of the Pesah-tradition. The paschal sacrifce was originally an apotropaic rite performed by shepherds, repeated annually in order to avert some mortal danger believed to be threatened by a fatal "Destroyer" who was thought to be abroad on a certain night. This rite is presumably of extreme antiquity. Israel's religion adopted this deeply rooted apotropaic-demonological tradition, but reduced its power by transforming it into a ceremony commemorating a one-time act of deliverance which occurred in the past, and by inserting this event firmly into its national history. The LORD delivered the Israelites from the "Destroyer" on the very same fateful night on which He slew the firstborn of Egypt, and this led directly to the Exodus from Egypt. The tendency to de-emphasize the demonological-apotropaic element and to historicize the ritual is epitomized in the book of Deuteronomy and in the writings of Philo, both of which describe the paschal sacrifice simply as a reminder of the Exodus without even incidental reference to the rescue of the Israelites from the "Destroyer".

Although the didactic psalms are silent about the Pesah, there is ample evidence that the original character of the ritual was not forgotten by the people. The most extreme example is the Midrash, which relates that the LORD stood at the entrance of the houses and warded off the "Destroyer". The book of Jubilees is more moderate; in it the LORD commanded the forces of Mastema to pass over the doors of the Israelites. Still more moderate is the account given by Josephus, who omits the "Destroyer", though he does retain some mention of the apotropaic character of the blood rite. Furthermore, as proven by Jubilees, despite the historicization of the Pesah, some awareness of the apotropaic power of the sacrifice remained even with regard to the annual Pesah. We have even seen that an appreciable segment of the tradition actually extended the role of the "Destroyer", recounting that the very same destructive angel who passed over the houses of the Israelites also smote the firstborn of Egypt, and thereby strengthening the link between these two legends and at the same time dissociating the LORD from the act of slaughter.

Our view necessitates a rejection of the scholarly consensus, namely, that the tradition of the slaying of the firstborn and that of the paschal sacrifice were originally one and the same and that this unity can be revealed by means of historical restoration. We reject this sort of restoration as harmonistic rationalism in the guise of historical criticism.

THE VERB *PĀSAḤ*

Of the two interpretations discussed above for the verbal root *psḥ*, "shield, protect" and "pass over", both of which have been current since Second Temple times, the former, as we have argued, is to be preferred as the more original. The latter, we have noted, is a theologically tendentious interpretation, designed to obscure the apotropaic character of the paschal sacrifice.[1] What is still lacking in our treatment of the issue is an examination of the apparent textual support which was adduced by proponents of the latter interpretation, "pass over".

The only early explanation of *psḥ* as "pass over" which seems to be philological in nature is that of R. Yoshiya (Mek. Bōʾ 7): "Read not *ūpāsaḥtī* but *ūpāsaʿtī*" ("I will step over"), since the Holy One, blessed be He, leaped over the houses of His children in Egypt".[2] Indeed, it would seem that no trace of the ancient, anti-apotropaic rationale for this interpretation can be detected here: R. Yoshiya's opinion is that of one individual, who lived centuries after the more ancient works containing the interpretation "pass over"[3] were composed.

More important, however, is the form of R. Yoshiya's comment. For even though the formula "Read not..." is clear evidence that what follows is not intended to explain the literal sense of the word, exegesis which associates *psḥ* with *psʿ*, and explains the latter to mean

---

1 See above, pp. 197-206. On the meaning "protect" as the more original, see also R. Weiss, *"psḥ = ḥml, ḥws"*, *Leš*, 27 (1964), pp. 127-130 [repr. in R. Weiss, *Studies in the Text and Language of the Bible*, Jerusalem 1981, pp. 255-258] [Hebrew].
2 This passage is discussed above, p. 201.
3 I.e., the LXX, Jubilees, and Philo; see above pp. 200-201.

"leap", should not be taken for granted. What has allowed the midrashic exegesis to develop is the weakening of the laryngeals and pharyngeals in the Hebrew of the Second Temple period, which led to the eventual disappearance of any distinction between *ḥet* and *ʿayin* in the spoken language.[4] Once *psḥ* had been assigned the meaning of the "homophonous" root *psʿ*, the jump from "step over" to "leap over, pass over" was a simple matter. Presumably, the more ancient exegetes did not sense, and they certainly did not call any attention to the fact, that they were assigning to the verb a linguistically inadmissible interpretation; it was only R. Yoshiya who later sensed the problem, as can be deduced from his use of the "Read not..." formula.

This reconstruction is indirectly confirmed by the LXX to Isa 45:23 ("By Myself have I sworn...to Me every knee shall bend, every tongue swear loyalty"), where the Hebrew word *tiššābaʿ* "shall swear loyalty" is rendered ἐξομολογήσεται "shall praise". Though the most obvious conclusion would be that the LXX misread *tšbʿ* as *tšbḥ*, M. Goshen-Gottstein has recently proven that the Rabbis midrashically interpreted *tšbʿ* in this passage to mean *tšbḥ*, which they pronounced identically, and has suggested, quite plausibly, that the LXX too actually read *tšbʿ* correctly and merely interpreted it, midrashically, to mean *tšbḥ*.[5] On the reason behind this exegesis, Goshen-Gottstein suggests:

> In parallelism to the "bending of the knee", swearing did not make perfect sense, especially after the swearing in the beginning of the verse. Therefore *nišbaʿ* was interpreted in the slightly cognate sense of *avowal* or *confession*, in short within the semantic field of Hebrew *hōdā*.[6]

Though the analysis of the exegetical considerations is convincing, the conclusion should be reformulated, i.e., *nišbaʿ* was interpreted in

---

4 See above, p. 201, note 27.
5 M. H. Goshen-Gottstein, "Theory and Practice of Textual Criticism", *Textus*, 3 (1963), pp. 156-158.
6 *Ibid.*, p. 157; italics in the original.

the sense of "praise". In other words, the combined effect of exegetical considerations and the weakening of the laryngeals and pharyngeals has been to create a new meaning for the verb *nišba^c^:* "praise". The same semantic leap is what has enabled the verb *pāsaḥ* to acquire the new meaning "step over, skip over, pass over".

CHAPTER SIX

THE EXODUS

I. The Time of Departure

The account of the Exodus relates that immediately after the slaying of the firstborn, which took place at midnight, Pharaoh ordered Moses and Aaron to appear before him (Exod 12:31). It must be assumed that they did so, despite the warning "None of you shall go outside the door of his house until morning" (Exod 12:22). The narrative states further that Pharaoh and his subjects urged the Israelites to leave in haste (vv. 33-34), and that they did indeed depart — presumably at once, without waiting for dawn.[1] This impression is corroborated by Deut 16:1, which expressly indicates that the LORD brought the Israelites out of Egypt *at night*.

Elsewhere, however, we are told that "It was *on the morning after the paschal offering* that the Israelites started out, defiantly, in plain view of the Egyptians" (Num 33:3). The mention of the paschal sacrifice in the verse may be taken as a mild allusion to the injuction forbidding the Israelites to leave their houses until morning, and the emphasis on their boldly defiant departure would appear to preclude anything but broad daylight.

Each of these two variants is the outcome of one of the two traditions we have been discussing thus far: the slaying of the firstborn and the paschal sacrifice. The latter, in which the Israelites are forbidden to set foot out of doors throughout the whole night of the paschal offering, necessitates a daytime departure, whereas the former,

---

1 This difficulty was first noted in the modern period by E. Meyer, *op. cit.* (Chapter Five, note 11), p. 34.

according to which the plague struck at midnight, implies that the journey was begun as soon as possible thereafter, during the night. On this point, the lack of coherence between the two traditions is unmistakable.

Jewish exegesis decided in favor of the daytime departure, explaining away all of the texts which state the contrary. Tg. Jonathan to Deut 16:1 translates "the LORD your God freed you from Egypt by night" with "the LORD your God freed you from Egypt; *you shall eat it* [the paschal sacrifice] at night", and Tg. Onqelos similarly renders "the LORD your God freed you from Egypt, *and performed wonders for you* at night". In the same fashion the Sifre (Rĕᵓēh 128) asks: "Did they actually depart at night? Surely they departed in the daytime, since the Torah states 'on the morning after the paschal offering' etc.! This verse is therefore intended to teach that they were *redeemed* at night". The midrashim on the book of Exodus also deny the nighttime departure, likewise basing their stand on the prohibition to leave the house before dawn, and/or on Num 33:3, "it was on the morning after the paschal offering".

The most far-reaching example of this exegetical tradition is the Mekilta deRabbi Šimᶜon bar Yoḥai, (Boᵓ12:31) in which it is stressed that even Moses and Aaron did not disobey the command not to leave their houses at night:

> "And he [Pharaoh] summoned Moses and Aaron at night" (Exod 12:31)...: But had they not already been told "None of you shall go outside the door of his house until morning" (v. 22)? The text thus indicates that they looked out from the balcony and told him "We are not going out at night. We shall depart at midday!"

This same view is discernible in Midr. Teh. to Psalm 113, which, instead of taking the verb *wayyiqrā*ᵓ in Exod 12:31 idiomatically ("summoned"), renders it literally: "called out":

> Pharaoh arose and went to Moses and Aaron at night, as it is said "he called out to Moses and Aaron at night", which means that Pharaoh kept knocking on the doors of Moses and Aaron,

saying to them "Up, depart from among my people" (Exod 12:31), to which they replied "Fool! Should we rise[2] (Yal.: should we depart) at night, leaving in the night like thieves? We shall depart in the morning, as the Holy One, Blessed be He, has instructed us "None of you shall go outside" etc.

Though the passage expressly mentions only the prohibition of going out of doors at night, the words "...like thieves" allude to Num 33:3.

A similar structure can be observed in those midrashic passages which avoid stressing that Moses and Aaron refrained from going out at night. An example is Mek. Bōʾ 13, which attributes to Moses the words "We are only forbidden to go out openly, as it is said 'None of you shall go out' etc." Here too, the word "openly" alludes to Num 33:3, but a new reason for the prohibition is implied: the Israelites were forbidden to leave their houses at night not only for their own protection but primarily in order that the departure might take place in broad daylight, in clear sight of the Egyptians. The combination of two reasons is explicit in Tan. Bōʾ 7: "Moses told him [Pharaoh]: The Holy One, Blessed be He, has commanded us, 'None of you shall go outside' etc. Are we thieves, that we should leave in the night? We shall leave only with open defiance, in the sight of all Egypt!", while Abot deRabbi Nathan (B, 29) quotes only the text of Num 33:3, giving as the sole argument of Moses and Aaron "Are we thieves, that we should leave in the night? Wait for us, until the Holy One, Blessed be He, brings us clouds of glory, with which we shall depart joyously and openly, as it is said, 'It was on the morning after the paschal offering that the Israelites started out, defiantly'".

Only in the Pentateuch itself are the traces of this problem to be detected. Outside of the Pentateuch, Israelite historiography, including detailed historical surveys, shows no interest in determining the precise time of day at which the Israelites left Egypt and whether it was before or after daybreak, satisfied with the mention of the simple fact that the departure from Egypt was a result of the slaying of the firstborn. Still, it would be incorrect to conclude that this, and the inconsistency in the Pentateuchal account, stem from the absence of

---

2 ʿōmĕdîn here is used in the sense of "rise"; see the lexica of rabbinic Hebrew.

an ancient tradition on the matter. Rather it seems that, as argued above, the tradition of the daytime Exodus evolved from that of the paschal offering, receiving additional corroboration from the tradition that the departure was a defiant one, and that the midnight departure tradition evolved from the story of the slaying of the firstborn.[3]

II. The Participants in the Exodus

According to Exod 12:37, "about six hundred thousand men on foot, aside from children" left Egypt. As glossed by Mek. Bō' 14, "aside from children" implies "aside from women, children and the aged"; this is echoed by Philo (VM I.xxvii, p. 104), who mentions that in addition to the six hundred thousand men who left Egypt there were not only children but also women and the aged. Josephus too states explicitly that the figure of six hundred thousand includes only males of military age (Ant.II.xv.1). This tradition of interpretation is evidently the plain meaning of the biblical text, since the round figure

---

3 R. Eleazar ben Azariah's interpretation of Exod 12:8 ("They shall eat the flesh on the same night" etc.) is another example of how the account of the slaying of the firstborn has influenced both the Pesah narrative and the laws of the paschal sacrifice. From the fact that the expression "on the same night" recurs in v. 12 ("I will go through the land of Egypt on the same night"), he concludes that, since the latter demonstrably refers to midnight (see v. 29), the former must have the same meaning, and infers that the paschal flesh is to be consumed by midnight (b. Ber. 9a; Pesah. 102b; Meg. 21a; Zebah. 57b; see also Mek. Bō' 6 and Tg. Jonathan to Exod 12:8). R. Eleazar's, however, is not the only view; other tannaim held that the paschal sacrifice may be eaten until dawn. Moreover, the Talmud attributes to the same R. Eleazar ben Azariah the view that the Exodus took place in the morning: "R. Abba said: Both (R. Akiba and R. Eleazar ben Azariah) agree that when the Israelites were *redeemed* from Egypt this took place in the evening, as Scripture says 'The LORD your God freed you from Egypt at night' (Deut 16:1) and that the actual departure took place during the day, as it says 'It was on the morning after the paschal offering that the Israelites started out, defiantly' (Num 33:3). On what matter do they differ? On the time of the 'haste'. R. Eleazar ben Azariah holds that the haste was on the part of the Egyptians (Rashi: who rushed [during the night], following the slaying of the firstborn, to drive them out of Egypt); R. Eleazar holds that the haste was that of the Israelites (Rashi: who did not heed them, leaving only in the morning [at which time they acted in haste])" (b. Ber. 9a).

of 600,000, which recurs in Num 11:21, corresponds to the more precise number of 603,550 Israelites able to bear arms, of whom a census was taken during the second year in the wilderness (Num 1:45), and to the 601,730 men fit for military service who were counted in the Plains of Moab (Num 26:51). Clearly, then, the number of those who participated in the Exodus, who are referred to as "all the troops of the LORD" (Exod 12:41; see also v. 17 "your troops" and v. 51 "troop by troop"), also pertains to men of military age. The scene is further depicted by Exod 13:18: "The Israelites went up out of Egypt *ḥămūšīm*", the meaning of which is stated correctly by the Mekilta (Bĕšallaḥ, proem): "The word *ḥămūšīm* here means armed, as in the passage 'but every one of you shall go across *ḥămūšīm*' (Josh 1:14), which is explained by 'The Reubenites, Gadites and the half-tribe of Manasseh went across armed...about forty thousand shock troops' (Josh 4:12-13)".

From these passages there emerges a picture of an ethnic group which migrated from its former place of habitation in order to conquer a new homeland. That their intent was one of conquest determines the unique character of the biblical account of their migration, in which they are depicted as warriors, and thus as armed. The tale of the migration of the Danites in Judges 18 reveals the typology of this pattern: "They departed from there, from the clan-seat of the Danites, from Zorah and Eshtaol, six hundred strong, girt with weapons of war" (Judg 18:11). Here too we are told of the departure of an entire ethnic group, including their womenfolk, children, and aged, and here too, since only the fighting men constitute the armed conquering force, only they are counted.

The close connection between the account of the Danite migration and the Exodus narrative may also be seen in the particularly interesting detail of the number recorded: in the case of the Danites, 600; in the case of the Israelites leaving Egypt, 600,000. The similarity of the two numbers becomes clear in light of the fact that, as shown by Malamat,[4] an Israelite "troop" (*gĕdūd*) contained six hundred men. Malamat suggests incidentally that the figure of 600,000 in the Exo-

---

4 A. Malamat, s.v. *"gĕdūd"*, *ʾEnṣīqlōpedīā Miqrāʾīt*, II, Jerusalem 1954, pp. 432-434.

dus can perhaps be viewed as a multiple of the number of men comprising a single troop. His suggestion can be confirmed in view of our typological comparison between the account of the Danite migration and that of the Exodus. The book of Judges relates that the Danites made up one complete troop; the figure in the book of Exodus means that the Israelites made up "a thousand" troops. A "thousand" was originally an indefinite number denoting a vast, innumerable multitude, but this typological number, which served in Israel's tradition to magnify the enormity of the event, gradually evolved into a precise number in the statistical sense of the word, employed in census passages as the basis for determining the exact number of warriors in each tribe. Most probably, the totals are more ancient than, and served as the basis for, the detailed enumeration,[5] as in the case of

5 Nineteenth-century scholars were aware of the unhistorical character of the figure 600,000. The fullest treatment of the topic is that of J. W. Colenso, *The Pentateuch and Book of Joshua, Critically Examined*, London 1862, who raised the question whether the round number of 600,000 is based on the more exact figures in Numbers 1 and 26 or vice versa. Those who held that the exact numbers, unhistorical as they may be, are the more ancient found various ways of supporting their claim. A. Knobel, *Numeri, Deuteronomium und Josua*, Leipzig 1861, attempted to find a basis for the exact numbers in later military censuses carried out by the Israelites in Canaan. Similarly W. F. Albright, "The Administrative Divisions of Israel and Judah", *JPOS*, 5 (1925), pp. 20-25, argued that the two censuses recorded in the Pentateuch are actually based on two sources describing David's census, which, he held, actually included the entire population, women and children as well as men of military age. However, this suggestion is unfounded. The passages referring to David's census (2 Sam 24:9 and 1 Chr 21:5) specify larger numbers and state explicitly that only military personnel were counted. Even if the exceedingly high numbers are admitted to be historically unreliable, there is no reason to question the statement that the census included only fighting men. After all, a comprehensive census, such as those practiced in modern times, is unheard of in the Bible and throughout the ancient Near Eastern sources.

A most original proposal concerning the census figures was made by W. M. F. Petrie, *Egypt and Israel*, London 1911, pp. 42-46. Petrie interpreted the word *ʾelep* ("thousand") in all the relevant passages to mean "family" in the narrowest sense — the total number of persons living in one tent. Such a verse as "those enrolled from the tribe of Reuben: forty-six *ʾelep* and five hundred" (Num 1:21) would thus mean that at the time of the first census the Reubenites comprised forty-six families, amounting to a total of five hundred persons. Hence, he concludes, the total number of Israelites at the time of the first census totalled no more than 5,500. We see that Petrie too assumed that the census included the entire population, an assumption which, as we have already stated, is anachronistic.

Petrie's influence can be detected in the study of G. E. Mendenhall, "The Census

the seventy persons who descended into Egypt (Gen 46:27; Exod 1:5; Deut 10:22), seventy being a typological number which, as proven by Cassuto,[6] antedates the detailed enumeration in Genesis 46.

While ancient tradition was untroubled by the number 600,000, it was perplexed by the statement that the Israelites were armed. The earliest evidence denying that they were is the LXX, which translates *waḥămūšīm* in Exod 13:18 with πέμπτη δὲ γενεά "the fifth generation". This translation is curious for two reasons: first, the Pentateuchal tradition recorded in the Covenant with Abraham states that "they shall return here in the fourth generation" (Gen 15:16); second, elsewhere the LXX itself translates *ḥămūšīm* with words meaning "armed, girt with weapons" — so in Josh 1:14 (εὔζωνοι), 4:12

Lists of Numbers 1 and 26", *JBL*, 77 (1958), pp. 52-66, even though Mendenhall is careful to avoid the error of turning a military census into a general one. He claims that the census figures in Numbers were taken from those of a military census carried out in the time of the Judges. Like Petrie, Mendenhall takes the word *ʾelep* as denoting a tribal sub-unit, though he believes it to be a somewhat larger one. He asserts that every such *ʾelep* was responsible for mobilizing a small unit, also called an *ʾelep*, for Israel's national army. From the verse above, therefore, Mendenhall would conclude that in the period of the Judges the Reubenites were divided into forty-six sub-units, which together contributed five-hundred soldiers to the Israelite forces. The average Reubenite *ʾelep* would therefore amount to eleven men.

Mendenhall further posits that the definition of *ʾelep* changed during the monarchic period, at which time it denoted a unit of 1,000 men. This new meaning, he believes, misled the redactor of the Pentateuch into calculating the total number of Reubenites as 46,500 men. The redactor erred further, Mendenhall concludes, by assigning the census to the wildernes period.

However, Mendenhall's reconstruction is entirely arbitrary. Nowhere does the Bible mention a general mobilization of all the tribes during the period of the Judges, nor is there any mention of the forty-six military units of the Reubenites. Nowhere is it intimated that the total number of soldiers in every *ʾelep* sub-unit was also called an *ʾelep*. Finally, Mendenhall is compelled to attribute the grossest misunderstandings to the redactor of the Pentateuch.

All in all, the various and repeated attempts to find a historical basis for the census figures in the Pentateuch fail to convince, and the opinion of those scholars who consider the round number of 600,000 to be the more ancient is to be preferred. This was indeed the view of G. B. Gray, *Numbers*, ICC, Edinburgh 1912. Admittedly, as long as the round figure of 600,000 is regarded as arbitrary and without significance, this interpretation is less than persuasive. Our interpretation of the meaning of the figure 600,000, i.e., a vast number of troops, removes this difficulty.

6 U. Cassuto, *Commentary to Genesis*, II, trans. by I. Abrahams, Jerusalem 1964, pp. 175-176.

(διεσκευασμένοι) and Num 32:17 (Heb. *ḥŭšīm;* LXX ἐνοπλισάμενοι). Only in Judg 7:11 did the LXX mistakenly render *ḥămŭšīm* as πεντήκοντα ("fifty"), an error easily explained as the result of the translators' having read *ḥămiššīm,* and bearing no resemblance to Exod 13:18 where the LXX reading seems to be deliberate. The translator was therefore presumably not ignorant of the meaning "armed"; rather, he rejected it as unreasonable, and endeavored to come up with another interpretation.

The same phenomenon can be found in the Midrash. As we have already had occasion to note, the plain sense of the text is often perfectly clear to the rabbis and is still rejected by many of them. The Mekilta deRabbi Šimᶜon bar Yoḥai on our passage presents what appears to be a compromise between the LXX and Gen 15:16: "Some of them went up after four generations, and some went up after five generations". Other midrashic interpretations include the idea that "five times as many aliens and slaves went up with them" and the suggestion that "only one fifth of them went up; others say, one fiftieth; others say, one in five-hundred". Particularly worthy of notice is Tg. Jonathan: "armed with good deeds".

It may therefore be concluded that the tradition belies a tendency to negate the scriptural assumption that the Israelites left Egypt armed. This negation would seem to have been prompted by two considerations.

The first is the fact that the Pentateuchal account neglects to indicate the source from which the departing Israelites obtained their arms. This difficulty is stated by the writer Demetrius, who in the third-century B.C.E. wrote:

> Someone asked how the Israelites had weapons, since they came out unarmed. For they said that after they had gone out on a three-day journey, and made sacrifice, they would return again. It appears, therefore, that those who had not been drowned (i.e. the Israelites) made use of the others' (i.e. the Egyptians') arms.
>
> (Eusebius IX:29, 16)

As they have come down to us devoid all of context, Demetrius' words are not entirely intelligible. Discernible in any case is the notion that the Israelites returned from Mount Sinai to the Red Sea in order to avail themselves of the weapons left by the drowned Egyptians. Josephus records the same tradition more simply, recounting that immediately after the Israelites crossed the sea the wind and tide swept the Egyptians' weapons into the Israelite camp. Recognizing the work of divine Providence, Moses collected the weapons and outfitted the Israelites with them (Ant. II.xvi.6). Thus, in eminently reasonable fashion, did Josephus solve the problem of Israel's obtaining arms in the wilderness.

The second difficulty with the statement that the Israelites had obtained weapons is that the account of the parting of the sea gives the distinct impression that the Israelites were unarmed. The LORD's miraculous deliverance of His people is immeasurably more credible when it is assumed that the Israelites were utterly helpless to defend themselves. The book of Exodus goes into lengthy detail concerning the Israelites' grumblings and Moses' reply, and throughout the exchange there is no mention of any means of defense in their possession. Not surprisingly, Ezekiel the Tragedian describes the scene as one of unarmed Israelites facing Pharaoh's army equipped with formidable weapons, stating explicitly that the Israelites were "all unprotected, without arms" (l. 210) while the Egyptians "trusted in their mighty armament" (l. 218). Similarly Philo comments on Exod 14:11 by saying that the Israelites were dismayed by the sight of Pharaoh's army at the Red Sea because they were unarmed, having left Egypt not for the purpose of making war but rather for resettlement! Philo goes so far as to ascribe to the Israelites the question "Can unarmed men fight against a fully armed enemy?" (VM I.xxxi, p. 108). Josephus too (Ant. III.i.4) explains the Israelites' complaint against Moses as the result of their being unarmed.

Now, since, as we have noted, a portion of the Hebrew midrashic literature categorically denied that the Israelites were armed at the time of Exodus, it stands to reason that they too would deny the existence of any Israelite arms at the parting of the sea. However, if any such tradition, parallel to that found in the Hellenistic sources, existed in the Midrash, it has not been preserved. All extant midrashic sources describing the events at the sea unanimously

affirm that the Israelites were armed, and this tradition has survived
in a more ancient form in Pseudo-Philo:

> Then considering the fearful situation of the moment, the chil-
> dren of Israel were split in their opinions according to three
> strategies. For the tribes of Reuben, Issachar, Zebulun and
> Simeon said: "Come, let us cast ourselves into the sea. For it is
> better for us to die in the water than to be killed by our enemies".
> The tribes of Gad, Asher, Dan and Naftali said: "No, but let us
> go back with them, and if they are willing to spare our lives, we
> will serve them". But the tribes of Levi, Judah, Joseph and
> Benjamin said: "Not so, but let us take up our weapons and fight
> with them, and God will be with us!"
>
> (LAB, X:3)

The same account appears in Midr. Wayyōšaᶜ:[7]

> When the Egyptians pursued Israel at the sea, the Israelites split
> into three divisions, the first saying: "Let us drown ourselves in
> the sea"; the second saying: "Let us return to Egypt"; and the
> third saying: "Let us wage war against them". To those who said
> "Let us drown in the sea", Moses replied, "Stand by, and witness
> the deliverance which the LORD will work for you today" (Exod
> 14:13). To those who said "Let us return to Egypt", Moses
> replied, "You will never see them again" (*ibid.*). To those who
> said "Let us wage war against them", Moses replied, "The LORD
> will battle for you; you hold your peace" (v. 14).

Most versions of this midrash[8] add here a fourth group, who proposed
that the Israelites should raise a battle-cry against the Egyptians in
order to disconcert them. To these Moses replied, "You hold your
peace". The evolution of the expansion can be inferred from Moses'
response: once the Midrash interpreted the several parts of Moses'

---

7 See A. Jellinek, *Bet HaMidraš*, I, Leipzig 1853, pp. 51-52; compare *Pirqē Rabbēnū
HaQādōš*, par. 35, in: A. Greenhut (ed.), *Sēfer HaYalqūṭīm*, III, (n. p.) 1899.
8 Mekilta deRabbi Šimᶜon bar Yoḥai, Bēšallaḥ 14:14; y. Taᶜaniyot, 2:5, 65b; Tg.
Jonathan to Exod 14:13-14.

reply to Israel's complaint (vv. 13-14) as addressed to separate portions of the community, it was felt necessary to account for the words "You hold your peace" in v. 14 by assuming a fourth group. Clearly, however, the original version concluded with the proposal of the large tribes to go to war, since this proposal is what restores Israel's honor.

To summarize, the Pentateuch portrays the departing Israelites according to an established literary pattern, a pattern designed to describe the migration of a tribe to conquer new territory. Hence the number of participants in the departure given by the Pentateuch refers to the fighting men alone. These men are armed, and even their number reflects that they constitute a vast quantity of troops. This pattern, however, does not cohere with the more ancient story, which cannot account for the source from which the Israelites obtained their weapons. It also disturbs the transition to the following narrative, that of the parting of the sea, in which no mention is made of any weapons and the distinct impression is created that only miraculous divine intervention can rescue Israel. Post-biblical literature has developed two methods of solving this literary tension. The more radical solution was to assert that the Israelites in fact left Egypt without any weapons, that they faced Pharaoh's host entirely unarmed, and that only thereafter did they confiscate the arms of the drowned Egyptians. The other solution, less logical but closer to the plain sense of the biblical text, was to admit that the Israelites left Egypt armed, to accept the implication that they were armed at the Reed Sea, and to give credit, at least to the bravest among them, for being prepared for battle.

CHAPTER SEVEN

THE PARTING OF THE SEA

I. The Parting of the Sea in the Exodus Tradition

Whereas the problems arising from the specifics of the Exodus are peculiar to the detailed narratives (and, later, to the Midrash, with its predilection for particulars), the didactic histories, which are aimed solely at glorifying the mighty acts of the LORD, were no more interested in the details of the Exodus than they were in the paschal sacrifice — which is treated in later tradition only insofar as it pertains to the regulations concerning the celebration of the festival. The absence of any reference to the paschal sacrifice in several of the detailed accounts — Artapanus, Philo, and Pseudo-Philo — should be seen in this light. In all these sources the plague narrative, which concludes with the departure from Egypt, is followed immediately by the account of the parting of the sea, and with this the story of the Exodus concludes.

The implication of all this is that only when the Egyptian army had perished did Israel's liberation from slavery become final and the Exodus from Egypt a permanent and irrevocable fact. And indeed, the Bible never again mentions the Egyptians. Neither the victories of Merneptah, whose stele boasts that Israel has been destroyed forever, nor the vestiges of Egyptian hegemony in Canaan, which persisted until the mid-eleventh century B.C.E., nor any other historical data which might tend to detract from the Exodus, are given any notice at all.

In biblical tradition, the tale of Israel's deliverance from slavery to freedom culminates in an episode of unsurpassed power and impact, in which the descent of Pharaoh's chariots and warriors into the depths of the sea is juxtaposed against Israel's safe passage through the sea on dry land. Not surprisingly, Israelite tradition throughout the generations has assigned to this episode particular pride of place, and all of the historiographical writings, detailed narratives as well as didactic histories, have shown a particular affection for this event.

II. The Biblical Tradition

A. The Tradition-History as Viewed by Scholars

In view of the above, the prevailing scholarly view, namely, that the core of the tradition is the tale of the Egyptians' descent into the sea, is quite inevitable. "The destruction of an Egyptian chariot force in 'the sea' forms the historical basis of the tradition," writes Noth,[1] thus granting the seal of historicity to the most ancient tradition, preserved in Josh 24:6-7:

> I freed your fathers from Egypt, and you came to the Sea. But the Egyptians pursued your fathers to the Sea of Reeds with chariots and horsemen. They cried out to the LORD, and He put darkness between you and the Egyptians; then He brought the Sea upon them, and it covered them. Your own eyes saw what I did to the Egyptians.

The assumption that the historical kernel of the tradition is the drowning of the Egyptians has occasionally led to rather farfetched conclusions. Most extreme is the theory propounded by E. Meyer,[2] that the Israelites never passed through the sea at all, nor even entered it, and that all that actually took place was the drowning of the Egyptians. As proof, Meyer adduces the Song of Moses, which contains no explicit reference to the Israelites' passage through the sea, and his own reconstruction of the ancient J account which was incorporated in the Pentateuchal narrative. And while Meyer's extreme view has

---

1 *Op. cit.* (Chapter Two, note 24), p. 120.
2 *Op. cit.* (Chapter Five, note 11), pp. 19-24.

found no further proponents, there are numerous scholars who view the Song of Miriam in Exod 15:21, which speaks only of the Egyptian demise, as the earliest source for the tradition of the parting of the sea.[3] Even the Song of Moses, which elaborates upon the drowning of the Egyptians and appends to it the mention of episodes from Israel's subsequent history, is held to be a later source. Nor would the refutation of this particular claim negate the theory itself, according to which the drowning of the Egyptians comprises the historical nucleus of the tradition.

This fundamental scholarly assumption presents the critic with clearly defined tasks. He must begin with the historical inquiry regarding the location at which the sea was parted and the natural phenomena reflected in the story. Here many scholars adhere to the traditional view, locating the crossing at the Gulf of Suez, while others prefer to place the event at one of the lakes to the north of the Gulf, or further north, towards the Mediterranean coast at the Nile delta, or at some point eastward along the coast as far as Serbonitis.[4] Tradition-history enters this historical and topographical investigation at two points. The first is the investigation of the sources from which the Pentateuchal account is composed. Scholarly consensus assigns the parting of the waters by an east wind and the motif of the pillar of cloud and fire to the J account; the remaining verses are assigned by some scholars to E and divided by others between E and P; still others despair of the attempt to distinguish between the later sources.[5] The second issue is the question arising from extra-Pentateuchal sources which depict the parting of the sea as a revival of the mythical conflict between God and the sea. These writings are generally regarded as a later mythologization of the early tradition

---

3 For a list of the proponents of this view, see M. Rozelaar in *VT*, 2 (1952), p. 226. Rozelaar himself should be included, and Lauha (*op. cit.* [Chapter One, note 14], p. 62), O. Kaiser (*Die Mythische Bedeutung des Meeres in Aegypten, Ugarit und Israel, BZAW*, 78, Berlin 1959, p. 130) and Noth (above, note 1, pp. 121ff.) should be added.

4 S. E. Loewenstamm, s.v. "*Yam Sūp*", *ʾEnṣīqlōpedīā Miqrāʾīt*, III, pp. 695-699 and bibliography cited.

5 For a survey of opinion see E. Galbiati, *La Struttura Letteraria Dell'Esodo*, Alba 1956, pp. 161f.; Kaiser, *op. cit.* (above, note 3), pp. 151ff.

which speaks only of the LORD's battle against the Egyptians and knows nothing of His war against the sea itself.[6]

B. The Absence of Reference to the Egyptians

The above approach, however, gives rise to grave doubts. First and foremost it must be pointed out that a considerable number of biblical texts refer to the parting of the sea without any mention of the Egyptians. Most prominent among these are the passages in which the parting of the sea appears in parallelism with the division of the Jordan, such as Joshua's address:

> Tell your children: "Here the Israelites crossed the Jordan on dry land". For the LORD your God dried up the waters of the Jordan before you until you crossed, just as the LORD your God did to the Sea of Reeds, which He dried up before us until we crossed. Thus all the peoples of the earth shall know how mighty is the hand of the LORD, and you shall fear the LORD your God always.
>
> (Josh 4:22-24)

6 This was taken for granted as early as Gunkel, *op. cit.* (Chapter One, note 4). Though Gunkel's pioneering study mentions the parting of the Reed Sea only incidentally, his brief references show conclusively that he regarded the connection between the sea-myth and the parting of the sea as a traditio-historically late combination of dissimilar elements. He considers it to be "extraordinary that once, in Isa 51:9, a past event, the story of the Exodus, is associated with the myth", and writes further that "Psalm 77 is typical of the manner in which a later period unorganically (*sic*!) connects traditional motifs. In vv. 17ff, imitating Psalm 18, the psalm describes a storm-theophany; here too the sea is intended, but the aim of the theophany is the parting of the sea in order for the Israelites to pass through it. In this way, echoes of the story of Creation and that of the Reed Sea have become intertwined" (pp. 90; 107-108). The most elaborate presentation of this view, which is still the accepted one, is that provided by Lauha, *op. cit.* (above, note 3), pp. 61-72. Lauha argues at length for the rationalistic character of the ancient tradition found in J, adducing numerous proofs for his assertion that "the Reed Sea tradition later came under the influence of mythological motifs" (p. 70). More recently, P. Reymond, *L'eau, sa vie et sa signification dans l'ancien testament, VTSup*, 6, Leiden 1958, p. 193, writes: "With the passage of time, and in particular due to the theological interpretation which arises from the historical fact of the crossing of the sea, the latter acquired such a considerable importance that, without actually becoming a myth, it at least assumed certain mythological features".

The same admonition to fear the LORD recurs in Psalm 66 in the form
of a hymn. The psalm begins with a call to praise God:

> Raise a shout for God, all the earth;
>> sing to the glory of His name,
>> make glorious His praise.
> Say to God:
>> "How awesome are Your deeds,
>> Your enemies cower before Your great strength;
>> all the earth bows to You;
>> all sing hymns to Your name".

(vv. 2-4)

Following the call there comes the explanatory statement:

> Come and see the works of God,
>> who is held in awe by men for His acts.
> He turned the sea into dry land;
>> they crossed the river on foot...

(vv. 5-6)

Though the name of the sea referred to is not mentioned, and one cannot fail to hear a strain of cosmogony[7] in the words "He turned the
sea into dry land", it is nonetheless certain that the specific historical
event referred to is none other than the parting of the Reed Sea. This
is clear from the parallel line "they crossed the river on foot", a clear
allusion to the division of the Jordan (even though it is the only passage which refers to the Jordan by the common noun *nāhār* river; see,
however, Job 40:23). God is to be held in awe for His acts not because
He vanquished the Egyptians but because He turned the sea into dry
land!

The exhortation to revere the LORD, which is quite explicit in the
above-cited passages, can be regarded as implicit in Psalm 114:

> When Israel went forth from Egypt,
> the house of Jacob from a people of strange speech,

---

7 Compare "Come and see what the LORD has done" in Psalm 46 (v. 9), a psalm
replete with mythological allusions (vv. 3-4, 7).

> Judah became His holy one,
> Israel, His dominion.
> The sea saw them and fled,
> Jordan ran backward....
>
> (vv. 1-3)

An echo of this tradition, which views the parting of the sea and the cutting off of the Jordan as two components of one episode, can be heard in the oracle of Isaiah 11, where Israel's future redemption is depicted in terms reminiscent of the Exodus from Egypt:

> The LORD will dry up the tongue of the Egyptian sea. He will raise His hand over the River with the might of His wind and break it into seven wadis, so that it can be trodden dry-shod. Thus there shall be a highway for the other part of His people out of Assyria, such as there was for Israel when it left the land of Egypt.
>
> (vv. 15-16)

To be sure, the "River" referred to here is the Euphrates, but the very notion that Israel's future deliverance will consist both of the LORD's raising His hand over the River, breaking it with His mighty wind into seven wadis, and His drying up the Nile, is intelligible only in light of what must have been a deeply-rooted tradition concerning similar acts performed at the time of the Exodus from Egypt. The war-like strain in the depiction of the future heptesection of the Euphrates also attests to the existence of a tradition in which the bisection of the Jordan was portrayed in patently mythological fashion.

To these passages, in which the parting of the sea is mentioned alongside of the division of the Jordan without any reference to the drowning of the Egyptians, we may add another set of verses which, though they speak only of the parting of the sea and not of the far less spectacular division of the Jordan, still lack any and all reference to the fate of the Egyptians. First among these is the admission of Rahab the harlot to Joshua's spies:

> I know that the LORD has given the country to you, because dread of you has fallen upon us, and all the inhabitants of the

land are quaking with fear before you. For we have heard how the LORD dried up the waters of the Sea of Reeds for you when you left Egypt, and what you did to Sihon and Og, the two Amorite kings across the Jordan, whom you doomed. When we heard about it, we lost heart, and no man had any more spirit left because of you; for the LORD your God is the only God in heaven above and on earth below.

(Josh 2:9-11)

The omission of the fate of the Egyptians is particularly remarkable here, since the mention of their destruction would seem to be the appropriate parallel to the mention of the fate of the Amorite kings, and would serve as further support for Rahab's statement that no nation will survive the Israelite onslaught. As it is, however, the text clearly presents the drying up of the sea as the crucial fact, whereas the historical, rationalistic argument, namely, the reference to the defeat of Sihon and Og, is simply an extra corroboration. The former alone was enough to prove that "the LORD your God is the only God in heaven above and on earth below". This reading is confirmed by Josh 5:1:

When all the kings of the Amorites on the western side of Jordan, and all the kings of the Canaanites near the Sea, heard how the LORD had dried up the waters of the Jordan for the sake of the Israelites until they crossed over, they lost heart, and no spirit was left in them because of the Israelites.[8]

---

8 In three different passages the book of Joshua accounts for the terror which struck the Canaanites. The Gibeonites state that they have come because "we have heard the report of Him; of all that He did in Egypt, and of all that He did to the two Amorite kings on the other side of the Jordan, King Sihon of Heshbon and King Og of Bashan who lived in Ashtaroth" (Josh 9:9-10). Here, the fate of the Egyptians is mentioned only in passing and the emphasis is on the defeat of the Amorite kings; this contrasts starkly with Josh 5:1, where the Canaanites are said to have been struck with dread by the cosmic power exhibited in cutting off the Jordan, whereby God demonstrated His sovereignty over the universe. Rahab's speech in 2:9-11 occupies an intermediate position: in place of the general reference to the Exodus, specific mention is made of the parting of the Reed Sea, so similar to the division of the Jordan which is to be recounted immediately thereafter, and the mention of Sihon and Og is appended.

Here, despite the stylistic and thematic similarity to 2:9ff, the rationalistic, military argument that the Canaanite kings have been instilled with the fear of Israel as a result of the defeat of Sihon and Og has disappeared. The only reason stated here for their fear is the drying up of the Jordan's waters.

A number of poetic passages, which invoke past acts of divine deliverance in order to arouse divine favor in the face of present adversity, may also be cited in this context. The statement in Isa 63:12-14 reminds the LORD that it was He who long ago

> ...made His glorious arm
> March at the right hand of Moses,
> Who divided the waters before them
> To make Himself a name for all time,
> Who led them through the deeps
> So that they did not stumble —
> As a horse in a desert,
> Like a beast descending to the plain,
> It was the spirit of the LORD that gave them rest;
> Thus did You shepherd Your people
> To win for Yourself a glorious name.

Though these words were uttered at a time when the LORD's Sanctuary had been trampled by His enemies (v. 18), the poet chooses to make no mention of God's victory over the Egyptians, sufficing instead with the parting of the sea and declaring that it was this and this alone which secured for the LORD an everlasting name.

In the preceding passage the parting of the sea served to illustrate God's shepherding care of His people; elsewhere in Isaiah (51:9-10) it is associated with the mythic battles He once fought:

> Awake, awake, clothe yourself with splendor
> O arm of the LORD!
> Awake as in days of old,
> As in former ages!
> It was You that hacked Rahab in pieces,
> That pierced the Dragon.

It was You that dried up the Sea,
The waters of the great deep;
That made the abysses of the Sea
A road the redeemed might walk.

Another passage designed to re-invoke God's past acts of salvation
in view of present adversity is Psalm 77, where the parting of the sea
appears within the context of a theophany:

You are the God who works wonders,
   You have manifested Your strength among the peoples.
By Your arm You redeemed Your people,
   The children of Jacob and Joseph.[9] Selah.
The waters saw You, O God,
   the waters saw You and were convulsed;
   the very deep quaked as well.
Clouds streamed water;
   the heavens rumbled;
   Your arrows flew about;
   Your thunder rumbled in the wheels;
   lightning lit up the world;
   the earth quaked and trembled.
Your way was through the sea,
   Your path, through the mighty waters;
   Your tracks could not be seen.
You led Your people like a flock
   in the care of Moses and Aaron.

(Ps 77:15-21)

Here we may conclude the discussion of texts in which the parting
of the sea is adduced without any mention of the Egyptians. Common
to all these texts, we may now assert, is the idea that the parting of
the sea alone was sufficient to achieve eternal renown for Israel's
God, and to demonstrate, both to Israel's satisfaction and that of the

---

9 The special mention given to the tribe of Joseph attests to the northern provenance
of the psalm; see S. Mowinckel, "Psalm Criticism Between 1900 and 1935", *VT*,
5 (1955), pp. 26-28.

entire world, that He alone is God in the heavens above and on earth below.

We turn now to a more thorough analysis of this fundamental belief. The passages which associate the parting of the sea with the division of the Jordan are presumably echoes of the Canaanite myth of Baal (i.e. Hadad) and his battle against the Prince of the Sea (Zbl Yam) and the Judge of the River (Ṭpṭ Nhr), a myth known from Ugaritic literature.[10] As discussed at length by Cassuto,[11] this myth is reflected in many biblical passages which have no connection with the Exodus, such as the opening lines of the theophany described in the prayer of Habakkuk (3:8):

> Are You wroth, O LORD, with Neharim?
> Is Your anger against Neharim,
> Your rage against Yam —
> That You are driving Your steeds,
> Your victorious chariot?

Similarly we read in Ps 74:13-15:

> It was You who drove back Yam with Your might,
> Who smashed the heads of the monsters in the waters;
> It was You who crushed the heads of Leviathan,
> Who left him as food for the denizens of the desert;
> It was You who released springs and torrents,
> Who made mighty rivers run dry.

Other passages exhibit these same motifs:

> He rebukes the sea and dries it up;
> And He makes all rivers fail.
>
> (Nah 1:4)

> With a mere rebuke I dry up the sea,
> And turn rivers into desert.
>
> (Isa 50:2)

---

10 Gordon, *op. cit.* (Chapter Four, note 30), text 68 (p. 150).
11 *Op. cit.* (Chapter One, note 10) pp. 83-84.

The rivers sound, O LORD,
    the rivers sound their thunder,
    the rivers sound their pounding.
Above the thunder of the mighty waters,
    more majestic than the breakers of the sea
    is the LORD, majestic on high.

(Ps 93:3-4)[12]

...who said to the deep, "Be dry;
I will dry up your floods."

(Isa 44:27)

The same motifs may underlie Isa 19:5 and Job 14:11.

Despite the affinity of these texts to the Ugaritic myths, however, it should be noted that the latter, few and fragmentary as they are, do not adequately account for the biblical use of these motifs. In particular, no precise parallel to the biblical idea that the LORD dried up the waters of the sea and the rivers has appeared so far in the Ugaritic literature, which states instead that Baal waged his war against the Prince of the Sea and the Judge of the River, who are portrayed as personal gods in their own right.[13] More importantly, the Ugaritic

---

12 The Canaanite background of this psalm has been explored by H. G. Jefferson, "Psalm 93", *JBL*, 71 (1952), pp. 155-160.

13 Ugaritic texts 137 and 68 leave room for doubt as to whether Yam and Nahar are one and the same deity or two separate gods. The former (see *ANET*², p. 130) speaks of *ml^ɔak ym t^cdt ṭpṭ nhr* ("the messengers of Yam, envoys of Judge Nahar"; l. 22) who begin their speech in the divine forum, in which they demand that Baal be surrendered to them, with the words *thm ym b^clkm ɔadnkm ṭpṭ nhr* ("message of Yam your lord, of your master Judge Nahar"; ll. 17, 33-34). In the latter text (*ANET*², p. 131), Baal's victory over this deity (or these deities) is depicted in such expressions as *hlm qdqd zbl ym bn ^cnm ṭpṭ nhr* ("strikes the pate of Prince Yam, between the eyes of Judge Nahar; ll. 21-22). In Anath III, the catalogue of Baal's enemies defeated by Anath (ll. 35-36) indicates that these two are separate deities. Among those listed are expression *mdd ɔil ym* ("El's beloved Yam") and *nhr ɔil rbm*. The latter is obscure; it has been variously translated as "El's Flood Rabbim" (H. L. Ginsberg, in *ANET*², p. 137), "the Great Rivers of El" (U. Cassuto, *op. cit.* [Excursus I, note 7], p. 93; this is unlikely in view of the fact that the remainder of the creatures dispatched by Anath are spoken of in the singular), "the mighty god Nahar" (G. R. Driver, *Canaanite Myths and Legends*, Edinburgh 1956, p. 87). Whatever the correct rendering may be, the Ugaritic epic clearly refers to separate, personal deities. The waters of Yam and Nahar are not mentioned, nor is their desire to inundate the earth or Baal's plan to dry them up.

myths ascribe cosmogonic significance to Baal's struggle with Yam and the rivers. Just such a view of the significance of LORD's battle with the sea is given in Psalm 104, which speaks of the wonders of Creation:

> He established the earth on its foundations,
>> so that it shall never totter.
> You made the deep cover it as a garment;
>> the waters stood above the mountains.
> They fled at Your blast,
>> rushed away at the sound of Your thunder.
>> — mountains rising, valleys sinking —
>> to the place You established for them.
> You set bounds they must not pass
>> so that they never again cover the earth.
>
> (Ps 104:5-9)

Here, the use of the general term "waters" is not intended to be non-specific; rather, it embraces the sea and the rivers (as in Ps 24:1-2: "The earth is the LORD's and all that it holds, the world and its inhabitants. For He founded it upon the seas, set it on the rivers").

It is also clear that the biblical tradition perceived the sea as constantly seeking to re-inundate the earth. Job asks "Am I the sea or the Dragon, that You have set a watch over me?" (Job 7:12; see also 38:10-11). This passage has rightly been compared to Enuma Eliš IV.139-140, where it is recounted that after defeating Tiamat, Marduk "pulled down the bar and posted guards; he bade them to allow not her waters to escape".[14] The same destructive ambition is attributed in biblical literature to the rivers. Jer 46:8 speaks of "Egypt that rises like the Nile, like rivers whose waters surge, that said, 'I will rise, I will cover the earth, I will wipe out towns and those who dwell in them'", and Isa 59:19 refers to the same motif: "...like a hemmed-in stream, which the wind of the LORD drives on". This being the case, the primordial battle between the LORD and the sea, recalled by Habakkuk, may, in the biblical view, someday be renewed. This

---

14 *ANET*[2], p. 67.

future struggle is alluded to in Isa 17:13, though it employs the more general image of "massive waters": "Nations shall rage like massive waters, but He will shout at them, and they will flee far away".

In light of all this, it becomes imperative to distinguish between the separate aspects of the common Canaanite-Israelite myth manifested in these texts. The battle waged by the god of heaven against the sea and the rivers may be associated on the one hand with the war against the sea monsters, which are reminiscent of Tiamat's henchmen and which appear, bearing their biblical names, in the Ugaritic literature. It is this personal aspect of the myth that is alluded to in the words of Ps 74:13-14 ("It was You who drove back Yam with Your might, who smashed the heads of the monsters in the waters; it was You who crushed the heads of Leviathan" etc.) and with even greater force in Isa 27:1:

> In that day the LORD will punish,
> With His great, cruel, mighty sword
> Leviathan the Elusive Serpent;
> He will slay the Dragon of the sea.

On the other hand, this same conflict is a cosmogonic one, a conflict which periodically renews itself even in the post-cosmogonic world, and which consists primarily of the drying up of the sea and rivers. Indeed, even as attested in Enuma Eliš, the myth exhibits this duality — though in a somewhat different fashion. The Akkadian myth opens with a personal conflict between Marduk and Tiamat and her henchmen, after which it proceeds to speak of the world order determined by Marduk, including reference to the fixing of boundaries for the sea. It may be assumed, therefore, that the ancient Israelite myth alluded to in the Bible also contained some similar duality. This assumption is corroborated by Psalm 74, where the drying up of the mighty rivers is mentioned alongside the crushing of Leviathan's heads.

A majority of the biblical passages discussed above, in which the parting of the sea and the division of the Jordan are featured, are to be understood against this mythological background which Israel inherited from the Canaanite peoples at the beginning of its history. It now becomes clear why these particular acts of deliverance were deemed to be the firmest possible basis for belief in the God of Israel, since even the Akkadian and Ugaritic forerunners of the Israelite myth include the notion that the conflict between the god of heaven and the great waters (or the anthropomorphic deities that represent them) anticipates the establishment of the victorious god's dominion. In parting the sea and the Jordan, Israel's God re-enacts the very heroic deeds He performed in primeval days, thereby proving Himself to be the Creator of the world who founded the earth upon the vanquished seas and rivers. The strength of such a claim, based on the LORD's defeat of superhuman powers, is infinitely greater than any argument stemming from His victory over mere mortals.

However, not all of the biblical references to the parting of the sea are to be accounted for in these terms. The inadequacy of the explanation is especially evident when the verses in Psalm 77 are considered. For although the words "The waters saw You, O God, the waters saw You and were convulsed; the very deep quaked as well" (v. 17) could be viewed as a reflection of the mythological tradition of the god of heaven and his battle with the great waters, what follows indicates clearly that such an interpretation is not sufficient. For if the reference to the quaking of the waters is evidence of God's war against them, the words "the earth quaked and trembled" (v. 19) would have to be taken to mean that a similar battle was waged against the earth. Such a conclusion would be entirely unacceptable, since no known myth contains such a motif. The reference to the terror-stricken waters cannot therefore originate, at least not exclusively, in the mythological tradition we have been discussing. It would thus seem preferable to approach the problematic Psalm 77 from another viewpoint, namely the possible connection between the tradition of God's conflict with the mighty waters and that of the theophany.

Two prominent motifs are featured in the psalm. The first is the description of the rain, thunder and lightning:

> Clouds streamed water;
> the heavens rumbled;
> Your arrows flew about;

Your thunder rumbled in the wheels;[15]
lightning lit up the world;
the earth quaked and trembled

(vv. 18-19)

The God who appears here is therefore the God who "makes clouds rise from the ends of the earth; He makes lightning for the rain; He releases the wind from His vaults" (Ps 135:7; compare Jer 51:16). Though these aspects of the divine do not pertain specifically to a theophany in the battle against the sea, they may certainly appear in such a context. The cosmogony of Psalm 104 is clear evidence of this, as the words "They fled at Your rebuke, rushed away at the sound of Your thunder" (v. 7) indicate that God's "rebuke" is none other than the sound of thunder; compare the above-cited passages in Isa 50:2 and Nah 1:4. Moreover, the theophany in Habakkuk, where the LORD's self-manifestation is compared with that which occurred when He waged His war against the sea and the rivers, contains expressions closely resembling Psalm 77, in particular, "A torrent of rain comes down; loud roars the deep....Your arrows fly in brightness" (Hab 3:10-11).

All these elements certainly originate in the traditions surrounding Hadad, the Canaanite god of thunder, lightning and rain. So influential were these traditions that they have even left their mark on the biblical account of the Sinai theophany (Exod 19:16), despite the fact that the Sinai events are not portrayed as a revelation of divine power in nature or in battle but rather as one of laws and statutes. In monotheistic religion, all of the divine characteristics which polytheistic tradition had distributed among various deities are concentrated in the one God, so that even when appearing as a Lawgiver He displays attributes pertaining to gods of war and fertility.

The second important motif in Psalm 77 is the violent effect of the

---

15 Heb. *baggalgal* "in the wheels" was already interpreted by Rashi to mean *kaggalgal* (NJPS: "like wheels"), and thus the text is frequently emended. Still, Ezek 10:2 would seem to indicate that the wheels were perceived as the source of the thunder and lightning, which militates in favor of MT; see also S. Mowinckel, "Drive and/or Ride in O.T.", *VT*, 12 (1962), p. 299.

appearance of God upon nature, described in vv. 17-19 ("...the waters saw You and were convulsed; the very deep quaked as well....the earth quaked and trembled"). As has been demonstrated at length elsewhere,[16] there existed in Israel a tradition concerning the upheaval of nature which accompanied the theophany. God's awesome self-manifestation was portrayed as sending a tremor throughout the natural elements, which are represented by the heavens, the earth and the mountains. It has also been pointed out that the very same pattern is recognizable in Akkadian hymns to Marduk, Adad, Ishtar and other warlike deities. The Akkadian hymns too describe at great length the terror which seized heaven, earth, mountains, and sometimes other natural elements at the appearance of the mighty god. This pattern was later transferred to the Assyrian chronicles, in which the kings of Assyria boast that when they appeared with their armies the world was terrified from one end to the other.

This idea of the upheaval of nature at the god's appearance is a tradition independent of the myth of divine battle with the sea. The majority of the Akkadian texts do not even include the sea among the natural phenomena which are disrupted by the divine revelation, and those few texts which mention the sea give it no particular emphasis. The Bible too refrains for the most part from mentioning the sea in this context,[17] only occasionally including the sea among the other

---

16 S. E. Loewenstamm, "The Quaking of Nature and the Appearance of YHWH", *David ben Gurion Volume*, Jerusalem 1964, pp. 508-520 [Hebrew].

17 Gunkel, *op. cit.* (above, note 6), pp. 104-105 proposed that those theophanies containing no mention of the sea originate in poetic accounts of the Sinai theophany. The absence of the sea would thus be easily accounted for, inasmuch as there are no bodies of water in the area of Sinai or any of the other locations at which the Israelites encamped. Similar views have been repeated in more recent scholarship; see A. Weiser, "Zur Frage nach den Beziehungen der Psalmen zum Kult: Die Darstellung der Theophanie in den Psalmen und im Festkult", *Festschrift A. Bertholet*, Tübingen 1950, p. 515, who writes, "It is generally accepted...that from the tradition-history point of view the accounts of theophanies derive from the Sinai theophany, which is their prototype". If this assumption is accepted, we shall have no difficulty understanding the cautious suggestion made by E. Pax, Ἐπιφάνεια, München 1955, p. 122, that in Psalm 77 "the passage through the sea is portrayed along lines unattested in the remaining traditions but which have apparently been influenced by the Sinai narrative". These statements all fail to take into account the antiquity of the theophany tradi-

terror-stricken natural phenomena, for instance, "I will shake the heavens and the earth, the sea and the dry land" (Hag 2:6). Unlike the Akkadian literature, however, the Bible does contain a few passages in which God's battle with the mighty waters is combined with a general upheaval of nature occurring at the same time as the war with the sea. This combination of motifs is not surprising: if nature is dismayed at the very appearance of the LORD, it stands to reason that it is shaken to its very foundations at the sight of the LORD engaged in dire combat with the sea. This is precisely what we find in the cosmogonic passage in Job 26:11-12: "The pillars of heaven tremble, astounded at His rebuke; by His power He stilled the sea; by His skill He struck down Rahab". The same motifs are juxtaposed in Nah 1:4-6, where "He rebukes the sea and dries it up, and He makes all rivers fail", is followed by "The mountains quake because of Him, and the hills melt" and then by "His anger pours out like fire, and rocks are shattered because of Him". The fullest integration of the two motifs is found in the prayer of Habakkuk, which likens the warlike appearance of God facing His enemies to His appearance in battle against the sea and rivers (3:8), hyperbolically describing the

---

tion and the Sinai narrative's dependence on that of the warrior-god's (especially Hadad's) theophany. This dependence is particularly evident in the case of the theophanies which do not mention the sea. In Akkadian literature too, only rarely is the sea included among the natural elements which quake in terror of the warrior-god, yet none would go so far as to contend that the Akkadian myths are derived from Israel's Sinai tradition!

The topic is approached from another angle by B. S. Childs, "The Enemy from the North and the Chaos Tradition", *JBL*, 78 (1959), 187-198. For no apparent reason, Childs restricts his study of the quaking of nature to the Hebrew root *r ʿš*, concluding that the mythological use of this term stems from an ancient tradition of the shaking of chaos which was eventually transferred to the theophany accounts. The single biblical passage in which Childs might find some support for his theory is Ps 46:2-4. He is probably right that "mountains quake in His/its swell" (Ps 46:4) refers to the swell of the sea and not to that of God, and that the intent of the psalm is that even if the mighty roaring of the sea (which symbolizes the powers of wickedness) should cause mountains to quake, "we are not afraid" since "God is our refuge and stronghold" (v. 1). Still, it cannot be denied that an echo of the tradition that the god of the sea too is included among, and no less powerful than, the other warrior-gods, can be detected. Akkadian literature too, in addition to the Bible, shows clearly that the motif of a theophany accompanied by the upheaval of nature does not originate exclusively in a tradition of the upheaval of chaos.

upheaval of nature in such statements as "The age-old mountains are shattered, the primeval hills sink low" (3:6) and "The mountains rock at the sight of You" (3:10). Moreover, a similar coalescence of ideas appears in connection with the Exodus in Ps 114:5-7: "What alarmed you, O sea, that you fled, Jordan, that you ran backward, mountains, that you skipped like rams, hills, like sheep? Tremble, O earth, at the presence of the LORD, at the presence of the God of Jacob".

Returning to Psalm 77, we note that it is the only passage in which the actual measures taken by God against the sea must be inferred from the mention of the sea's own terrified reaction: "The waters saw you, O God, the waters saw you and were convulsed; the very deep quaked as well" (v. 17). The emphasis placed upon the convulsive quaking of the water is not a customary feature of descriptions of the upheaval of nature caused by the theophany, and is no mere coincidence here. Rather, it is an intentional reference to the parting of the Reed Sea, a reference completed in the psalm's concluding verses: "Your way was through the sea, Your path, through the mighty waters; Your tracks could not be seen. You led Your people like a flock in the care of Moses and Aaron" (vv. 20-21). The psalmist has purposely refrained from stating simply that the LORD parted the waters of the sea for the benefit of the Israelites and that the latter subsequently passed through on dry land. At the same time he has succeeded in arousing the listener's recollection of this wondrous occasion upon which the LORD displayed to all nations His might. The author of Psalm 77 is thus the only biblical poet to have portrayed the parting of the sea indirectly. His sophisticated poetic artistry has enveloped this miraculous event in a cloud of mystery, as is particularly evident in the words "Your tracks could not be seen".

The passages cited combine to form a multicolored portrait of a tradition which tells of the parting of the sea but passes silently over the drowning of the Egyptians. Here and there the mythological motif of God's war with the sea appears intact, with all the features of the original myth still evident, but it is also discernible in passages where the mythological coloring has faded. An example of the latter is the statement of Rahab the harlot, in which the fact that the LORD dried up the Reed Sea for the Israelites is taken as proof that He is God in heaven above and on earth below. A similar instance of the mythological motifs' appearing in a somewhat obscured fashion is the didactic history in the book of Judith, where the parting of the sea is alluded to in the brief statement "their God dried up the Reed Sea for them" (5:13).

The aforegoing survey is sufficient grounds for calling into question the view that the defeat of the Egyptians is the core of the Reed Sea tradition, since the bold assertion that the tradition which speaks of the parting of the sea without mentioning the fate of the Egyptians is a later one can hardly be accepted. To this tradition, as we have seen, belong not only passages containing mythological depictions but also a number of passages in which, though the mythological aspect has been attenuated and the main emphasis has been placed on God's acts of deliverance, the Israelites' rescue from the Egyptians is still not mentioned. In light of this consideration, the weight of the evidence is shifted in favor of the opposite assumption, namely, that the original nucleus of the Reed Sea tradition is none other than the act of parting the sea itself.

C. The Association of God's Victory Over Egypt With His Victory Over the Sea

It is immediately to be added that the theory we have just advanced receives support from two biblical passages, both of which are of a composite nature. While both passages mention the fact that the Egyptians perished in the sea, they nevertheless preserve at one and the same time the tradition that the LORD vanquished not only the Egyptians but the sea itself as well. The first passage in which this tradition seems to be preserved is Ps 136:13-16, where "Who split apart the Sea of Reeds" etc. is followed by "and made Israel pass through it...Who hurled Pharaoh and his army into the Sea of Reeds". The other passage, where the motif of the LORD's victory over the sea is certainly present, is Ps 106:9-12. Here, "He rebuked the Sea of Reeds; it became dry; He led them through the deep as through a wilderness" is followed immediately by "He delivered them from the foe, redeemed them from the enemy. Water covered their adversaries; not one of them was left. Then they believed His promise, and sang His praises."

D. The Defeat of the Egyptians is not the Nucleus of the Reed Sea Tradition

The commonly held scholarly view, which negates any original connection between the parting of the sea and the LORD's battle with the sea, viewing instead the drowning of the Egyptians as the original nucleus of the story, is the result of the following three presuppositions:

(1) The Pentateuch contains no trace of the idea that the sea offered any resistance to the LORD's action.

(2) The J narrative, which is the earliest prose description of the parting of the sea, relates that the sea was torn by a wind from the LORD; that is, that the event had a natural, or at least quasi-natural cause. Only the later sources add the mythological motif of Moses' rod.

(3) The earliest literary source referring to the parting of the sea is the Song of Miriam (Exod 15:21), whose antiquity is proven by its brevity, and this source mentions the drowning of the Egyptians.

As we shall now proceed to demonstrate, however, the arguments based on all three of these assumptions fail to convince.

1. The Sea's Resistance Not Mentioned in the Pentateuch. Though it is indeed the case that the Pentateuch contains no reference to the sea's resistance, the assumption that the Pentateuch is evidence for the earliest tradition is easily impeached. The simple fact that the Pentateuch was uncomfortable with the more ancient tradition that God created His world by vanquishing the sea and the rivers is too obvious to be ignored. The Creation account in Genesis makes this especially apparent: the contrast between "God said: Let the water below the sky be gathered into one area, that the dry land may appear" (Gen 1:9) and the cosmogony in Ps 104:5-9 is clear enough indication of the reworking of mythological traditions carried out by the Pentateuch, the objective of which was without a doubt to eliminate the motif of God's struggle against the forces of nature. This Pentateuchal tendency has been discussed by Cassuto, who adduced as an instructive example the case of Gen 1:21 "God created the sea-monsters, and all the living creatures of every kind that creep".[18] Here we have an implied rejection of the myth of God's conflict with the sea-monsters, attested in passages such as "It was You...who smashed the heads of the sea-monsters in the waters" (Ps 74:13).[19]

With regard to cosmogonic traditions, scholars have long agreed that the accounts of mythological battles are more ancient than the Pentateuchal cosmogony, which depicts the forces of nature as subservient to their Creator and according to which any uprising on their part would be quite unimaginable. Hence it logically follows that the traditions concerning God's victory over the Reed Sea have undergone a theological adaptation, similar to that of the tradition of His primeval victory over the sea. To be sure, the Reed Sea tradition has not been reworked as thoroughly as the cosmogony, since the Pentateuch does not relate that the Reed Sea was parted at God's spoken command,[20] nor does it speak simply of the feat without describing the manner in which it was accomplished. Rather, the Pentateuch speaks unabashedly of God's use of the wind, and of Moses' use of a rod. Still, the recognition that the Reed Sea tradition has not been theologically reworked as extensively as the cosmogony does not alter the basic fact that the adaptation of the two traditions represents a single theological tendency: to avoid any account of the battle between God and the forces of nature.

This approach has enabled us to evaluate holistically the relation-

18 Op. cit. (above, note 11), p. 101.
19 Compare Isa 27:1; Job 7:12.
20 To be sure, even the notion of God's acting by means of speech alone has its roots in Near Eastern myth; see L. Dürr, *Die Wertung des göttlichen Wortes im Alten Testament und im Antiken Orient*, Leipzig 1938, pp. 1-180. In Israel, for obvious reasons, this motif did not encounter the same opposition as did the motif of the divine battle. The idea of God's being victorious in battle is to some extent a limitation on His power since, though He triumphs over His opponent, both He and His enemy meet on the same battlefield; God too must fight, and not merely issue a decree, in order to obtain His victory. The motif of God accomplishing His will by mere speech, on the other hand, attributes to Him unlimited supernatural power, immeasurably greater than that associated with a warrior who triumphs over his foe.

ship between the Pentateuchal traditions, which deny the existence of a struggle between God and nature, and the other sources, which admit that such a struggle took place. It also explains the similarity between the traditions concerning the parting of the sea and the splitting of the Jordan by providing them with a common background, namely, the divine victory over sea and rivers — precisely the motif which appears in the passages discussed above.

The scholarly reluctance to admit the antiquity of this tradition is to be explained in part by the fact that the miraculous nature of the splitting of the Jordan is less impressive than that of the parting of the Reed Sea. The difference, however, is understandable as the result of two factors. The first is that God's victory over Yam, the sea-god, is considerably more wondrous than His victory over Neharim, the river-god. This is reflected in the Ugaritic myth, where the Judge of the River is always mentioned after the Prince of the Sea, and finds expression in Midr. Teh. on Psalm 114, which asks why the Jordan "ran backward" (Ps 114:3) when the Reed Sea was parted, that is, long before the Israelites arrived at its banks, and replies, "Once the head of the army had fled, all of the army had to flee as well".[21] The second factor is the different ways in which the two traditions developed. Only the Reed Sea tradition includes the idea that by parting the waters God saved His people from their foes and destroyed the pursuing oppressor. Not only is the miracle itself, therefore, immeasurably greater in the case of the Reed Sea tradition, so too is the deliverance it brought about. These two factors, however, are of a secondary nature, and do not obscure the fact that both traditions have the same mythological background.

2. J's Supposed Naturalistic Description of the Parting of the Sea.
The argument advanced by scholars is that not only the J narrative but also the Song of the Sea in Exodus 15 depict the parting of the sea in naturalistic, or at least semi-naturalistic, terms, since they

---

21 The term used in the Midrash is ʾummānūt, = Akk. ummānāte "army"; see the remarks by J. Barth, *Etymologische Studien*, (= *Beilage zum Jahresbericht des Berliner Rabbiner-Seminars 1891-1892*), Berlin 1893, p. 61, on the Mishnaic reference to "brothers who were jointholders, one of whom is taken into public service" (m. B. Bat. 9:4).

speak of a "wind" of God as causing the waters to part. This argument is untenable on several grounds. First of all, the assumption that in J miracles are always performed by means of natural forces, employed by God for a certain purpose and at a particular time and place, runs into inescapable complications the moment the account of the slaying of the firstborn is considered. Here, this assumed policy of J is offset by another consideration: J's insistence that God acts alone, without the aid of angel or messenger. The Pentateuchal account leaves no room for doubt that the slaying of the firstborn was carried out by the LORD alone, and it is equally certain that this plague was not performed by means of any natural phenomenon. This alone is sufficient justification for rejecting the argument that the J narrative admits of no miracles other than those brought about through natural causes.

More important is the fact that the "wind of the LORD", which is said to have parted the sea in the Pentateuchal account, is itself an outgrowth of mythological tradition. Though this mythological element is not particularly prominent in the narrative statement that "the LORD drove back the sea with a strong east wind" (Exod 14:21), it is clearly perceptible, as has often been pointed out, in the poetic portrayal in the Song of the Sea: "At the blast of your nostrils the waters piled up" (15:8). Nor is this surprising, since the wind is a common manifestation of the warrior-god; the theophany in 2 Sam 22:14-16, with its evident similarity to the Reed Sea tradition, may be compared:

> The LORD thundered forth from heaven,
> The Most High sent forth His voice;
> He let loose bolts, and scattered them;
> Lightning, and put them to rout.
> The bed of the sea was exposed,
> The foundations of the world were laid bare
> By the mighty roaring of the LORD
> At the blast of the breath of His nostrils.

It should be added that winds are included among the attendants of Baal in the Ugaritic myth, and that they appear as the weapons of

Marduk in his battle against Tiamat in Enuma Eliš IV.96-100.[22] The parallel between the latter and the Reed Sea tradition has been rightly noted by Pedersen.[23]

The narrative portrayal of the parting of the sea being carried out by a blast of wind from the LORD is thus firmly rooted in the mythological tradition of the warrior-god. Moreover, the same is true with regard to the tradition that the sea was parted by Moses' rod. As we have argued at length in Chapter Four,[24] Moses' rod was originally the rod of none other than the LORD Himself, a staff bequeathed by God to His faithful servant to be used in the performance of his emissarial tasks. Assuming all this to be correct, it necessarily follows that the tradition that Moses divided the Reed Sea with his rod is no more than a transformation of the original tradition that God Himself did so with His rod. This tradition, and the closely related tradition that God parted the sea with a blast of His "wind", have their counterparts both in the Akkadian epic, where Marduk wages war against Tiamat with the aid of the winds and crushes her head with his rod (Enuma Eliš IV.130),[25] and in the Ugaritic epic, where Baal, Lord of the winds, smites the Prince of the Sea with his rods.[26]

In brief, both variants — the wind of the LORD and the rod of the LORD, evolved from the same mythological tradition; both winds and rods belong to the stock of traditional weapons used by the warrior-god in his battle against the sea.

3. The Evidence of the Song of Miriam. Scholars argue that the Song of Miriam (Exod 15:21) is the earliest source in which the parting of the sea is portrayed, and that this source speaks solely of the drowning of the Egyptians. However, since the text of Miriam's song is nothing more than a verbal repetition of the opening line of the Song of the Sea sung by Moses, the more likely conclusion is that this is intended to indicate that Miriam recited the Song in its entirety. This conclu-

22 For the Ugaritic material see Gordon, *op. cit.* (above, note 10), text 67, V, 1. 7 (p. 149; *ANET*², p. 139); for the Akkadian text see *ANET*², p. 67.
23 *Op. cit.* (Chapter Five, note 13), p. 729.
24 Above, pp. 147-154.
25 *ANET*², p. 67.
26 Gordon, *op. cit.* (above, note 10), text 137 (pp. 167-168; *ANET*², p. 131).

sion was reached long ago by Philo: "[the Hebrews] set up two choirs, one of men and one of women, on the beach, and sang hymns of thanksgiving to God" (VM I.xxxii, p. 109). It is echoed in Mek. Běšallaḥ 10: "'And Miriam responded to them' (Exod 15:21): This indicates that just as Moses recited the Song to the men, Miriam recited it to the women, saying 'Sing to the LORD' etc." This traditional interpretation accords fully with the biblical text, and it may well be that the critical scholar has nothing more to add to it. The most he can do is to suggest the possibility that there initially existed two traditions, one that the Song of the Sea was recited by Moses and the Israelites, the other that it was recited by Miriam and a choir of women, and that a redactor eventually combined the two traditions, noting that Miriam and the women actually repeated the Song which had been sung by Moses.

In addition to all of this, the brevity of the Song of Miriam is to begin with no proof at all of its antiquity. The one poetic passage in the Bible which is universally considered to be ancient is the Song of Deborah, which is not brief at all but quite lengthy. Nowhere in the Bible is there a poem whose form corresponds to what scholars assume to be the case with the Song of Miriam: an introductory "Sing" or "I shall sing" which is not followed by the appropriate sequel, that is, the elaboration of what is to be sung about. A Ugaritic text containing two poems, both opening with "I shall sing", one ten lines long and the other thirty-nine lines long,[27] provides additional confirmation. The assumption that the brevity of Miriam's Song is evidence for its antiquity is the result of arbitrary fragmentation of the Song and unfounded a priori judgments, not of the empirical study of ancient poetry.

27 *Ibid.*, text 77 (p. 153).

E. The Sources of the Pentateuchal Account of the Parting of the Sea

1. The Song of the Sea. (a) Date. Having established that there never existed a brief version of the Song, sung by Miriam, and that the one-line poem attributed to Miriam is simply an abbreviation for the entire Song, we must confine the critical inquiry to the question of the Song's date. Considerable scholarly controversy surrounds this issue. Although recent critics agree that the Song contains no features connecting it with Second Temple times, some would still place it as early as the period of the Judges, while others would assign it to the end of the United Monarchy or even to the end of the First Temple period. Lately there has been a revival of the attempt to dissect the Song into separate components and to assign each one to a different period.[28]

A *terminus a quo* for the Song is often suggested on the basis of v. 17: "The place You made to dwell in, O LORD, the sanctuary, O LORD, which Your hands established". Lauha even argued that these words are an indication of Deuteronomistic thought. Scholars who assign the Song to a more ancient period deny the reasoning behind this claim; Cassuto, for instance, viewed v. 17 as a reference to a *future* sanctuary,[29] whereas Cross and Freedman take it as a reference to God's celestial habitation. In light of these possible interpretations, it is evident that the mere mention of the word "sanctuary" is not suf-ficient proof of the Song's late date, and can only be considered as part of the contextual analysis of the Song in its entirety.

As has long been realized, this contextual analysis reveals that the author of the Song held the anachronistic view that the Philistines dwelled in Canaan at the time of the Exodus, whereas in actual fact they did not settle there before the twelfth century B.C.E. This is only

---

28 Mention may be made of the following studies of the Song: Lauha, *op. cit.* (above, note 3), pp. 61-64; W. F. Albright, *op. cit.* (Chapter Four, note 106), pp. 3-5; F. M. Cross-D. N. Freedman, "The Song of Miriam", *JNES*, 14 (1955), pp. 237-250; J. D. W. Watts, "The Song of the Sea — Ex. XV", *VT*, 7 (1957), pp. 371-380; S. Mowinckel, *op. cit.* (above, note 9), pp. 26-28; Rozelaar, *op. cit.* (above, note 3), pp. 221-228.

29 Commentary on Exodus (see Chapter Four, note 36), p. 177.

one part of a thoroughly anachronistic picture, since the Song (Exod 15:13-16) also places the Conquest of Canaan immediately after the Exodus and the crossing of the sea, never pausing to refer to any of the vicissitudes faced by Israel in the wilderness. More importantly, the Conquest is portrayed as a miraculous event, parallel to the parting of the sea itself. The Israelites are depicted as making their way safely through the midst of the Canaanite peoples (including the Edomites!), all of whom are stunned into silent trembling, just as they had made their way safely through the Reed Sea on dry land as the waters stood still. The inhabitants of Canaan are "still as stone" (v. 16), just as the Egyptians "sank like lead in the majestic waters" (v. 10). God's guidance of His people to His holy abode (v. 13) is none other than a repetition of the miracle of the crossing of the sea.

The LORD's victory over the Egyptians is not presented in the Song for its own sake; rather it is the prototype of the subsequent victories bestowed by God upon His people when they conquered their land. The only possible light in which to view this portrayal of the Conquest of Canaan is the Davidic conquests; it is their echo which can be heard in the triumphant shout of the Song. It follows ineluctably that the Sanctuary whose establishment is referred to in v. 17 is the triumphal climax of David's victories, and must therefore be none other than Solomon's Temple, the construction of which was considered to be the crowning achievement of the new era authored by David.

These considerations clear the way for an appreciation of the Song's literary integrity. The entire Song is a hymn celebrating the establishment of the LORD's reign as King. It appropriately opens with the parting of the sea, since this is the paradigm of divine might and had served as a basis for divine kingship even in ancient mythological tradition. The other events described in the Song proceed directly from the parting of the sea: hearing of the miraculous deliverance of the Israelites, the Canaanites were terrified; thus not only the Egyptians but the Canaanites as well were paralyzed by one and the same event. The Conquest has ceased to be an independent historical episode and has become a consequence of the miracle performed at the Reed Sea. The climax of this Conquest, for its part, is the building of the Temple, which signifies the final stage in the establishment of the LORD's kingship on earth, since kingship is not complete without a royal palace. To ask why this Song opens with the miracle at the sea and proceeds to speak of events only tenuously connected with it is to ignore the artistic logic of the poem, which incorporates separate events, from the parting of the sea until the building of the Temple, viewing them as a continuous, unified process by which God's earthly reign was established.

We may therefore assert with some confidence that the Song of the Sea reflects the enthusiastic optimism of the latter days of the United Monarchy.[30] The claims of those who would assign the poem to a later period are not convincing. No trace of the Deuteronomic outlook can be detected in a passage which portrays the parting of the sea as the first in an unbroken chain of victories leading directly to the building of the Temple, and there is no linguistic affinity between the Song and Deuteronomistic phraseology. Nor is there any substance to the reasoning advanced for placing the Song's composition in the time of the Judges, such as the argument adduced by Cross and Freedman that the Song contains no mention of Ammon. Why Moab is mentioned and Ammon is not cannot be established with certainty, but it does bear mentioning that the itinerary of Num 33:40-49 speaks specifically of Edom and Moab without any reference to Ammon. It would appear that an earlier tradition that the Israelites merely attempted to traverse the territories of Edom and Moab has evolved into a secondary tradition that they actually did so, and this later tradition may have left its mark on the Song of the Sea. There is no known tradition of any attempt by Israel to pass through the land of Ammon. As for Albright's claim that the similarities between the Song and the Ugaritic literature, which extend to matters of syntax as well as idiom, we would point out that the Canaanite literary tradition, as rightly stressed by Mowinckel, remained alive in Israel for many centuries.

(b) The Parting of the Waters as the Nucleus of the Song's Tradition. The Song ends with the words "The LORD will reign for ever and

---

30 This has also been argued by M. Weinfeld, *op. cit.* (Chapter Five, note 41), p. 11, where additional literature is cited.

ever!" (Exod 15:18) — meaning, of course, that He will reign forever in the Sanctuary He has established on Mount Zion. No more fitting prelude to this hymnodic account of the process culminating in the establishment of God's kingly abode than the parting of the sea could possibly be suggested. This event, a display of strength reminiscent of that employed in Creation, succeeded in humbling mighty Egypt and struck terror into the hearts of all the inhabitants of Canaan, the land where He was to establish His abode. This explains the Song's shift in emphasis, from the actual parting of the waters to the death of the Egyptians. For this poem, it is not merely the fact that at a blast of His nostrils the waters piled up in a heap and stood straight like a wall (v. 8) — alluding to the safe passage of the Israelites through the sea — that is worthy of special attention. Rather, it is the even more marvelous fact that at the same time God's blast of wind sank the pursuer in the majestic waters: "I will sing to the LORD, for He has triumphed gloriously; *horse and driver He has hurled into the sea*" (v. 1).

Yet despite this particular emphasis placed on the destruction of the Egyptians in the Song, an emphasis which stems from the Song's literary and historical context, it would still appear that the original miracle is simply the parting of the waters. Psalm 78 provides clear evidence that this is indeed the more ancient belief. Here, the destruction of the Egyptians is alluded to in the words "He led them to safety; they were unafraid; as for their enemies, the sea covered them", which occur late in the psalm (v. 53), whereas the distinction "marvels" is reserved for the actual parting of the sea: "He performed marvels in the sight of their fathers, in the land of Egypt, the plain of Zoan. He split the sea and took them through it; He made the waters stand like a wall" (vv. 12-13).

Consideration of the matter from another viewpoint will lead us to the same conclusion. The final words of the Song, "The LORD will reign for ever and ever", are based on all that precede them, but they are most specifically the logical conclusion to the Song's account of the parting of the sea and of the building of the Temple. The latter's connection with the establishment of the LORD's "reign" is self-evident. Yet the former too would seem to be a necessary prelude to the theme of kingship. For the prose account of the Reed Sea episode ends in a manner similar to the poetic passage, in the words "When Israel saw the wondrous power which the LORD had wielded against the Egyptians, the people feared the LORD; they had faith in the LORD and His servant Moses" (Exod 14:31). "Faith" in the LORD is none other than the belief in His rule; the rational, theological concept of "faith" corresponds to the mythological concept of the submission to "kingship". And although the scope of events upon which the Israel-ites' "faith in the LORD" is based is narrower in the prose account than in the Song, the prose account does include both the parting of the sea and the destruction of the Egyptians.

And here too we are justified in asserting that the basis for the acceptance of the LORD's kingship, or, in other words, the basis for "faith in the LORD", has been broadened by later tradition. As noted above,[31] Isa 63:12 voices the belief that the parting of the waters alone was sufficient grounds for the LORD to achieve "an everlasting name", and the book of Joshua (2:11; 4:21-24; 5:1) posits that the parting of the Reed Sea and the division of the Jordan succeeded in striking terror into the hearts of foreign nations. Therefore, though the king-ship of God as reflected in human belief is grounded in some passages on the parting of the sea alone, in others on the drowning of the Egyp-tians as well, and in one — the Song of the Sea — on a long series of later historical episodes including the building of the Temple, the core is always the same common feature: the parting of the sea.

The Midrash, commenting on the daily liturgy, made the point quite aptly: "Why must mention of the parting of the Reed Sea be included in the benediction following the recitation of the Shema (which is recited as a formal declaration of the acceptance of God's rule)? Because Israel believed in the LORD after He split the sea for them, as it is written: '...they had faith in the LORD and His servant Moses' (Exod 14:31)" (Exod. Rab. Běšallah 22:3). It is to be noted that, in addition to the belief in the LORD, the belief in His servant Moses too is grounded upon the parting of the Reed Sea.

(c) Mythological Strains in the Song. In light of all that has been

31 See p. 240.

said, it is no wonder that the mythological background of the Song
has also left its mark on its linguistic features. The only scholar to
have studied the language of the Song from this viewpoint is
Cassuto,[32] who began by noting that the words *gāʾō gāʾā* ("triumphed
gloriously") in v. 1 seem to imply that though the sea "swelled" (*gāʾā*;
see Ps 87:10; compare 46:4 and Job 38:11), the LORD rose even
higher, exceeding the surging of the sea. Cassuto further suggested
that the expressions *sūs wĕrōkĕbō* ("horse and driver") in the same
verse and *markĕbōt parʿō* ("Pharaoh's chariots") in v. 4 have replaced
the horses and chariots of the warrior god (see Hab 3:8 and Enuma
Eliš IV.50-55). He also compared *ʿozzī* ("my strength") in v. 2 with
Isa 51:9 and Ps 89:11,14, and *yĕšūʿā* ("deliverance") in the same
verse with the parallel usage in Hab 3:8; he further viewed the portrayal of the LORD as an *ʾīš milḥāmā* ("warrior") in v. 3 as corresponding to God's mythological depiction.

Cassuto pointed out the same feature in such expressions as
tĕhōmōt ("the deeps") in v. 5, which appears in a clearly mythological
context in Isa 51:10, Hab 3:10, and Ps 77:17, and *mĕṣūlōt* ("the
depths") in the same verse, the similar backgound of which is attested
in Isa 44:27 and Zech 10:11. He also compared the LORD's "right
hand" in v. 6 with Ps 89:14 (which is the sequel of v. 11), and associated the expression *neʾdārī bakkōaḥ* ("majestic in power") in the same
verse with *mayīm ʾaddīrīm* ("majestic" waters) in v. 10 — the idea
being that the LORD is even more "majestic" than the "majestic"
waters, as stated explicitly in Ps 93:4: "more majestic than the break-
ers of the sea is the LORD, majestic on high". To the "blast of Your
nostrils" (*rūaḥ ʾappekā*) in v. 8, Cassuto compared the "blast" and
"raging of His nostrils" in the mythological battles described in 2 Sam
22:16 (*rūaḥ ʾappō*), Hab 3:8 and Job 9:13 ([*ḥārā*] *ʾappō*), and with
the waters, which in the same verse are said to have stood as still as
a wall (*nēd*), he associated God's cosmogonic power when he "heaps
up the ocean waters like a wall (*nēd*)" (Ps 33:7).[33] The mythological

32 *Op. cit.* (above, note 11), 99-101.
33 Cassuto's interpretation implies his rejection of the reading *nōʾd* found in the Versions for MT *nēd*.

character of the expression *pele⁾* (v. 11), clear from Pss 77:12, 89:6, and Job 37:5, as is the connection between the verbs *ḥyl* and *rgz* in v. 14 and passages in Jer 5:22, Hab 3:10, Ps 77:19. The connection between the mention of God's "arm" (v. 16) and the divine arm mentioned in Isa 51:9 and Ps 89:11,14 was also adduced by Cassuto, who concluded by noting that the declaration "the LORD will reign", with which the poem ends, is to be viewed in connection with the tradition that God ascended His throne after having subdued the forces of the sea (Pss 29 and 93:1).

Not all of the passages cited by Cassuto are of equal weight. It could be pointed out that the image of God's "raging nostrils" is associated not only with His anger at the sea but also, in innumerable references, with His wrath at men, and that the image of God's "arm" is not restricted to passages connected with the parting of the sea; similar reservations could be voiced about other texts. Moreover, a more general objection could be levelled against Cassuto's entire theory, namely, that the very fact that the Song speaks of the LORD's defeat of the Egyptians is enough to explain the use of many of the above expressions — even though they themselves may have originated in the warrior-god tradition. All of this notwithstanding, however, the large concentration of linguistic usages found in passages depicting the LORD's battle with the sea, along with other expressions of a more particular nature, such as "depths", "majestic waters", and "the deeps", and especially the concluding reference to the establishment of God's sanctuary and His reign, all attest to a connection between the Song of the Sea and the mythological tradition too close to be fortuitous.[34] In view of our earlier discussion, we may go beyond Cassuto's suggestion, and postulate further that the connection between the Song and the myth is not only linguistic but also thematic, that is, that the Song itself evolved from an earlier version of the tradition, one in which the sea resisted being parted.

2. The Prose Narrative. Unlike the Song, which enumerates a series of events commencing with the parting of the sea, the narrative account in Exodus 14 is confined to this event alone. For this reason,

---

34 *Ibid.*, p. 101.

no historical perspective which might enable us to fix the date of the prose narrative can be discerned. As discussed above, however, the nucleus of the account is the fact that the waters were parted, and this served as the primary event upon which the belief in God and in His servant Moses, which corresponds to the acceptance of God's kingship in the poetic account, was founded. As we have also established the mythological background of the twin motifs of God's rod and His wind, it remains only to complete the picture along these lines.

Turning first to the divine "wind", it was sensed long ago by the Midrash that the specific mention of an east wind in Exod 14:21 is not merely incidental. Rather, as pointed out in Mek. Běšallaḥ 4, the east wind appears here because it is one of the LORD's traditional weapons, as evidenced by Jer 18:17 "Like the east wind, I will scatter them", Ps 48:8 "You will shatter the Tarshish fleet with an east wind", Hos 13:15, where the east wind is called "the wind of the LORD", and Isa 27:8, which speaks of God's waging war "with His pitiless blast on a day of east wind". The Midrash then asserts that the "blast of God" and the "breath of His nostrils" mentioned in Isa 27:8 and Job 4:9 are none other than the east wind, and deduces further, on the basis of Jer 18:17, that the word "scatter" in Gen 11:8 also implies that God made use of an east wind to disperse the builders of the Tower. Whether or not we accept the interpretation offered by the Midrash for those passages which do not specifically mention an east wind, the fact remains that Israel's mythological tradition attached greater importance to the wind coming out of the east than to any other.

The words used in the prose account for "dry ground", *yabbāšā* (Exod 14:16,22,29), and especially *ḥārābā* (v. 21; see also Josh 3:17; 4:18; 2 Kgs 2:8) would also have recalled the mythological tradition to those familiar with it, since, although these words are not actually used in any of the texts possessing mythological overtones, the two sets of verbs *yābaš/hōbīš* and *ḥārab/hĕḥerīb*, which occur occasionally in parallelism, feature prominently in these texts.[35] This is so

---

35 For *ḥrb* see Isa 44:27; 50:2; 51:10; Nah 1:4; Ps 106:9; compare Isa 19:5; 37:25; Job 14:11. For *ybš* see Isa 44:27; Nah 1:4; Zech 10:11; Ps 74:15 and compare Isa 19:5; Job 12:15; 14:11.

despite the fact that the mythological strains in Ezek 30:12 "I will turn the channels into dry land (*ḥārābā*)" and in Ps 66:6 "He turned the sea (referring to to the parting of the Reed Sea) into dry land *yabbāšā*" are somewhat faint.

Another trace of the mythological tradition may perhaps be discerned in the words "the waters were split" (*wayyibbāqěʿū*) in Exod 14:21. To be sure, it is not certain that the verb *bqᶜ* was employed in ancient Israelite epic poetry to refer to the parting of the waters and their transformation into dry land.[36] But the following points should be borne in mind: (1) Gen 7:11 indicates conclusively that the verb *bqᶜ* was used by Israelite epic poetry, although in a different sense; (2) this verb also denotes the slashing of a body in two, as in the Ugaritic *bhrb tbqᶜnn;*[37] (3) biblical references to the parting of the sea which are independent of the Pentateuchal account also use the verb *bqᶜ;* here we would include Ps 78:13 "He split (*bāqaᶜ*) the sea and took them through it", whose independence of the Pentateuchal narrative has been demonstrated above,[38] thus enabling us to posit a common poetic source for both the Pentateuch and the Psalm, and Isa 63:12 "Who divided (*bōqēᵃᶜ*) the waters before them", whose independence of the Pentateuchal narrative requires no proof; (d) the Midrash

---

36 Though Cassuto, *op. cit.* (Chapter Four, note 105), p. 12 believed that in a few passages this is indeed the case, all his examples are doubtful. "By His knowledge the depths split apart (*nibqāᶜū*)" (Prov 3:20) may indeed be interpreted to mean that God dried up the watery depths, but the second hemistich "and the skies distilled dew" does not confirm this reading; compare "All the fountains of the great deep split apart (*nibqěʿū*), and the floodgates of the sky broke open" in Gen 7:11. It is more probable that the verse speaks of God as providing water for the earth from streams and fountains rising from the deep, and dew from the skies. The parallelism in "It was You who split (*bāqaᶜtā*) springs and torrents, who made mighty rivers run dry" (Ps 74:15) would seem to support Cassuto's view, but since there is still no evidence that drying up springs and torrents is counted among the LORD's mighty acts in the same sense that drying up the rivers is so considered, some uncertainty remains. Cassuto's interpretation of Hab 3:9, which he reads as "The rivers (that is, the spirit who personifies the rivers) Thou didst shatter (*tēbaqqaᶜ*) upon the ground", is particularly attractive. The suggestion is based on Ugaritic text 68, ll. 22-23 (Gordon, *loc. cit.* [above, note 10]; *ANET*[2], p. 131), where the defeated Prince of the Sea and Judge of the River fall to the ground, but it nevertheless remains no more than a fascinating conjecture.

37 *Ibid.,* text 49, II, ll. 31-32 (p. 138; *ANET*[2], p. 140); see also Ezek 29:7; Amos 1:13.

38 Above, pp. 71-79.

deduces from the words "the waters were split (*wayyibbāqĕʿū*)" that "all the waters in the world, the waters above and the waters beneath" were split (Mek. Bĕšallaḥ 4). This surprising assertion, which lacks all foundation in the literal sense of the biblical text, goes so far beyond the historical account of the Pentateuch that it is safe to assume that it harks back to the original intent of the phrase, which presumably was used in connection with the LORD's cosmogonic power.

F. The Course of Events in the Pentateuchal Sources

We may now proceed from the discussion of the tradition itself to the detailed analysis of the Pentateuchal sources which relate how the waters of the Reed Sea were parted.

1. The Song. The course of events described in the Song of the Sea is internally consistent. Just as a blast of God's breath divided the waters, at which they "piled up" and "stood straight like a wall", and "the depths froze in the heart of the sea" (v. 8), so did the process reverse itself: "You blew with Your wind, the sea covered them; they sank like lead in the majestic waters" (v. 10). The waters do not simply re-converge; a second act on the part of the LORD, an *actus contrarius*, the counterpart of the initial act by which they were divided, is necessary to re-unite them. This feature of the poetic account is the result of the Song's overall aim of representing the drowning of the Egyptians as God's victory over them, an aim which cannot be achieved unless the victory itself is accomplished by means of a divine act performed for this specific purpose.[39] From the

---

39 The words "You put out Your right hand, the earth swallowed them" (v. 12) also allude to the drowning of the Egyptians in the re-converging waters. The Midrash was uneasy with this verse, construing it as a contradiction to the previous verses which depicted the Egyptians as being swallowed by the sea and not by the earth; see Y. Komlós, "A Fragment from the Targum Yerushalmi to the Song of Moses", *Sefer Seidel*, Jerusalem 1962, pp. 7-11 (Hebrew) and literature cited. The same issue is raised by modern commentators; see Heinisch, *op. cit.* (Chapter Five, note 30), p. 126, who believes that the Song's description of the parting of the sea is concluded in v. 11 and that the account of subsequent events opens in v. 12 with an occurrence similar in nature to the drowning of the Egyptians, namely, the death of Dathan and Abiram (who were swallowed by the earth). Lauha, *op. cit.* (above, note 3), p. 89 refrains from deciding whether the verse comprises an oblique refer-

tradition-history standpoint, however, the motif of the *actus contrarius* would seem to be secondary, just as it is in Artapanus' account of the plagues, discussed above,[40] where Moses is said to have smitten the Nile twice — once in order for it to flood its banks, and again to return it to its channel. Further evidence of the secondary character of this feature is the account of the division of the Jordan in Joshua, where the waters re-converge spontaneously.

2. *The Prose Account.* Because the prose narrative of the parting of the sea is apparently an amalgamation of several versions of the story, it is considerably more complex than the poetic account. Obviously, no certain reconstruction of the process by which the poetic text evolved can be obtained, since the text combines three separate elements: the LORD's "wind", Moses' rod, and the pillar of cloud and fire. But of these three, the first two may be functionally distinguished from the third: the first two are naturally suited to be employed in

---

ence to the death of Dathan and Abiram or a stylized reference to the Reed Sea event. Watts too (*op. cit.*, [above, note 28], p. 374) appears to be equally uncertain; his noncommittal formulation asserts that the verse was originally intended as a reference to the Korah rebellion and was later combined with the account of the defeat of Pharaoh at the sea. Nonetheless, there is certainly no place for any comment on the death of Dathan and Abiram in this description of the parting of the sea and Israel's subsequent victorious campaign of conquest; the verse refers exclusively to the drowning of the Egyptians. To be sure, the poet has in fact already concluded this section of the poem in v. 11, but before moving on from the sad fate of the Egyptians to the dazzling destiny of Israel, he once more recapitulates what has preceded. The resumption leads into the transition: thus did the Egyptians perish, while "in Your love You led the people You redeemed" (v. 13). The seemingly anomalous statement that "the earth" swallowed the Egyptians has been explained by some in accord with Ps 148:7 "Praise the LORD from the earth, all sea monsters and ocean depths", i.e., "earth" is taken to be a general term incorporating the sea as well. Preferable, however, is Gunkel's suggestion (*op. cit.* [above, note 6], p. 18) that "earth" here means the netherworld, an interpretation for which he adduced the evidence of Isa 14:12; 29:4; 44:23; Ezek 26:20; 31:18; 32:18,24; Qoh 3:21 and the similar use of the Aramaic ʾarʿā in the Targumim. The primary meaning of Hebrew ʾereṣ, as correctly stated by Gunkel, is "that which is underneath", a concept which, when used in contrast to the heavens, encompasses both the face of the earth and its interior. As further pointed out by Cassuto ("Biblical and Canaanite Literatures" [1941-1943], in U. Cassuto, *Biblical and Oriental Studies*, II, trans. by I. Abrahams, Jerusalem 1975, p. 35 n. 36), Ugaritic ʾars and Akkadian erṣitu function in this same double sense; see *CAD*, E, p. 210.

40 See p. 125.

the actual parting of the waters and in the *actus contrarius* of their reunification, whereas the third, the firecloud, is assigned two other tasks, which differ not only from the above but also from each other. First, it acts as a partition, keeping the Egyptian and Israelite camps apart so that Pharaoh's speedy chariots do not succeed in overtaking the marching Israelites; in this the firecloud alternates with God's angel. Second, it causes the Egyptians to panic and flee.[41]

Omitting for the moment the auxiliary function of the firecloud, that of keeping the two camps at a distance from each other, we are left with the following portrayal of the actual parting of the waters:

> "...And you lift up your rod and hold out your arm over the sea and split it, so that the Israelites may march into the sea on dry ground."...So Moses held out his arm over the sea and the LORD drove back the sea with a strong east wind all that night, and turned the sea into dry ground. The waters were split, and the Israelites went into the sea on dry ground, the waters forming a wall for them on their right and on their left.
>
> (Exod 14:16,21-22)

Here, the parting of the waters by means of Moses' rod has been transformed into a stage merely preparing the way for the divine action, in a manner similar to what is related of the arrival of the hail (Exod 9:22-23) and especially reminiscent of the plague of locusts:

---

41 An exhaustive study of the firecloud would require a comprehensive treatment of the wilderness traditions, and this lies beyond the scope of the present discussion. For attempts to find some basis for the firecloud tradition in some natural phenomena, see Gressmann, *op. cit.* (Chapter Two, note 1), pp. 112f., and especially C. S. Jarvis, *Yesterday and Today in Sinai*, Edinburgh and London 1933, p. 179. The idea of God appearing in fire and cloud presents no difficulty at all, nor does the idea that God threw the Egyptians into a panic by looking down upon them from His pillar of cloud and fire. It is rather the fact that this momentary theophany has been transformed into a permanent manifestation of His presence, materialized in the form of the firecloud by means of which He leads the Israelites through the wilderness, which is problematic. The motif of the cloud serving to keep the warring armies apart, though it is employed only in the Reed Sea narrative and is without parallel in the Bible, also becomes fully intelligible once it is realized that the cloud signifies the LORD's protective care of His people throughout their wanderings.

The LORD said to Moses, "Hold out your arm over the land of Egypt for the locusts, that they may come upon the land of Egypt"...So Moses held out his rod over the land of Egypt, and the LORD drove an east wind over the land all that day and all night; and when morning came, the east wind had brought the locusts.

(Exod 10:12-13)

The question whether this amalgamation of two fundamentally distinct motifs ought to be regarded as the work of a redactor whose intent was merely to preserve two traditions, or whether it may be evidence for a peculiar theological viewpoint, has been discussed above.[42] In any case the originally independent character of the motif of Moses' rod alone being used to part the waters is clearly evident here, since the command to Moses (v. 16) does not simply say "Hold out your arm over the sea" but rather includes the explicit order "and split it". In fact, as we shall see below,[43] a number of sources, beginning with Isa 63:12 and culminating in the Midrash, preserve the tradition that Moses parted the waters with his rod.[44] The accepted critical view which distinguishes between two traditions — the one, that the waters were parted by Moses' rod while a divine emissary kept the two camps apart; the other, that the LORD Himself both parted the waters (with His breath) and kept the camps a distance from each other (by means of the firecloud) — may thus be upheld. At the same time it may be admitted that variants can be discerned within the firecloud tradition itself. Exod 14:19b-20 reads as follows:

...the pillar of cloud shifted from in front of them and took up a place behind them, and it came between the army of the Egyp-

---

42 See pp. 130-134.
43 Section III.
44 Galbiati (*op. cit.* [above, note 5], p. 161) attempts to obscure this issue by claiming that "Moses' gesture...is not conceived of as a magical act; Moses gives the signal, apparently for the people, tangibly proclaiming to them the advent of divine, supernatural intervention, which, in response to the signal, then arrives in the form of an extraordinary south wind". It goes without saying that this explanation ignores both the plain sense of the text and its tradition-history.

tians and the army of Israel. Thus there was the cloud with the darkness, and it lit up[45] the night.

Now, whereas the words "Thus there was the cloud with the darkness" are consistent with Josh 24:7 ("He put darkness between you and the Egyptians"), the words "and it lit up the night" are associated with the earlier notice that "the LORD went before them in a pillar of cloud by day, to guide them along the way, and in a pillar of fire by night, to give them light" (Exod 13:21).

In contrast with this account of the passage of the Israelites through the parted waters, the analysis of which, despite the few difficulties encountered, is still relatively straightforward, the account of the Egyptians' demise presents us with an inconsistency. In order for the drowning of the Egyptian army to be parallel to the earlier part of the narrative, the LORD would at some point have to command Moses once again to hold out his arm with his rod over the sea, which would cause the "wind from God" to blow once more, returning the waters to their former condition and thereby drowning the Egyptians. Instead of this, the text relates that "at the morning watch, the LORD looked down upon the Egyptian army from a pillar of fire and cloud, and threw the Egyptian army into panic", and that "He locked the wheels of their chariots" so that they fled in dismay (Exod 14:24-25). Only then did God order Moses once more to stretch forth his arm, presumably with rod in hand, and this act alone re-unites the parted waters, thereby drowning the Egyptians as they flee (vv. 26-28).

45 Tg. Onqelos renders here "Thus there was cloud and darkness for the Egyptians, while the Israelites had light the whole night". More elaborately, Tg. Yer. II reads "Thus there was a cloud; half light and half darkness: the light shone upon the Israelites, and the darkness enveloped the Egyptians". This midrashic notion is without basis in the narrative, however, and should not be considered as an actual tradition but merely as an attempt to alleviate a textual problem. More recently E. A. Speiser, "An Angelic 'Curse' in Exodus 14:20", *JAOS*, 80 (1960), pp. 198-200, has proposed rendering "and it cast a spell upon the night", taking *wayyāʾer* as Hiphʿil of *ʾrr* "curse". Proceeding to explain his rationale, Speiser writes "The celestial barrier made the resulting darkness so thick that the two camps were effectively sealed off from each other. To the Egyptians it was black magic. But for the Israelites it was benign and protective intervention". The idea that the cloud "cursed" the night is too extravagant, however; it was against the Egyptians, and not the night, that the action of the cloud was directed.

As generally agreed by scholars, the implication would seem to be that one of the traditions which preceded the final text recounted this episode according to the *actus contrarius* pattern, whereby the waters were both parted and restored by Moses' rod. Only the latter half of this tradition has been preserved intact; of the former half only traces may be discerned, but these make the restoration quite certain. Much less certain is any attempt to reconstruct the original context of the alternate tradition of the pillar of cloud and fire that threw the Egyptians into panic and caused them to flee. Only with some hesitation can we accept the prevailing view, that from the outset this firecloud tradition diverged from the *actus contrarius* pattern and related that the "wind from God" only parted the waters, after which, at the morning watch, the pillar of cloud and fire, which had separated the two armies, caused the Egyptians to flee, whereupon they drowned in the waters which were meanwhile re-converging of their own accord. Though this assumed tradition placed stress upon the firecloud, symbol of God's immanence and providence, it too maintained that a specific and deliberate divine act brought about the demise of the Egyptians. At the same time it regarded this very act as having been put into effect by the firecloud, which both caused the Egyptians to flee and also retarded their progress, so that when, in the morning, the LORD's wind subsided and the parting of the waters ceased, they sank into the sea.

Three separate traditions regarding the parting of the sea and the drowning of the Egyptians therein should thus be distinguished: (1) A blast of wind from the LORD divided the waters, and His firecloud separated the armies, terrified the Egyptians and put them to flight in the morning, whereupon they were drowned in the spontaneously re-converging waters. (2) The *actus contrarius* pattern: a blast of wind from the LORD parted the waters and re-united them. (3) Another version of the *actus contrarius* pattern: Moses parted the sea and re-united it with his rod. As later elaborated upon, this final tradition also maintained that an angel of God meanwhile kept the two armies apart.[46]

46 As already noted, the results of our analysis overlap to a considerable extent the findings of classical source criticism; see, for instance, H. Holzinger, *Exodus*,

III. The Extra-biblical Tradition[47]

A. Artapanus

Turning to the post-biblical sources, we find that Artapanus contains two separate traditions concerning the parting of the sea. One, he relates, was current among the Jews of Memphis; the other in the community at Heliopolis.

"The Memphites say that Moses was familiar with the countryside and watched for the ebb tide and he conveyed the multitude across through the dry sea" (Eusebius IX:27, 35). This tradition, which, it should be noted, makes no mention of the fate of the Egyptians,

Tübingen 1900, p. 44, whose reconstruction of the J account closely resembles our tradition (2) above, particularly in the fact that, in his view, J speaks of the waters as spontaneously re-converging. The only real difference between our analysis and the classical one concerns the words "the waters forming a wall for them on their right and on their left" (Exod 14:22), which Holzinger fails to assign to J. His position is understandable in light of the source-critical assumption, refuted above, that J invariably treats miracles as taking place by means of natural phenomena. Here too, the unprejudiced reader will admit, the theological bias of the critic interferes with his analysis. The words "the waters forming a wall" etc. are in full accord with the Song's poetic depiction "At the blast of Your nostrils the waters piled up, the floods stood straight like a wall" (Exod 15:8), and this is incontrovertible evidence for the existence of a tradition according to which the divine wind caused the waters to pile up like a wall. In principle it is immaterial whether the Song too imagines two walls, between which the Israelites passed, or whether perhaps it pictures the waters piled up as a wall to one side only; there can still be no denying that the tradition of God's "wind" envisions the waters as forming a wall.

Mention may be made of an attempt by J. R. Towers, "The Red Sea", *JNES*, 18 (1959), pp. 150-153, to find in the biblical narrative traces of the Egyptian myth according to which the soul of the deceased is purified in the Reed Sea before ascending to heaven. Towers reasoned that just as the Egyptian dead were obligated to perform this ritual of purification before ascending to heaven, so were the Israelites required to undergo a similar purification before embarking on a new stage in their national existence. While we are unable to evaluate the Egyptian texts upon which Towers relied, we may state categorically that his suggestion has no basis whatsoever in Israelite tradition. Not only is the notion that crossing the sea could have purified the Israelites from the defilement of Egypt nowhere even intimated at in the Bible, it cannot even be ventured as a conjecture, since Israelite tradition is unanimous in its agreement that the Israelites crossed the Reed Sea on dry land and therefore could not possibly have been cleansed by its waters!

47 For the bibliographical references pertaining to the extra-biblical sources, see Chapter Four, notes 1-5.

is a clear reflection of the enlightened Hellenistic rationalism of Memphis, with its refusal to believe in wonders and its determined search for naturalistic explanations for the miraculous. Such heretical views, needless to say, are unprecedented and utterly without foundation in earlier tradition.

The Jews of Heliopolis, on the other hand, say "that the king rushed down with a great force" upon the Israelites, who were in possession of the property they had appropriated from the Egyptians, "but a divine voice came to Moses to strike the sea with his rod and divide it. When Moses heard, he touched the water with the rod and thus the flowing water separated and the host went through a dry path" (35-36). This Heliopolitan tradition, which preserves the ancient motif of Moses' parting the waters with his rod, speaks of the drowning of the Egyptians as well: "When the Egyptians went in with them and pursued, fire shone out from in front of them and the sea again flooded the path. All the Egyptians were destroyed by both the fire and the flood" (37).

Though the appearance of a fire confronting the Egyptians accords with the Pentateuchal account of the firecloud by means of which God looked out upon the two armies, namely, in front of the Egyptian camp, the notice that the Egyptians also perished by this fire as well as by the swelling waves is somewhat cryptic. As formulated, Artapanus' words may be interpreted to mean that some Egyptians perished by fire, others by water; however, since this is unattested elsewhere it is more likely that the intent is simply to say that in the course of fleeing from the fire they perished in the sea.

As no explanation is given as to how the waters re-converged, the implication would seem to be that they did so of their own accord. In this regard Artapanus resembles the ancient tradition whose existence was posited above: namely, that the Egyptians, escaping the LORD's firecloud, drowned in the spontaneously reconverging waters. The absence of the "wind" motif is a pronounced deviation from the Pentateuchal tradition, while the absence of the secondary motif of the separation of the two camps by means of the firecloud is not so remarkable, and may indeed simply be a function of Artapanus' laconic style.

B. Ezekiel the Tragedian

Our interpretation of the brief notice found in Artapanus is supported
by the lengthier account of Ezekiel the Tragedian which, despite its
similarities to Artapanus, mentions the firecloud which kept the two
armies apart. Following his description of the Egyptians' approach,
Ezekiel relates:

> And thereupon commenced divine portents
> full wondrous to behold! And, all at once,
> a mighty column stood, of cloud and fire,
> midway between the Hebrew camp and ours.
> And then their leader, Moses, taking up
> the rod of God by which he'd lately wrought
> such evil signs and ills on Egypt's land,
> did smite the Red Sea's surface, and the depth
> was rent asunder, so they as one
> with haste went forth along that briny path.
> We quickly sped along in that same route,
> foll'wing their track; by night we entered in,
> in close pursuit with shout; then all at once,
> as if with chains our chariot wheels were bound.[48]
> From heaven, then, a shining light like fire
> appeared to us, so we were led to think
> that God was their defense. For when they reached
> the farther shore a mighty wave gushed forth
> hard by us, so that one in terror cried,
> "Flee back before the hand of the Most High;
> to them He offers succor, but to us,
> most wretched men, destruction does He work."
> The sea-path flooded, all our host was lost.

(ll. 220-242)

---

48 Compare LXX to Exod 14:25, reading *wy'sr* "were bound" instead of MT *wysr*,
similarly Sam.

Here, as in Artapanus, Moses parts the sea by striking it with his rod, and no mention is made of the LORD's "wind". Here too the pursuing Egyptians are confronted by some sort of fiery apparition, and the waters of the sea re-converge unaided. The account diverges from Artapanus' in that it makes explicit reference to the pillar of cloud and fire which separated the two camps. Moreover, Ezekiel's description relates precisely how the Egyptians perished in the sea, diverging from the Pentateuch not only in substance but in the orderly progression which characterizes the sequence of events. The first sign heralding the Egyptians' imminent demise is the refusal of their chariot wheels to turn; only thereafter does the fiery light from heaven appear, indicating that the LORD has entered the battle against Egypt. Not until the Israelites have finished passing through the divided waters do the Egyptians hear the approaching mighty wave closing in on them, whereupon they try in vain to flee and are overpowered by the sea.

C. Philo

In contrast to the coherent, logical account given by Ezekiel, Philo's narrative attests clearly to the presence of various and conflicting traditions concerning the parting of the sea. The passage begins:

> ...at sunset a south wind of tremendous violence arose, and, as it rushed down, the sea under it was driven back, and, though regularly tidal, was on this occasion more so than usually, and swept as into a chasm or whirlpool, when driven against the shore. No star appeared, but a thick black cloud covered the whole heaven, and the murkiness of the night struck terror into the pursuers. Moses now, at God's command, smote the sea with his staff, and as he did so it broke and parted in two.
>
> (VM I.xxxii, pp. 108-109)

In what follows, Philo presents a dramatic description of the rearing of the waters to a vast height and their standing motionless as a wall.

Two totally disparate elements can be distinguished, easily and with absolute certainty, in Philo's version of the story. According to one tradition, a strong southerly (!) wind intensifies the force of the ebbing tide, causing the sea to disappear entirely. This may be viewed as somewhat of a compromise between the Memphite tradition, reported by Artapanus, that the sea dried up at low-tide, and the tradition that the LORD's "wind" split the sea in two. The blatant heresy of the Memphite tradition has been eradicated by God's mighty wind, which, by blowing at just the right moment, provides the clearest evidence of divine providence. At the same time, the miraculous event approximates the natural order as much as possible, and the wind referred to is devoid of any mythological character.

The other tradition reflected in Philo's account is that of Moses' striking the sea with his rod, whereupon the waters stand still as a wall. As in the Pentateuch, both the wind and the rod have roles to play in parting the waters. However, while in the Pentateuch Moses does not strike the water, and his outstretched arm is merely a prelude to the onset of the gust of wind from God, according to Philo the wind first begins to blow, after which Moses strikes the water.

So completely has Philo developed each of the separate motifs that he has created an inescapable paradox: Moses strikes water which is no longer there! Clearly enough, Philo's account is not based on the Pentateuch but is rather the outcome of the quite mechanical combination of traditions current among his contemporaries — as evidenced by Artapanus.

Philo goes on to speak of the cloud which served to separate the two camps, merging this motif with that of the cloud which caused the Egyptians to panic. As described by Philo, only at the actual moment of the crossing did the cloud appear behind the Israelite camp, spurring the Israelites quickly to procede onward and retarding the advance of the Egyptians. Confounded by this spectacle, the Egyptians attempt to flee, drowning in the waters of the sea which have meanwhile been re-united by a powerful northerly (!) wind. No role is assigned to Moses' rod in the re-convergence of the waters; rather, the *actus contrarius* motif is evident in the appearance of the north wind as counterpart to the southerly wind which had split the waters. The motif is somewhat adulterated, however, since the drying up of the sea is only partially accomplished by the south wind.

D. Josephus

The same process of blending separate motifs, which in Philo's account has led to an incoherent and illogical narrative, has resulted in Josephus in a completely consistent picture. The passage opens with Moses' prayer (Ant. II.xvi.1), after which we read:

> After this solemn appeal to God, he smote the sea with his staff. And at that stroke it recoiled and, retreating into itself, left bare the soil, affording passage and flight for the Hebrews. Moses, beholding this clear manifestation of God and the sea withdrawn from its own bed to give them place, set the first foot upon it and bade the Hebrews follow him...
>
> (Ant. II.xvi.2)

After recounting the Egyptian pursuit into the sea, Josephus continues:

> When, thereupon, the entire army of the Egyptians was once within it, back poured the sea, enveloping and with swelling and wind-swept billows descending upon the Egyptians: rain fell in torrents from heaven, crashing thunder accompanied the flash of lightning, aye, and thunderbolts were hurled....Thus perished they to a man.
>
> (Ant. II.xvi.3)

Josephus, then, portrays Moses as parting the sea by striking it with his rod, while it is God's wind, described here no less graphically than in Ps 77:16-20, that causes the waters to re-converge. The firecloud is not mentioned, and the simplest solution possible has been provided for the tension created by conflicting motifs of the rod and the wind: the rod parted the waters, the wind blew them back.

E. Pseudo-Philo

In contrast, Pseudo-Philo reverts to the *actus contrarius* pattern, employing it in an otherwise unattested fashion.

> And God said, "Why have you cried out to Me? Lift up your rod

and strike the sea, and it will be dried up". And when Moses did all this, God rebuked the sea and the sea was dried up. And the waters of the sea[49] piled up and the depths of the earth were visible, and the foundations of the world were laid bare by the fearful din of God and by the breath of the nostrils of the Lord.[50] And Israel passed through the middle of the sea on dry ground. And the Egyptians saw this and continued following them. And God hardened their perception, and they did not know that they were entering the sea. And while the Egyptians were in the sea, God again commanded the sea and said to Moses, "Strike the sea yet once more". And he did so. And the Lord commanded the sea, and it started flowing again and covered the Egyptians and their chariots and horsemen.

(LAB, X:5-6)

Moses' actions, both when the waters are parted and when they are re-united, are a prelude to the main event: the action of the LORD. The latter, however, is depicted according to two different schemes. The parting of the waters is described, in terms which amount to a free paraphrase of Ps 106:9 and 2 Sam 18:16, as a divine "rebuke", whereas the return of the sea to its bed is seen as an act of compliance with God's command. This divergence from the *actus contrarius* pattern was unavoidable, since the divine "rebuke" of the sea, resulting in its fleeing and drying up, was a well attested motif in Israelite tradition (see Isa 17:13; 50:2; Nah 1:4), whereas the idea that another "rebuke" was needed for the sea to return to its own natural course is implausible. It is instructive to note that the author has apparently not sensed this discrepancy, so obvious to the modern reader, since he introduces the second divine action with the words "God again commanded the sea". For the author, God's "rebuke" of the sea, accompanied by thunder, lightning and the fiery breath of His nostrils, and His "command" that the sea return to its former condition, are one and the same type of action. Here then, the "rebuke" has

---

49 The Latin text has *maria aquarum* "the seas of water".
50 Here the Latin text reads *Domini mei* "of My Lord".

become nothing more than a picturesque expression for the divine command that the sea clear a path to make way for the Israelites.

F. The Midrash

The mythological background of the tradition surrounding the parting of the sea is exhibited with extraordinary clarity in the midrashic literature. Reference has already been made to one midrashic passage in which the east wind is shown to be among the divine weapons and in which explicit reference is made to the patently mythological motif that when the Reed Sea was parted so were all the seas of the world.[51] It may also be mentioned in this context that all of the midrashic discussion on the question of whether the sea was parted by God Himself or by Moses is based on the assumption that in either case the sea resisted being split. Moreover, these midrashic passages invariably refer to "the sea" and not "the Reed Sea".

A few brief midrashim attribute the parting of the sea to God alone and omit all mention of Moses. Such is the case in Exod. Rab. Běšallaḥ 24:1:

> "They rebelled at the sea, at the Sea of Reeds" (Ps 106:7): "at the sea", that is, while still on the shore of the sea; "at the Sea of Reeds" is intended literally: when they were *in* the sea. That moment, the Prince of the Sea became incensed with them and wished to overwhelm them with his flood, but the Holy One, blessed be He, rebuked him and dried him up; thus Scripture says, "He rebukes the sea and dries it up" (Nah 1:4); "He rebuked the Sea of Reeds; it became dry" (Ps 106:9).

To this the following comment (Midr. Teh. to Ps 114:3 "The sea saw and fled") may be compared:

> The sea was unwilling to be parted since the Israelites were acting rebelliously. It protested: They act rebelliously, and I should part? But the Holy One, blessed be He, rebuked it, as Scripture

---

51 See above, p. 265.

says, "He rebuked the Sea of Reeds; it became dry" (Ps 106:9). Seeing this, the sea fled at once.

Similar is the answer given by R. Nehemiah to the question posed by the words "The sea saw and fled" (Ps 114:3): "What was it that the sea saw?" Adducing the words of Ps 77:17 ("The waters saw You, O God"), R. Nehemiah reasons: The sea, as it were, saw the very hand of God, and split in two, as Scripture says "the waters saw You and were convulsed" (Yal. Sim'oni to Psalm 114).

In the vast majority of midrashic passages, however, Moses is mentioned. This is even the case in the lengthy midrash on Psalm 114 appearing in Mekilta deRabbi Šim'on bar Yohai, Běšallah 14:21,[52] even though Moses' name does not appear in the psalm itself:

> When "Moses held out his arm over the sea" (Exod 14:21), the sea began to rise up against him. To what may this be compared? To a mortal king who had two gardens, one within the other, and sold the inner garden and not the outer. When the purchaser attempted to enter, the sentry would not allow him to pass. He said, "In the name of the king!" but was still not admitted. He showed the sentry his ring, but to no avail. Then the king himself drove by. Seeing the king, the sentry began to flee. The purchaser asked him, "Why do you flee?" He replied, "I am not fleeing from you but from the king". In the same way, when Moses stood at the sea and ordered it to part in the holy name of God, the sea refused; Moses showed the sea his rod but it still refused. Only when God Himself appeared to him, "the sea saw and fled" (Ps 114:3). Said Moses: "I ordered you to part in the name of God and you refused; I showed you my rod and you refused. 'What alarms you, O sea, that you flee' now (Ps 114:5)?" Replied the sea: "I flee not from you, O son of Amram, rather 'at the presence of the LORD, Creator of the earth' (Ps 114:7)".

Though this passage states unequivocally that it was God and not Moses who caused the waters of the sea to part, the author's ambiva-

---

52 J. N. Epstein and E.Ẓ. Melamed, *Mekilta D'Rabbi Šim'on b. Jochai*, Jerusalem 1955, p. 61.

lence is unmistakable. Every possible emphasis is given to Moses' intimate relationship with the LORD: by comparing the floor of the sea to the king's innermost garden and asserting that the king has sold it to a purchaser, the author implies that God has admitted Moses to His innermost domain and granted him full authority over the sea. Moreover, the sea itself knows full well that it is bound to part at Moses' command; its consciousness of its wrongdoing is evident the moment the Holy One, blessed be He, appears on the scene and the sea is terror-stricken. With extreme caution, then, the motif of Moses' parting the sea is avoided here, and at the same time it is stressed that Moses was certainly worthy of performing the feat.

In view of the reservations in the midrashic literature which may be inferred from the above passage, it is only to be expected that elsewhere the Midrash states openly that the sea was split by Moses' rod. R. Nahorai, responding to the same question posed above by R. Nehemiah regarding the words "The sea saw and fled" (Ps 114:3): "What was it that the sea saw?" answers: "It saw the ineffable Name engraved on Moses' rod, and split apart" (Yal. Šim'oni to Ps 114:3). Still, though the focal point has been shifted to Moses' own actions, the decisive role assigned to the divine Name retains at least a trace of the tradition that the LORD parted the waters.

In light of the fact that midrashic comments on Psalm 114, in which Moses' name does not occur, contain variant traditions on the issue of who parted the sea, it should not be surprising that midrashim which expound upon Isa 63:12, where the parting of the sea is presented in the biblical text itself as a result of Moses' and God's interraction, exhibit the same trait. As we might expect, some of these passages accentuate God's role, while others give prominence to that of Moses. As recounted in Exod. Rab. Běšallaḥ 21:6, God ordered Moses to part the sea:

> Moses immediately hearkened to God and went to divide the sea, but the sea refused to comply, exclaiming, "Shall I split at your behest? Am I not greater than you, since I was created on the third day and you on the sixth?" When Moses heard this, he went and reported to God, "The sea refuses to part". What

did God do? He placed His right hand on the right hand of Moses, as Scripture says "Who made His glorious right hand march at the right hand of Moses" (Isa 63:12).

While the stress which is here laid on the sea's obstinacy serves to enhance the power of God's own action, elsewhere the same verse is expounded in order to focus on Moses' role. In Tan. Wā'ethannan 6[53] we read that when Moses was about to die,

> He went to the shore of the great sea, and asked it to intercede on his behalf. The sea replied: "Son of Amram, what is so special about today? Are you not the same son of Amram who came to me with your rod, smote me and split me into twelve parts, and was I not unable to withstand you because the Presence of God accompanied you, as Scripture says 'Who made His glorious right hand march'" etc.?

This passage enlarges upon its scriptural basis by adding the motif of Moses actually striking the sea with his rod and not merely holding it aloft; though this is unusual in the midrashic literature it is well enough attested in the Hellenistic sources discussed above. To the motif of the sea's having been split into twelve channels, compare Tg. Jonathan to Exod 14:21 ("The waters were split"): "The waters were split into twelve parts, corresponding to the twelve tribes of Jacob".

Even here, however, it is still maintained that the sea did not agree to be parted by Moses, and that it was rather the appearance of the divine presence on the scene which made it comply. This final qualification is revoked only in the later Midr. Wayyōša', where we read as follows:

> "Go to the sea as My agent, and say to it: I am the messenger of the Creator of the universe, (who orders you): 'Show My children the way through you'". Moses then went to the sea and conveyed these words to it, but the sea said: "I will not do as you, a mere mortal, tell me, especially inasmuch as I am three days older than you, having been created on the third day whereas

53 Ed. S. Buber, Vilna 1895, *Sēder Dĕbārīm*, p. 12.

you were created only on the sixth!" Moses relayed the sea's words to the Holy One, blessed be He, who responded by asking, "What is done to a servant who disobeys his Master?" Moses replied, "He is beaten with a rod". Said the Holy One, blessed be He, "Then you, too, must 'lift up your rod and hold out your arm over the sea and split it'". Whereupon "Moses held out his arm over the sea" (Exod 14:15, 21) and split it.[54]

Though the argument given by the sea in support of its defiance is the same as that appearing in the more ancient midrashim, the reply given by God is new.

All of the midrashic passages adduced thus far assert that the sea was unwilling to be parted; its refusal is the common point of departure for various types of midrashim. In contrast to this essential unanimity, variant traditions appear with regard to the question of whether the sea was finally parted by God or by Moses: those passages which aim at stressing the role of Moses occasionally retain even the ancient motif of striking the water with the rod; those passages which speak of the waters having been split by God eliminate even the wind, even though midrashic literature recognized the wind as a divine weapon.[55] In most of the midrashic accounts, however, and especially the longer and more thoroughly developed passages, the very appearance of the divine presence serves to make the sea "flee"; the LORD's supremacy is so absolute that He has no need for any weapon.

An original solution to the conflict between the tradition that Moses parted the sea and the tradition that the LORD Himself did so is attested in an aggadic composition, in the form of an alphabetic acrostic, which was inserted in the Targum to the reading of the Pentateuch on the seventh day of Pesah. It appears in Maḥzor Vitry,[56] and was subsequently published, almost in its entirety, on the basis of manuscript evidence and with important textual variants, by Y. Komlós.[57] The translation which follows is based on the text as it

54 J. D. Eisenstein, *Ozar Midrashim*, New York 1915, p. 148.
55 See above, p. 265.
56 S. Hurwitz (ed.), *Machsor Vitry*, Nürnberg 1923, pp 306-307.
57 Y. Komlós, "The Targum Text of the Parting of the Reed Sea", *Sinai*, 45 (1959), 223-228 [Hebrew].

appears in Maḥzor Vitry. Komlós' manuscript, which is quite defective, particularly at the beginning of the passage but also elsewhere in the text, has been used only in order to cite a few variants which are of interest.

1 "Go, Moses, stand by the sea and say to it: 'Retreat from the divine presence!'

2 In My name, go and say to the sea: 'I am the messenger of the Creator of the universe;

3 Clear your path for a short while so that the redeemed of the LORD may pass through you.[58]

4 For the tribes of Jacob are in distress, and their enemies pursue them,

5 So that if[59] you close yourself off in front of them, and evil Pharaoh will fall upon them from behind'".[60]

6 So Moses went and stood by the sea and said to it: "Retreat from the divine presence!"[61]

7 The sea moved away from Moses when it saw the wonder-working rod in his hands.

8 The sea boiled and raged, and was rising to turn backward.

9 But it then argued: "Son of Amram, am I not more powerful and older than you?[62]

10 I am three days older than you, since I was created on the third day and you on the sixth!"

11 When Moses saw that the sea refused and that its waves surged, he said to it:

12 "This is not a time for argument; Israel is in distress!"

---

58 Of the first three lines, only a fragment of l. 2 is preserved in Komlós' MS.

59 Missing in Komlós' MS and best deleted.

60 Following Komlós, we may compare Mekilta deRabbi Šimᶜon bar Yoḥai, Běšallaḥ 3 (to Exod 14:15): "'Moses, My children are in distress — the sea is closing in, and the enemy pursues them — and you stand by in prayer?! Why do you cry out to Me?' — which teaches that there is a time to be brief and a time to speak at length".

61 Repeating the formula used in l. 1; Komlós' MS has "from My Presence", anticipating l. 7. As Moses is God's emmissary, the two are not entirely distinguishable; this accounts for the variant.

62 Following Maḥzor Vitry; as noted by Komlós, the text of the MS in this line is plainly corrupt.

13 Moses replied to the sea: "I am here on behalf of the Creator of the universe."[63]

14 Hearing his words, the sea turned, and was about to do the will of the LORD of Heaven.

15 But the sea then said to Moses; "I submit not to the will of a mortal".

16 Moses replied, "A Master greater than both of us will force you to submit".

17 Moses opened his mouth in song and spoke words of praise;[64]

18 Moses' prayer ascended; in supplication and entreaty he spoke his words;

19 He called: "You promised me[65] in the book of the Law, 'Now you will see what I will do to evil Pharaoh';[66]

63 In response to the sea's claim (l. 10) that it is older than he, Moses makes the assertion (l. 13) that he is the agent of God. What intervenes (ll. 11-12) would seem to be Moses' response to what is depicted in l. 8. Thus Moses first argues that since the Israelites are in distress the time is not right for arguing (l. 12; cf. l. 4), but later realizes that the sea will not give in unless its claim is refuted.
   Komlós' MS has the much lengthier "God answered, exclaiming and saying to it: 'Be off!'" at the end of l. 11. But this reading is suspect on two grounds; first the Hebrew *klk* ("Be off!") is inappropriate in this Aramaic text (despite the appearance of the Hebrew *yôṣēr bĕrēʾšît* "Creator" in ll. 2 and 13, which is a technical term); we should rather expect the Aramaic root ʾzl as in l. 1. Second, the statement is out of place: if God had immediately rebuked the sea Himself, the sea would certainly have surrendered immediately, precluding any further activity on the part of Moses — particularly his claim that he is God's agent! It may be that the reading has been influenced by the midrash cited above (note 60), to the effect that God addressed Moses in an effort to urge him to act quickly, which in turn brought about Moses' response to the sea (l. 13).

64 "Song" and "praise" here may allude to the Song of the Sea; cf. Tg. Onq. to Exod 15:1: "With that Moses and the Israelites offered this praise before the LORD". In what follows, however, Moses offers a prayer of supplication; the content of his song of praise is not described. The intent may be to portray Moses as leading up to his petition with words of praise; in any case the passage remains somewhat unclear.

65 Following Komlós' MS; Maḥzor Vitry has "him".

66 Komlos holds that the reference is to Exod 14:13, but it appears more likely that Exod 6:1 is intended. Despite the absence of direct reference to the parting of the sea in the latter passage, the Rabbis may have interpreted it as an allusion to the drowning of the Egyptians in the Reed Sea; see b. Sanh. 111a: "You shall see what I will do to Pharaoh: the war against Pharaoh you yourself will witness, but the war against the thirty-one Canaanite kings you will not witness".

20 Master of the universe![67] Do not deliver Your people into
the hands of evil Pharaoh".
21 The Most High gave him[68] the wonder-working rod to
destroy all the rebellious ones.
22 The sea heard the voice of the holy spirit speaking with
Moses from within the fire;
23 The sea turned, its waves were calmed, and the Israelites
proceeded across.

This Targumic interpolation would seem to agree that the sea split
in two at the sight of Moses' rod. However, it adds the sequel, unattested elsewhere, that the sea then changed its mind, echoing the
claim so well attested in the Midrash, that it is older than Moses.
Moreover, the process repeats itself: Moses counters with the fact that
he is God's agent, the sea acquiesces, and once again immediately
revokes its consent, this time repeating the argument that no mere
mortal will subdue it. Moses entreats God, and only when the sea
hears the divine voice conversing with Moses from within the fire
does it finally open a path for the Israelites.

Here a unique solution is proposed to the problem of conflicting
traditions. From a literary standpoint, the parting of the waters has
become a three-part ascending series: the sea is hesitant about splitting apart at Moses' command; submits, changes its mind, submits
again, changes its mind again, finally surrendering when it hears the
voice of God. God, however, does not speak to the sea but rather to
Moses, which is what proves to the sea that Moses is indeed God's
own agent. Thus, by inference, the sea's final capitulation is not so
much to God as it is to Moses. At the same time, the alternative motif
of the sea's refusal to clear a path for the Israelites until God Himself
appears on the scene is retained.

Mythological elements are attenuated. Reference to the tradition
that the rod of Moses was employed to part the sea is confined to the

---

67 In place of this, Komlós' MS reads "Holy one, blessed be He!". Thus the acrostic
in Maḥzor Vitry includes two lines beginning with *rēš*, and that in the MS has two
lines beginning with *qōp*; both readings are equally suspect.
68 Or "me", if "him" in both texts is emended; see note 65.

mere mention of the rod; no action against the sea is attributed to it. God's "rebuke of the sea" has been transformed into a divine response to Moses' prayer, serving merely as proof that Moses is God's messenger. Still, the basic notion that the sea resisted being split is given every possible emphasis; mention is made even of its raging and of the surging of its waves in its angry resentment.

Another type of midrashic passage depicts the parting of the Reed Sea as a re-enactment of the cosmogony. Put simply by R. Meir:

> The Holy One, blessed be He, said to Moses: "There is no need for the Israelites to entreat Me. If I created dry land for Adam, who was the only human, as Scripture says, 'Let the water below the sky be gathered into one area, that the dry land may appear' (Gen 1:9), how much more should I do so for an entire holy nation destined to say 'This is my God and I will adore Him' (Exod 15:2)?"
>
> (Exod. Rab. Běšallaḥ 21:8)

Later midrashic opinion, however, did not find this formulation satisfactory. Some authorities were disturbed by the imperfect comparison between the parting of the Reed Sea and Creation, observing that the cosmogonic parting of the waters was permanent while the parting of the Reed Sea was a momentary miracle. Others ignored this difficulty and concentrated on a far more serious issue: If the existing world was complete at the conclusion of the six days of Creation, can the process of Creation be re-opened at all?

The first of these two problems is discernible in a passage which has been interpolated into the section from Mekilta deRabbi Šim'on bar Yoḥai quoted above.[69] The interpolation appears to be a re-working of the very same comment on Isa 63:12 adduced above in the formulation appearing in Exod. Rab. 21:6.[70] In its later form, it reads as follows:

> When Moses came and stood at the sea, he said to it: "A message for you from the LORD: Make a road for the redeemed to walk

69 See p. 281.
70 See pp. 282-283.

288

(cf. Isa 51:10)". The sea replied to Moses: "Son of Amram, was not Adam created at the end of the six days of Creation, not at their beginning, while I was created earlier? Since I am therefore greater than you, I shall not part at your command". Moses reported to the Holy One, blessed be He: "The sea has said thus-and-such; Master of the Universe, it is indeed more prestigious and will not part at my behest. If You command it, however, it will part". The Holy One, blessed be He, said to Moses: "If I tell the sea to part, the world will never recover. Rather, you command it to part, so that you may also provide the remedy. Here at your side is a reflection of My Power". Moses thereupon went, with Power marching at his right side, as Scripture says "Who made His glorious arm march at the right hand of Moses" (Isa 63:12). When the sea saw that Power stood at Moses' right side, it said to the earth: "Make me cavities, so that I may enter your channels[71] [and thus flee] from the Presence of the Lord of all, blessed be He!"[72]

Though the issue of renewing the cosmogony is not explicitly mentioned, it is still present in the notion that the sea can be repaired only if split by Moses with the aid of a mere reflection of the Power of God, but not if it were to be torn apart by God's Power itself, which split the sea at Creation.

Weightier still is the second argument, advanced by another late midrashic selection, against the idea that even the Creator Himself has the right to make alterations in Creation. In the passage, it is Moses who gives voice to this view, challenging God as follows:

"You order me to part the sea and turn it into dry land, but Scripture says 'I, who set the sand as a boundary to the sea, [as a limit for all time, not to be transgressed]' (Jer 5:22); You have thereby sworn that You will never tear it apart". R. Eleazar Ha-kappar explained: Moses said to Him: "Did You not say that

71 Compare Philo (above, p. 276).
72 The passage does not appear in the Epstein-Melamed edition (see above, note 52), but is found in the edition of D. Hoffmann, *Mechilta de-Rabbi Šimon b. Jochai*, Frankfurt am Main 1905, pp. 49-50.

the sea can never become dry land, as Scripture says 'I, who set the sand as a boundary to the sea', and it is further written 'Who closed the sea behind doors' (Job 38:8)?"

The answer provided is characterized by the same concern for the theoretical problem as that which is found in the question:

> The Holy One, blessed be He, replied: "Have you not read the opening words of the Torah: 'God said: Let the water below the sky be gathered' (Gen 1:9)? It was I who laid down the provisions for the sea; I stipulated from the outset that I would eventually rend it apart, as Scripture says 'At daybreak the sea returned to its normal state' (Exod 14:27): instead of the word *l'ytno* ('to its normal state') read *ltn'o*, 'to its provision', i.e., the provision which I had stipulated from the beginning".
>
> (Exod. Rab. Běšallaḥ 21:6)

The essence of this midrash may also be found in the statement attributed to R. Yohanan in his comment on Gen 1:9 (Gen. Rab. 5:5): "The Holy One, blessed be He, stipulated in advance that the sea would part for the Israelites, as Scripture says 'At daybreak the sea returned *l'ytno*, meaning *ltn'o*". Thus the midrashic solution is that the parting of the sea did not entail either a re-opening of the process of Creation or any spontaneity on the part of God. Rather, all was pre-ordained; the parting of the sea and its return to normal were envisaged in the original act of Creation.

This same denial of the concept of the miraculous as that which God performs counter to the laws of nature appears in the words of a later Talmudic authority, R. Yirmiah b. Eleazar:

> The Holy One, blessed be He, made provisions in advance not only for the sea but for all that was created in the week of Creation, as Scripture says: "My own hands stretched out the heavens, and I commanded all their host" (Isa 45:12): I commanded the sea to part, and the heavens to stand silent before Moses — "Give ear, O heavens" etc. (Deut 32:1); I commanded the sun and the moon to stand still before Joshua...
>
> (Gen. Rab. 5:5)

In place of the simplistic perception of the parting of the sea as a new act of creation, the Midrash has provided a philosophical doctrine denying the possibility of any exception to the natural order and maintaining that the universe is eternally bound by the provisions set down for all time at Creation. Not by chance did Maimonides adduce this passage in his discussion of miracles and the natural order, asserting that "all this is an evasion of the idea that anything new can come into existence" (Guide, II:29).[73]

And yet, though from the standpoint of canonized philosophical theory there can be no distinction between the parting of the sea and other miracles, it cannot be taken as merely coincidental that the authoritative philosophical statement of this principle takes the parting of the sea as its point of departure. The very existence, in ancient tradition, of the idea that when the sea was parted the process of Creation was re-awakened posed the acute theoretical question of whether allowance has been made in the universe for any form of spontaneous new creation. An answer in the negative leads inescapably to the categorical denial of all possibility of change in the natural order. The history of the motif of the parting of the sea confirms an important principle in the humanistic disciplines regarding the history of thought: the philosophical evolves from the mythological. The circle is closed: the final stage of the motif of the parting of the sea in Jewish philosophy bears testimony to its origin.

IV. Summary

The discussion of the multifaceted tradition of the parting of the sea, characterized throughout by the tension between historical and mythological perceptions, may here be concluded. Myth has become history; not the history of happenstance, of events transient as the waves of the surging and subsiding sea, but rather the history which retains the enduring, transcendent nature of myth, a living symbol for future

---

73 See also m. ʾAbot, 5:6 and Maimonides' commentary ad loc.

generations. To put it quite plainly, the historicization of the myth is also, simultaneously, the mythologization of history.

At the beginning of this evolutionary process there may have stood an actual historical event. Even so, it remains an open question whether those sources which tell of this event in a manner stressing its historical nature are in fact directly based on the event itself or whether they draw on a mythological tradition which had long ago discarded its ancient form. In this study we have attempted to advance the latter position, distinguishing three stages in the development of the story: first, the myth of God's primordial battle against the sea; second, the historical-mythological account of God's re-enactment of Creation, brought about by parting the sea for the Israelites; finally, the added motif, that the outcome of this feat was that the Egyptians then perished in the depths of the sea.

KEY TO ABBREVIATIONS

A partial listing of the more frequently recurring abbreviations is given below; the complete key, including the abbreviations for Biblical, Apocryphal and Rabbinic works, may be found in the Journal of *Biblical Literature*, 107 (1988), pp. 579ff. See also the Key to Extra-biblical Works, pp. 295–296.

*ANET*² James P. Pritchard (ed.), *Ancient Near Eastern Texts Relating to the Old Testament*², Princeton, NJ 1955

Ant. Josephus' Antiquities

b. Babylonian Talmud

BASOR *Bulletin of the American Schools for Oriental Research*

BDB F. Brown, S.R. Driver, C.A. Briggs, *A Hebrew and English Lexicon of the Old Testament*, Oxford 1953

BZAW *Beihefte zur Zeitschrift für die alltestamentliche Wissenschaft*

CAD *Chicago Assyrian Dictionary*

CT *Cuneiform Texts from Babylonian Tablets in the British Museum*

GKC *Gesenius' Hebrew Grammar*, ed. E. Kautzsch, trans. A. Cowley, Oxford 1910

HTR *Harvard Theological Review*

HUCA *Hebrew Union College Annual*

IEJ *Israel Exploration Journal*

JBL *Journal of Biblical Literature*

JPOS *Journal of the Palestine Oriental Society*

JThS *Journal of Theological Studies*

l., ll. line, lines

LAB Pseudo-Philo's *Liber Antiquitatum Biblicarum*

Leg. All. Philo's *De Legum Allegoriarum*

Leš *Lĕšōnēnū*

LXX Septuagint

m. Mishnah

MGWJ *Monatschrift für Geschichte und Wissenschaft des Judentums*

MS, MSS Manuscript, Manuscripts

MT Masoretic Text

NJPS	*Tanakh--A New Translation of the Holy Scriptures According to the Traditional Hebrew Text*, Philadelphia: The Jewish Publication Society, 1985
PEQ	*Palestine Exploration Quarterly*
RB	*Revue Biblique*
Spec. Leg.	Philo's *De Specialibus Legibus*
VT	*Vetus Testamentum*
VTSup	*Vetus Testamentum Supplements*
v., vv.	verse, verses
VM	Philo's *Vita Mosis*
WS	Wisdom of Solomon
y.	Talmud Yerushalmi
ZAW	*Zeitschrift für die alttestamentliche Wissenschaft*

KEY TO EXTRA-BIBLICAL WORKS

Bibliographical data generally appear in the footnotes accompanying the first reference to each work; works for which no explanatory footnote is given are indexed below.

Aquila	In *Origenis Hexaplorum quae supersunt*, ed. F. Field, Oxford 1867, 1874
Babylonian Talmud	*Talmud Babli*, ed. Romm, Vilna (frequently reprinted)
Diodorus	*Diodori Siculi Bibliotheca*, Parisiis 1878
Eusebius	Eusebius, *Praeparatio Evangelica*, K. Mras (ed.), *Eusebius Werke*, Achter Band, Berlin 1954
Gen. Rab.; Exod. Rab.; Num. Rab.	All cited according to Vilna, 1921 edition (frequently reprinted)
Herodotus	*Herodoti historiarum libri IX*, Lipsiae 1926
LXX	Septuagint (ed. A. Rahlfs, Stuttgart 1935)
Mek	*Mekilta deRabbi Yišma^cel* (ed. H. S. Horovitz and I. A. Rabin, Frankfurt am Main 1930)
Mekilta deRabbi Šim^con bar Yoḥai	Ed. J.N. Epstein and E. Z. Melamed, Jerusalem 1955
Midr. HaGadol	*Midraš HaGadol* to Exodus (ed. M. Margaliot, Jerusalem 1956)
Midr. Teh.	*Midraš Tehillim* (= *Midraš Šōḥēr Ṭōb*, ed. S. Buber, Vilna 1891)
Mishnah	cited according to *Talmud Babli*, ed. Romm, Vilna (frequently reprinted)
Mišnat R. Eliezer	*Mišnat Rabbi Eliezer* (= *Mišnat Šělōšīm Uštayīm Middōt*, ed. H. G. Enelow, New York 1934)
Pausanias	Pausanias, *Graeciae descriptio*, Parisiis 1882
Peshitta	Cited according to *Biblia Hebraica³*, ed. R. Kittel, Stuttgart 1937
Pirqe R. El.	*Pirqe Rabbi Eliezer*, Warsaw 1852
Sam	Samaritan Pentateuch (ed. A. von Gall, Giessen 1914-1918)
Sifre	Ed. M. Ish-Shalom (Friedmann), Wien 1884
Symmachus	In *Origenis Hexaplorum quae supersunt*, ed. F. Field, Oxford 1867, 1874
Tan.	*Tanhuma* (ed. S. Buber, Vilna 1891)

Extra-biblical works

Tg. Jonathan	To Pentateuch: Pseudo-Jonathan (ed. M. Ginsburger, Berlin 1903)
	To Prophets and Hagiographa: Targum Jonathan, in Rabbinic Bible
Tg. Neofiti	Targum Neofiti (*Neofiti I. Targum Palestinense*, ed. A. Diez Macho, Madrid-Barcelona 1968-1978)
Tg. Onqelos	Targum Onqelos (ed. A. Berliner, Berlin 1884)
Tg. Yer. II	Targum Yerushalmi II (*Fragmententargum zum Pentateuch*, ed. M. Ginsburger, Berlin 1899)
Vg	Vulgate (*Biblia Sacra iuxta Latinam Vulgatam versionem ad codicum fidem isussu Pii XI*, 1926ff.)
Yal. HaMakiri	*Yalqut HaMakiri* (ed. S. Buber, Berditchev 1900)
Yal. Šimᶜoni	*Yalqut Šimᶜoni* (cited according to Warsaw 1876-1878 edition, frequently reprinted)
Yerushalmi	*Talmud Yerushalmi*, Zhitomir 1860-1867 (frequently reprinted)

INDEX OF AUTHORS CITED

INDEX OF PASSAGES CITED

GREEK AND HELLENISTIC LITERATURE

PUBLICATIONS OF THE PERRY FOUNDATION FOR BIBLICAL RESEARCH
IN THE HEBREW UNIVERSITY OF JERUSALEM